Running BOARD MEETINGS

Running BOARD MEETINGS

3rd edition

How to get the most from them

200201

Patrick Dunne

KOGAN PAGE

London and Sterling, VA

First published in 1997
Second edition 1999
Third edition 2005

Apart from any fair dealing for the purposes of research or private study, or criticism or review, as permitted under the Copyright, Designs and Patents Act 1988, this publication may only be reproduced, stored or transmitted, in any form or by any means, with the prior permission in writing of the publishers, or in the case of reprographic reproduction in accordance with the terms and licences issued by the CLA. Enquiries concerning reproduction outside those terms should be sent to the publishers at the undermentioned addresses:

120 Pentonville Road
London N1 9JN
United Kingdom

22883 Quicksilver Drive
Sterling VA 20166-2012
USA

www.kogan-page.co.uk

© Patrick Dunne, 1997, 1999, 2005

The right of Patrick Dunne to be identified as author of this work has been asserted by him in accordance with the Copyright, Designs and Patents Act 1988.

British Library Cataloguing in Publication Data

A CIP record for this book is available from the British Library.

ISBN 0 7494 4347 2

Typeset by Jean Cussons Typesetting, Diss, Norfolk
Printed and bound in Great Britain by Creative Print and Design (Wales), Ebbw Vale

Contents

Foreword

My predecessor as Chairman of 3i Group, Sir George Russell gave me a copy of *Running Board Meetings* when it was first published in 1997. He described it as a thought provoking and unstuffy book and one which would be of use to directors of businesses and organizations of all shapes and sizes. George was absolutely right and it has been clear from its success that others agreed. The demand for a third edition also proves that there is as much need today.

In his foreword to the first edition George said that:

'The focus on corporate governance in the last decade has delivered some very positive effects. However, we all need to be careful that the debate, the new processes and the substance of what happens in practice remain well balanced. Boards must not lose sight of their real commercial purpose.'

I couldn't agree more and was delighted to be asked to write the foreword for this third edition which has been significantly updated from the second edition which was published in 2000.

So much has happened since 2000 to influence the job of the director in companies large and small. There have been the highly publicized collapses of some major companies across the world. The Sarbanes–Oxley act, the Higgs review, the Smith report and the many reviews of financial markets and corporate governance have also led to a significant increase in the regulation that directors have to comply with and understand.

Alongside this, the expectations that institutional shareholders, the media, government and employees have of their directors has continued to rise – as have the risks of failing to meet these expectations. The legal, financial and reputational risks inevitably are starting to deter some people from taking on public company board positions. Although in some cases this is probably a healthy development, we all need to be careful that the balance of risk and reward is sufficient to attract the best to fulfil these ever more demanding roles.

At 3i we are that lucky the strength and breadth of the relationships we have across the world gives access to some terrific people who meet those defining characteristics of effective directors that Patrick talks about in the book:

'Good judgement, superb interpersonal skills and finely tuned antennae'.

We are also fortunate in gaining enormous benefit from the pioneering work, led by Patrick, that has been done in the area of developing practical board skills. The courses we run for our staff, for the directors of our portfolio companies and the industry as a whole continue to be popular. Boardroom skills can always be developed no matter how experienced you are.

Whether you are an aspirant or highly experienced director I think you will find this book of use; and I am sure you will enjoy reading it.

Baroness Hogg

Acknowledgements

I have been very fortunate to have had the help of so many people in putting together the three editions of this book. I would like to thank and pay tribute to the following:

At home: My amazingly tolerant wife Rebecca. Our three boys who have all contributed. Patrick for his penetrating questions, Nicholas for his great sense of fun and engaging personality and Rory for giving me the natural deadlines of his birth to start the first edition and his first birthday to finish it.

At 3i: It seems a long time since the 'Running Board Meetings' project was begun and so there are a few people I need to thank who have now retired. Our former Chairman Sir George Russell, who gave me not just the benefit of his wisdom but also tremendous encouragement. Brian Larcombe, who was CEO from 1997 to 2004, and Ewen Macpherson, CEO from 1992 to 1997. Two very different characters and two people who taught me a great deal. Richard Summers, my boss at the time of writing the first edition, for being open minded enough to let me have a go. The final retirees are David Wilkinson, Roger Lawson and Eric Barton in the UK, and Frederic De Broglie in France and Gabriel Gutterez Ugalde in Spain for their trailblazing work at 3i as directors of our portfolio companies.

Others at 3i today include our Chairman Sarah Hogg who not only sets a terrific example but whose razor sharp intellect provides tremendous constructive challenge. Brian Larcombe's successor as CEO, Phil Yea, who has skilfully inducted himself into the 3i board. Michael Queen, who now heads up our growth capital business but was Finance Director from 1997 to 2004. Few people I know possess

Michael's wonderful combination of intellect, humility, decency and resilience. Our Company secretary Tony Brierley and his teammate Sabina Dawson have provided excellent advice to me over many years. Sergio Sambonet who runs 3i in Italy and Ere Kariola in Finland, who have both been especially enthusiastic on the subject of developing best practice in their countries over many years.

In my time at 3i in the many roles I have had since embarking on the 'Running Board Meetings' project I have enjoyed some fabulous secretarial and administrative support. I would have to single out Cordelia Brunt, Helen Jones, Karen Wolstenholme, Alex Robb and last but not least Lorene Gibbons. All of them combine great efficiency with charm. The success of 3i's Independent Directors Programme would not have been possible without a great team and I would like to pay tribute to Pat Hayward, Cindy Thorneycroft, Dorothea Kronenburghs in Germany, Jean Louis Grange in France and Bruno Pastore in Italy.

Others at 3i I must thank are Carol Brennan and Charles Richardson.

Wise elders: Sir Adrian Cadbury, Lord Cuckney, Sir Christopher Hogg, Sir Denys Henderson, Lord Alexander, Jon Foulds, Sir Derek Birkin, Raymond Seitz, Sir Max Williams and Tim Melville-Ross know that I mean it with great respect. They all gave me terrific pearls of wisdom at one time or another.

At the Federal Reserve System: Former Secretary William Wiles, current Secretary Jennifer Johnson and Carolyn Doying.

At Leap: Pete Lawson for his wonderful chairing skills, Helen Carmichael, our former CEO, for just being a joy to work with as a trustee and Jenny Rogers, her successor, likewise, and Janet Cummins for setting such a high standard as a board member.

At Harvard business schools: Professors Jay Lorsch and Jay Light.

At Cranfield: Murray Steele, Ruth Bender and Leo Murray.

At INSEAD: Manfred Kets de Vries and Jean Claude Larreche

At UBC Vancouver: Dan Muzyka

Elsewhere in the USA: John Shane, Barbara Thomas, Norton Reamer, Con Hurley, Charles Carter, Alan Ferguson, Peter Bollier, Bob Monks, Hugh Parker, Stan Lukowski, Jeer Thompson and John Ward.

In mainland Europe: Frederic de Broglie, Andrew Richards and Solveig Nyvold.

All of 3i's Independent Directors Programme members: Over the thirteen years I was responsible for this activity we made over 2,000 board appointments through the programme and had tremendous fun as we learnt how to make boards work more effectively all over the world. The members of the programme gave me terrific support and it is unfair to single out any in particular, but I feel I must pay a special tribute to Bernard Norman, Hugh Stewart, Robert Wright, Wayne Bradley and Derek Wooler.

Others who fit no neat category are: Peter Brown from Independent Remuneration Solutions, Sally Field, Janet Morgan, Gerry Acher, David Bishop, Mike Rake and Sean O'Hare.

And finally: John Hawkins, my friend and expert proof reader, Michelle my niece for her cartoons and the Suzy Lamplugh Trust for their excellent guides and work.

Introduction

Why on earth did I decide to write the first edition of this book in 1997? Interest in the subject, arrogance, rampant egomania? Well I suppose all were possibilities. Happily for most things in life you can construct a wonderfully convenient post-rationalisation as to why you did them. This is especially true in business. So perhaps in this particular case, the fact that there was virtually nothing then written already on a subject of importance to all company directors might have moved me in a moment of inspiration, opportunism or pomposity to get scribbling. Coming clean, I was really spurred into action by a series of circumstances.

One of the joys of my job at 3i then was finding chief executives, independent directors and chairmen for companies undergoing significant change. Of most interest were the companies that needed to undergo some dramatic change but hadn't quite spotted or come to terms with it yet. These 'It'll be all right on the nighters' would often say that 'We're really on the edge of something big'. Something big to them meant a business wonderland. Yet in reality it was something really big such as a Grand Canyon style cliff. A good first step in such situations is to attend the next board meeting. Doing this provides a deeper understanding of the issues facing the company and, more importantly, the characters involved in addressing them. As a consequence I've attended many a fun eight-hour session listening to a board discussing the car policy or what type of coffee machines they should have whilst their business runs out of cash. People usually put on a pretty good show for a bit, but normally as long as you are quiet and not distractingly attired they revert to their normal behaviour patterns. These behaviour patterns cover an extraordinary range, and not just for the individuals but for the group as a whole. Few boards, particularly ones that aren't getting on together or are under pressure, can keep up a show for long.

It was after one such marathon session where its length seemed to be in inverse relationship to its result that I wondered 'is there a book on running board meetings that I can give to Fred to help him?' I rushed into the local bookshop the next morning to buy this gift. No luck. Lots on meetings, plenty of sound advice for project meetings and business meetings in general but nothing that really met Fred's need. Fred, I should hasten to add, is a really decent chap who had built a great business and then let it get too much for him. This would have been alright if he had built a strong team around him. Alas, he hadn't. His non-executives were also committing the cardinal sin of not telling him what he needed to hear. This was in no way through fear – it was more because he was such a nice chap they couldn't bear to tell him. As one of them said, 'After all, it's his family's company, not ours.' Result, the wrong people discussing the wrong things in a terribly cosy fashion. Meanwhile the company was in desperate need of radical change.

It did seem somewhat odd to me that nothing much had been written on board meetings so I had a formal literature search done both here and in the USA. Not much again – how puzzling. Board meetings ought to enhance the success of a business and for thousands of companies they do. Yet for many these meetings are viewed as irrelevant, which is bizarre when you consider the amount of effort, cost and stress involved.

With all the discussion and debate over the probity of boards it was worrying me that the important topic of what boards actually do was becoming overshadowed. 'Business is about making money, having fun and doing both in a responsible way.' Yet there was the prospect that they might become considerably less fun. To balance this we had been running a series of case study sessions on board issues with directors of 3i investee companies. Themes included dealing with board disharmony, retaining high quality people, picking independent directors and so on. It was at some of these events that I mentioned my puzzle of there being nothing much available on the board meetings themselves. The reaction was unanimous: do a session on it and write something.

To gather material and ensure that what was going to be written bore some resemblance to the real world, I gathered together groups of 30 to 50 seasoned campaigners for brainstorming sessions and interviewed some well-known masters of the art. The brainstorming sessions included chairmen, managing directors, independent directors and company secretaries from companies big and small, thriving and struggling. A highly sophisticated structure was chosen 'Before', 'During' and 'After'. Quite quickly the importance of preparation and planning came through and we had to assemble more groups on the 'Before'. With this material, a growing collection of anecdotes and the help of the wonderful 3i calendar cartoons, the six-page flyer *Running Board Meetings* was born. Over 10,000 of these were issued. We seemed to have struck a chord.

Case study events for members of our independent director's programme were then arranged. The majority of our then 325 members came. Flushed with this success, we ran identical evenings for 3i investee and potential investee companies. Chemco, the case study we used for the events, is included as an appendix. This is for those of you who want to try it for your board. I have also included a Convo case study on board disharmony. *Directors' Dilemmas*, also published by Kogan Page, contains over twenty case studies with analyses and descriptions of the outcomes in each situation.

Why go on then and write a book? Firstly because enough people whom I respect thought there was a receptive market. Secondly because I thought it might be fun to do it.

Some of the fun was in looking at international comparisons. 3i is a very international business and our research into board structures for our own business and that of our investee companies provided an insight into how things differ in North America, Asia and right across continental Europe. My team of encouragers also encouraged me to go to the United States to see how things compared. American friends and a number of people I'd previously met who sit on both US and UK boards introduced me to a broad mix of US board members. These covered the range from those at fledgling early stage businesses to those at major banks and pension funds. I was also lucky enough to meet William Wiles (now retired) and his team at the Federal Reserve System in Washington. Board meetings at the Fed are about as professional and well organised as you could imagine. Even though most of us don't have quite the same operating environment, the approach they adopt and the rigour they apply to their board meetings is most instructive.

This third edition has been updated significantly to reflect how things have changed in the past Enron and Parmalat era. It also contains a 'rough guide' to the Higgs review of 2003.

My objective in writing this book is nothing more than to provoke thought. There is no universally applicable model or code of practice for running board meetings. One of the fantastic things in business is the variety of situations companies find themselves in. More fantastic are some of the collections of people thrown together to deal with these situations – a sort of corporate Brownian motion I suppose, with thousands of molecules swirling around and colliding into each other, some with a happy union, some with an explosion.

The book has been written for busy people. Each section stands on its own. This combined with a 'Before, 'During' and 'After' the board meeting structure should make it easy for you to dip in and out.

I hope you enjoy it.

Before ...

'The Preparation'

TRIANGULATION

Weird as it may sound, as a kid I was fascinated by triangles and amazed at how useful they were in so many different contexts. I was nuts about aviation and loved to read biographies. Trigonometry seemed so useful to the great aviators like Lindbergh and Bleriot, to pioneering explorers and astronomers and to history's great builders. In my early days in the chemical industry, when I was working on lots of logistical challenges, I would often use triangles to help me work through issues or problems.

When I first started to work in earnest with dysfunctional boards as a venture capitalist, I was learning on the job and felt each situation was quite different. As of course they are. However, combining this with experience of high performing boards I began to recognise patterns and remembered my triangles. It struck me very clearly one day when trying to explain to a very frustrated chairman who had been intro-duced to turn a business around that pretty well all the issues he had with his board were to do with people, purpose and process, three things.

I drew the triangle below and we quickly worked out that although the board did have people and process issues, before we started anything we had to be sure what we thought the board was for. Only then could we really know that we had a board team fit for purpose and a set of simple board processes to achieve that purpose.

Before embarking on any journey it is helpful to know where you are starting from, where you want to get to and to have some idea of how you are going to get there. I have found my little triangle very helpful

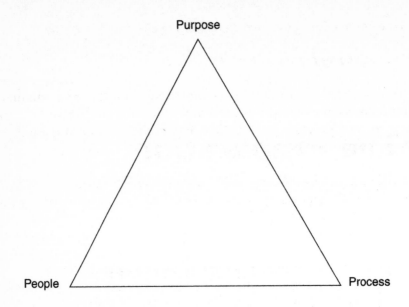

over the years, all over the world, in crystallising thoughts and gaining clarity on what really needs to be done. Not just in a board setting either. It has been tremendously helpful when taking on new roles, especially the ones requiring a major change programme.

WHAT'S THE POINT?

So what's the purpose of a board?

You might expect to get a broadly similar response to this question. You don't. For many it's simply to go through the procedural formalities necessary to comply with the Companies Act and other regulations. So it's all fairly dull and over as quickly as possible with the chairman priding himself that:

'Our board meetings never last more than half an hour.'

For others it's about discussing and taking the key strategic decisions. The ever patient and methodical company secretary or finance director will cover the rest. Perhaps the less enlightened feel it's simply a means of communication with non-executives, joint venture partners, a family that aren't involved in the business or other irritant groups. There's also the occasional chief executive or chairman that thinks it's really the best forum for clearing the in-tray.

Jon Foulds, former chairman of Halifax plc, once asked me:

'Is it a creative process or not?'

The masters of the art that I have interviewed for the three editions of this book seem to broadly agree that for the most part a board meeting is a creative process. 'Why bother having the meeting if it isn't!' For them the point of the meetings is to:

- agree a strategy and regularly assess its effectiveness;
- within the strategy establish and maintain clear policy on relevant operational issues;
- consider and enable successful succession planning throughout the organisation;
- gain external input and calibration for executive decisons;
- ensure the company effects all necessary procedural and compliance items across the range from health and safety issues to Stock Exchange compliance matters.

In running training sessions around the world over the past 15 years I have found the following shorthand helpful when describing the role of a board and the purpose of board meetings:

- *Right strategy*
  Ensuring that the right strategy is in place and that it is being executed. Also ensuring that there is a good process in place for developing and monitoring strategy.
- *Right resources*
  Making sure that there are the appropriate resources in place to fit with the agreed strategy. The most important of these are people and money.
- *Keep out of jail*
  By this I mean that the board needs to ensure that the company complies with the appropriate laws and regulations relating to its industry and location. In other words, 'all the governance stuff'.

You would also have to think that a board that had clarity and agreement about what its purpose was would be much more likely to get a better result than one that didn't. Naturally, though, many boards have developed over time without really thinking about what the point really is. After all why should board meetings be that different from other rituals developed over centuries? Considering this fundamental question usually results in getting rid of a lot of the claptrap that clutters up board meetings. It also helps in deciding what people you need. Often as a consequence the requirement for a decent team worrier or administrator in smaller companies will be highlighted. Another typical output is clarification as to what should go on the agenda. Of which more anon.

WHO?

One of the first masters of the art I discussed this subject with when writing the first edition of this book was Lord Cuckney. Well known for running efficient and effective board meetings, I felt he was bound to give me some useful tips. His wide range of experiences in public bodies and major international corporates and his work marshalling the Maxwell Pension Trustees gave him an unusually broad perspective. I expected he would have a huge amount to pass on. I was right.

The most critical thing in his view was to have the right people on the board.

'All the chairing skills in the world are useless if you don't.'

Obvious, I suppose, but who are the right people? Well that clearly depends on the situation. Before you start worrying, there won't now be a complete regurgitation of all that's been written on teambuilding. It is interesting, however, and possibly a bit scary sometimes, when you sit down and analyse what skills, knowledge and experience you need to meet the challenges ahead. If you then look at the skills you have in the present boardroom team you will usually find a few gaps and overlaps, particularly given how quickly things change.

The defining characteristics of great directors, whether they are executive or non-executive, have always been for me:

■ great judgement;
■ superb interpersonal skills; and
■ finely tuned antennae.

You generally make a lot more money and have a lot less bother with colleagues who have a fine sense of judgement of people and commercial situations. However, in order for them to bring those judgements to bear they need strong interpersonal skills. Being irritatingly right

RETIRED EXEC LOOKING FOR AN OFFICE PARTY

frequently means you are not listened to. In order to make great judgements you need to have the right inputs, hence the antennae (see page 28).

Something which struck me as pretty peculiar when first becoming involved in helping people find non-executives was how the previous ones had been chosen. There was one FTSE 100 company that picked a non-executive on the basis of its chairman meeting the individual at a cocktail party. The pair then met the next week for a cuppa and, following a board lunch towards the end of that month which enabled him to meet the rest of the team, his appointment was confirmed. Now of course most chairmen of FTSE 100 companies have to be very good at picking people. This one is clearly inspirational. It also seems odd when you consider that to get into the same company as a graduate there's a fearsome application form, a battery of psychometric tests and role plays together with several days' worth of interviews. Of course I'm not suggesting that any less rigour should be taken in recruiting graduates, though as an aside I do think some overzealous human resource directors have gone a bit far. As a further aside it seems quite important if you are going to have a human resource function that it's staffed with humans who are resourceful. There are many that are neither. Returning to the point it has to make sense to take at least the same amount of care when selecting board members as with other appointments.

For smaller companies it can help focus the mind to consider the cost of a board member in relation to their contribution. Remembering, of course, that sometimes particularly non-executives can be a bit like American footballers – they turn up at each game, may spend most of their time on the touchline but are essential at those vital moments when you need someone to score a major goal.

A piece of wisdom from teambuilding research is that it's no good just picking members in isolation. You need complementary skills and people who can work together. Good chemistry is vital and there must be a balance of perspectives in the team. The saying that 'every business needs a dreamer, a businessman and a son of a bitch' encapsulates this well. It's also possible when constructing your fantasy boardroom team to end up with a board that's too clever or cocky for its own good. That great footballing teambuilder the late Bill Shankly's immortal saying that 'as he had no education he had to use his brains' has given hope to as many as it has prevented others from over-sophistication. Shankly also believed passionately in the principle 'that a highly committed team of average ability players who can work together will outdo a bunch of clever prima donnas any day.'

A board that becomes too comfortable with itself also spells danger. Some element of flux and a mix of ages, sexes and backgrounds is healthy. I think it was JP Morgan who said:

'If two people on a board always agree with each other then one is unnecessary.'

Homogeneity of thought is perhaps why many boards which have hitherto enjoyed a golden period develop feelings of invincibility just at the wrong time.

Chief executives and managing directors today may find their position somewhat lonely and isolated. This is despite the fact that most of the people they come into contact with are terribly nice to them face to face. A sycophant appears for them around almost every corner. In smaller companies where there is only one non-executive, the main reason the MD really wants one is that they want someone to talk to. It can be difficult for even the most open of chief executives or managing directors to share their worst fears or highest hopes with their immediate colleagues. It can be even more difficult sometimes for their colleagues to do the same for them.

The mix of characters on the board will clearly have a big influence on its effectiveness. You might think that its size must do as well. Too big might be too formal – real debate may become inhibited. Too small and the broader perspective could be missed. Small boards are also more prone to become dominated by one individual, although I have to say I've seen many experts from the 'divide and rule' school on bigger boards. The American branch of this school is considered to be much larger because of the tradition of having few executive directors on board, the president/chief executive and chief financial officer frequently being the only two. Ironically many of the outside directors I talked to in the United States felt that this gave the executives more power rather than less. In the worst cases the president was normally the only source of information for the busy outside directors. It is much easier to put your own own slant on issues without any of your other executive colleagues around to give it away in their body language, a point endorsed by Professor Jay Lorsch at Harvard Business School.

The religious difficulty many senior business people had with the separation of Chairman and Chief Executive roles does seem to be waning in the wake of Enron, Worldcom and other big US governance scandals.

IT'S LONELY AT THE TOP

At 3i we have tended to focus on four key board roles, believing that if we get these right then they will ensure the other board members will also be right:

- Chairman
- Chief Executive
- Finance Director
- Independent Director/s.

It is interesting to note that many boards are now moving to a model of having only the Chief Executive and Finance Director as executives on the board. For this model to work the Chairman and the independent directors need to find effective and time-efficient ways to get to know the rest of the senior executive team. Otherwise succession and calibration of information can be tricky.

Because of the way boards evolve, few are the size they are for a particular reason. For most, the reality is that it just happened that way. In the 2003 Higgs Report a census was done of the 1700 or so UK listed companies and some interesting demographic statistics emerged. There were 5172 executive and 4610 non-executive directors on the boards of these companies. Of the 3908 individuals who held non-executive directorships in UK listed companies, 80 per cent had only one post. Ten per cent held two and only 7 per cent held an executive position as well. Thirteen per cent of Chairmen held more than one Chairmanship.

Only five FTSE 100 companies had a joint Chairman but 24 of the FTSE 100 chairmen were formerly the chief executive of the same company. Only 4 per cent of the executive director posts and 6 per cent of the non-executive director posts were held by women. Few boards were bigger than twelve.

There does seem to be a general consensus that a board bigger than twelve forces the board into procedural/governance mode. This is particularly true if there were only four executives or less. I've asked a number of people for tips on this issue of size. A favourite response was from someone who reckoned they knew a board was too big if it needed nameplates at its meetings. In his view it meant they either didn't know each other, couldn't remember who they were, or were possibly a different group each time.

There are numerous studies available on the backgrounds of UK and US board members although they are usually confined to the major companies. Fifty-something males from middle to upper socioeconomic groups still dominate the top group but women are breaking through at last. The rise of the female finance and marketing directors suggests that it will probably be only a matter of time, albeit not overnight, before women are proportionately represented. However, studies in the USA at the Kelly School of Business suggest that the number of women with executive positions in US boardrooms is lower

'He's young ... I don't like that in a man.'

in the late nineteen nineties than in the late nineteen eighties. There are numerous books on the subject. Howeer, as I write this book 3i Group is still the only FTSE 100 with a female chairman.

Overseas nationals are also making an impact and growing in number in many countries. However, there still aren't enough young people being given the opportunity to serve on the board. Of course, no one should be on a board as a token youngster, woman or anything else. They should be there because they are able to add something to the result. There must, however, be the potential to liven up a boat of boards by taking a risk and having a better mix of ages. It is easier to balance a bit of naive vigour than it is to invigorate a tired and out-of-date board.

One group of younger people in Europe and the States who do attain board roles early in their careers are venture capitalists and private equity directors and people responsible for joint venture relationships. It is common practice in the venture capital industry to appoint the director who puts the transaction together as a non-executive upon completion of the deal.

Four reasons are normally put forward as to why it is appropriate for an investing institution to appoint an investor representative to the board:

> *'Monitoring and influencing investments is easier when you sit on the board.'*

> *'They will add considerable value by bringing a new dimension to the board's thinking.'*

> *'Gaining additional board experience is developmental for the individual investor.'*

> *'In some markets it would be considered as an insult not to do so.'*

Some alternative perspectives –

On monitoring and influencing:

> *'We don't need to be on the board to monitor our investment or enjoy a good relationship with the people we have backed. Experience has enabled us to find more productive ways to keep track of what is happening and to communicate our views on matters of relevance. In fact by not being on the board it is sometimes easier to be more objective and avoid conflicts of interest especially at times of difficulty, when a bid is received or further money is required.'*

'It is inherently difficult for any board to strike the right balance between strategic, operational and governance issues. Board meetings that become a show or a talking shop for investors make it even harder.'

On the investor's ability to add value:

'If you developed a specification for what you wanted in a non-executive for a particular situation you'd be jolly lucky if it matched perfectly the guy who happens to be handing over the cheque.'

'Whilst there are many excellent venture capital directors they usually, though not always, are the industry's most seasoned campaigners.'

'I wonder if they might add more value to the investing institution by spending more time on their day job, ie finding, negotiating and managing investments. It is a question of playing to strengths.'

On developing the careers of investors:

'We only want people on our board who are going to do something constructive. Investors might be better developed through board positions in non-institutionally backed businesses.'

On insulting management teams:

'Any management team will naturally be insulted if the investor appears disinterested and is unsupportive. Being on the board may not necessarily make them any more interested or supportive. It will, however, highlight their real level of interest. The guy who turns up late, immediately gets on the phone about another deal and then asks a question covered half an hour before he arrived insults me more.'

The reality today is that most investing institutions in majority-controlled buyouts or syndicate-controlled venture deals will require board membership. The key therefore is ensuring that you get the right person to fulfil the role for your specific situation.

HOW OFTEN?

Most boards meet monthly and for approximately two to three hours. But does this suit the business? For numerous people current board schedules have become the corporate equivalent of a hamster wheel. Fortunately many are now challenging this ritualistic approach and having less frequent but more focused meetings. There is no rule that says you have to have them monthly. At many of the speeches, workshops and board awayday presentations I've run since the book was originally published I've asked the question: 'Who has monthly board meetings?'

About three quarters of the audience will usually put their hands up at this point.

'Quarterly?'

Typically the balance respond although you always get a few who are either terribly shy, think it's not worthy of an answer or maybe can't remember.

If you then follow up with asking them, 'Why?'

'Because we always have,' tends to be the most common response.

Perhaps questioning this approach would enable boards to focus on the few really big issues to get right and force the many inappropriate items off the agenda which consume so much time and sap energy and interest. Increasing use is made of the board calendar as a way of planning ahead and allocating time appropriately. Sir Christopher Hogg, former Chairman of Reuters, shared this view. When asked about it he said:

'I've now retracted from monthly board meetings wherever I can. In fact I'm deeply suspicious of boards that have them. It tends to allow you to waste time and forces focus on monthly reports at the cost of time for strategic issues.'

His preference was for bi-monthly meetings. This view seems to be held by many chairmen, and I know many at 3i were pleased when Sir George Russell reduced the number to seven annually plus a strategy away day. Those who find it too big a shock to the system to go from monthly to bi-monthly in one go may get there in stages, first by moving to nine meetings a year. Sir George, well known for his ability to focus on the basics and concentrate people on what matters, feels pretty strongly about this.

'Each board meeting will typically involve an executive board member in three days' work in preparing for it and dealing with the aftermath. Do you really want your top players tied up for 36 days a year with board meetings?'

Tim Melville-Ross, former Director-General of the Institute of Directors, has some concerns about a less frequent meeting:

'It's important to meet frequently to build a good team spirit. My experience is that monthly boards are much more use'.

In 2002 the Top Pay Research Group and 3i published a survey of 1200 independent directorships. We received the response shown in Figure 1 to the question: 'How many times a year does the board meet?'

Eight-three per cent of the companies also met for separate budget or strategy meetings. These gatherings are generally held in delightful little sunny spots enjoying the most pleasant of views. Ironically the conference rooms used rarely have windows and little time is given up to enjoy the place. The degree of preparation for such events varies widely. Making them work requires a lot of forethought and effort from the chairman, chief executive and the company secretary.

In a similar survey by Independent Remuneration Solutions in 2005 covering 1200 companies there was more conformity around 8–9 formal board meetings and 2 days for strategy awaydays.

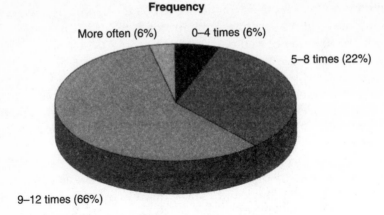

Figure 1   *How many times a year does the board meet?*

HOW LONG?

The effectiveness of discussion will probably vary according to the pressure the Board is under. This is shown in Figure 2.

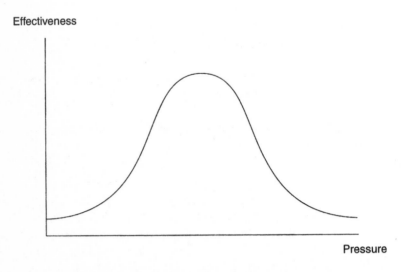

Figure 2   *Effectiveness and pressure curve*

Too little pressure leads to sloppiness, whilst too much can result in hasty and ill thought-through decisions. What are the causes of pressure? Time is an obvious one. Two to three hours was the norm in the companies I talked to who were both happy and effective. The less harmonious and ones with some problems take much longer. As one person told me:

'We have to have a lot of long board meetings to try to put right what we mess up the rest of the time.'

It seems to me to be mad to be overly prescriptive about the length of time a board meeting should take or to suggest that they should always last a uniform time. There has to be a balance.

The Top Pay/3i survey of 1200 directorships in 2002 found the spread of time taken for board meetings shown in Figure 3. Between three and four hours is the average.

Duration

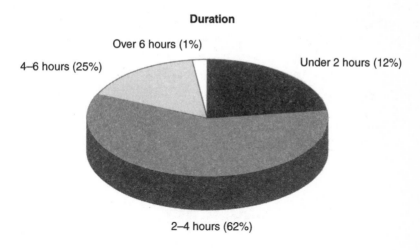

Figure 3   *Time for a full board meeting*

What else causes pressure? Well, it might be easy to think that the company's position must be the main contributor, ie if you're highly successful, it's pretty smug and relaxed; if you're staring a receivership in the face, it must be unbearably stressful. Surprisingly this is often a fallacy. Many of the most successful companies are just as paranoid about falling off their perch. Ever restless, they tend to be continually asking themselves what they're going to do for their next trick. They will on average employ higher quality people so there may be a more competitive environment between board members. Although what I am going to say may not seem right to many, I think the relationships between board members actually cause more pressure than the company's health. Think about the pressure caused in a successful business when someone takes all the credit and the contributions of others aren't recognised. Just look at the pressure caused by searching for a scapegoat when it's not going well. This often prevents a board getting on and sorting out the problem. Conversely many overcome some horrendous external shock or threat because they are well led and galvanised into action. Rates of change in the sector, the prevailing economic climate and a whole host of other obvious factors will also raise pressure. The major components, though, are people or issues you can't stand, a vicious cocktail of 'no point, no action, no fun', or worse, a ritual beating or bleating.

An interesting exercise is to ask each board member to put a mark where they think the board is on the effectiveness and pressure curve in Figure 2. You may find some surprisingly different points of view. Yet more instructive is to go a step further and ask those not on the board to mark where they think the board is. The chairman normally thinks his board's about three-quarters of the way up the left-hand side of the curve. Analysts or investors often think the board is only half-way up the same side (ie: fat cat territory). Meanwhile, the employees and frustrated customers or suppliers would put their mark way over on the right-hand side (ie: the land of the headless chickens). The power of 'seeing ourselves as others see us' is, as ever, especially useful.

WHERE?

Companies sometimes have a preference for holding meetings at locations other than their head office, perhaps a subsidiary location or overseas operation. There are mixed views on the wisdom of this approach. If the objective is to inform the board about a part of the business or meet the people, is this the best way to do it? The diversion of effort to a subsidiary location can be significant, the cost high and the logistical challenge over-demanding. Many board members and particularly canny independent directors may find visits of a different nature more useful for obtaining a deeper understanding.

WHAT ABOUT THE BOARDROOM ITSELF?

At one board more than slightly reluctant to accept change, I was sat down at a very cramped table and introduced in the following way: 'And now we're going to hear why we need another non-executive.' He might as well have added 'from this clever dick sitting on my right'. This was approximately three hours into the meeting. Regrettably we were only half way through the agenda. Perhaps the cramped seats or maybe the boredom led to my somewhat aggressive response: 'I'm terribly sorry. I thought I was here to talk about replacing non-executives, not adding more. Anyway the table's not big enough for anyone else.' Suddenly the three septuagenarian non-executives sat bolt upright in their chairs. One of them rather supportively from my point of view said: 'The lad's right you know, we can't afford a new table.'

Boardrooms obviously must suit their purpose. Light, airy and erring on the cool side seems to represent a general preference. As is an uncramped, dark and highly polished table which is wide enough and not creaking. A good measure of wide enough might be 'where you can't kick the person opposite'. Some, however, prefer a horseshoe shape facilitating the use of visual aids for those presenting to the board. In choosing this style you need to be careful not to lose some of the intimacy of the oval approach.

With regard to temperature you can always borrow the well-known airline hostess trick of turning the heat up or down to get the passengers asleep or awake at the right time. Not having the plugs, projectors, light and other basics in the right place also crops up surprisingly frequently as a minor irritant.

Of more importance are the chairs – comfortable, but not soporific, quiet and certainly not those 'slippy hot ones' or the terribly low ones which make shorties like me end up with our chins where our elbows should be. Deciding where people sit is another issue. Should they always sit in the same place? You also need to avoid interruptions, welcome though they occasionally might be. In summary it's important to get all the domestic arrangements right otherwise 'people can waste a lot of time moaning about the coffee' or worse, can become downright grumpy.

WHERE TO SIT?

In smaller companies with three or six board members this clearly isn't an issue. When the numbers are greater where people sit can affect the effectiveness of the meeting. Figure 4 shows a model which seems popular amongst boards of around ten. Don't forget though that quite a lot of grown ups, particularly those possessing moderate egos, aren't always comfortable with being told where to sit. Just as many people prefer the random method as those with a passion to plan as much as possible.

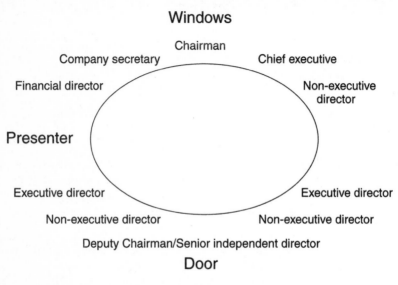

Figure 4   *Where to sit?*

The seating plan in Figure 4 has been designed with the following in mind:

- The chairman and the deputy chairman should have a complete field of view, almost windscreen-wiper like.
- They also should be opposite each other for increased 'winkability'.
- The company secretary should be between the chairman and the finance director to provide papers and prompts when required.
- A chairman always has their back to the window. Being opposite the door they can see all comers and goers.
- The chief executive sits next to the chairman to emphasise unity.

- To avoid the non-executives sitting as a group, a noughts and crosses method has been used to mix them up with the remaining executives.
- For convenience keep the positions of the chairman, deputy chairman, chief executive, finance director and company secretary the same at each meeting but change the positions of the rest.
- If you have a board lunch before or afterwards have completely different positions.

WHAT INFORMATION BEFOREHAND?

Many famous disasters including the Charge of the Light Brigade have occurred because of erroneous information. Many more have been made on the basis of no information. It's clearly vital for a board to get the right information at the right time and in a form it can digest at appropriate speed. The right information appears to be accurate and concise fact, ensuring the directors know the current and most likely future position of the company, plus enough supporting information to enable proper debate and decision on discussion items. The right time appears to be at least a week ahead of the meeting, but not so far ahead that too much time is spent at the meeting providing updates.

The right manner is in short succinct reports with as much represented graphically as possible and the real issues made abundantly clear. Using colour coding so that different items are always easily picked out is also popular, ie agenda white, financial papers always in yellow and so on. Beware, though, because quite the prettiest board papers I've ever seen turned out to be the most misleading. There's something magical about a computer-generated graph that takes many of us in. Changing the format from meeting to meeting whilst carefully avoiding confusion or generating suspicion can provoke a better understanding. Some boards now use pre-board briefings for those not up to speed on a particular issue. This obviously needs care as it can be used as an excellent way for an overly autocratic chief executive to get the right answers from the board.

So what is the typical length of board papers and what do they consist of in effective and happy boards?

The regular items usually consist of:

- *an agenda* (one page – you know you've got problems if there are more);
- *minutes from last time* (two or three pages);
- *management accounts pack* (ten pages);
- *papers relating to specific agenda items* (anywhere from 1 to 20 pages each).

An amusing fact emerged when I was researching this area. When asked what they consider to be the ideal length of board papers in total for a meeting, most chairmen gave me a number half the size their own were in practice.

A good company secretary will guide a novice in preparing a board paper on a specific item, giving useful advice as to the format, length and style required. In looking at board papers used by a whole range of companies a typical profile of 'Purpose', 'Background', 'Issues' and 'Recommendations' was clear.

WHEN SHOULD BOARD MEMBERS RECEIVE THESE PAPERS?

Most boards circulate papers a week in advance of the meeting. However, I do remember being chastised by one managing director for introducing 'a hopeless independent director'. His complaint was that the board's latest member hadn't read his board papers before the meeting. Worse, this was the second time it had happened. I was particularly concerned by this as it seemed most unlike the individual concerned who in my view was a highly diligent character. Perhaps the papers were just too long or not relevant? I diplomatically enquired whether this was the case. 'Of course not,' came the response. So I asked, 'Well, when did he get the papers, he wasn't away on holiday was he?' 'No, of course not, they were at reception for him to collect as normal just before the meeting.' You will no doubt be thinking that the independent director is still at fault for allowing this to happen. You're right. In the early 'getting to know you' stages of a new appointment this is an easy trap to fall into, especially when trying to build a rapport. Hindsight usually suggests though that is is well worth the pain and the risk of upsetting the relationship at a delicate stage to set the tone and establish the ground rules. By using a clear appointment letter from the company to the independent director this and other related pitfalls can be neatly avoided. A copy of a menu-style appointment letter is included in Appendix III.

HOW DOES A BOARD CALIBRATE THE INFORMATION IT IS PROVIDED WITH?

'The addition is correct, Wilkins, but where is the money?'

Of course there are some canny operators who have an uncanny knack of knowing when the most eloquently presented and well researched proposals just don't make sense. Getting the green light – sorry, gaining board approval – for a new product launch or major capital project is where these people prove invaluable. Their most telling questions tend to be 'Who says?' 'What are the competition working on?' 'Why will anyone buy it?' 'Who's building/supplying it?' 'Do they know what they're doing?' and my favourite 'But what's it for?'

9-5

'I find it simply amazing that what we know as just good business is perceived by the public as greed.'

Even if you are lucky enough to have a board of innately shrewd operators it is still vital to get your perspective right. In this situation the 'who says?' question proves particularly powerful. Questions which focus on the way in which the research, market or otherwise, has been conducted can also produce amusing responses. Most of our decisions are still based upon too much internal information and not enough calibration with the real world. The rapid rise in corporate tourism and the greater degree of openness these days is an interesting and healthy development. People love talking about their business, especially if it's successful. We all have learned the power of 'talking to our customers'. Some have even listened. The really smart people have also avoided giving them questionnaire fatigue in the process. I am not sure, though, that we have gone quite as far along this learning curve with suppliers, customers and employees. We often have an unrealistically high or low view of them and it may be far too general and not based on any real hard fact. Independent directors can clearly bring experiences from the other situations they are involved in. What surprises me is how few boards have other external visitors to broaden their view.

Another increasingly critical area relates to decisions made on major investments in information technology. In a sense this is back to who sits on the board. There is bound to be considerable anxiety over the big IT decisions. We are always anxious when the importance of a decision is high and our understanding of the subject is low, since the whole of the business will know if we've got it wrong. Most of us are also naturally suspicious of the IT salesmen and consultants whose advice is laced with vested interest. Surprising then that so few boards ensure they have enough IT awareness amongst the boardroom team and they receive so little IT training. By implication most IT decisions are really taken by the IT director who is often the finance director as well. We then sack them when they get it wrong. The sacking makes us feel less guilty but the business is still left with the same system. This is not to suggest that the whole of the board should become computer freaks or nerds, merely that they need to be aware of the possibilities and the risks in a bit more depth. Growing numbers of business people at all levels are visiting other companies to see their systems in operation – another healthy trend.

A large amount of time is spent in producing analysing and reading board papers in the belief that they are the key input to a fundamental decision. As a consequence there is little chance of the average board member running out of reading material. Yet for many it is what they hear before, during or after the meeting that will really drive their thinking, not what they read. Having the discipline to go through the process of writing a detailed board paper providing an analysis of options, costs, risks and rewards on a subject ought to be useful. What matters is not necessarily what you see written before you but the rigorous process the operators have had to go through to persuade. There is, however, a dilemma here in the word processor, spreadsheet driven, multi-media age we live in. When canvassing views of people on this subject there was considerable support for the more disciplined approach from board members. Less so from the producers of such reports. Funny that. A slightly paternal or matriarchal feel emerged – board members complaining that this will hurt us more than it will hurt you and so on.

Although they were in a very small minority several people I talked to who were just below main board told me some slightly disturbing things. The most extreme of these said:

> *'It didn't matter what the facts were. As long as you put it in a form the old buffers could easily digest, they would approve what you wanted. They never argued with spreadsheets or computerised graphs – only opinions. So the trick is to work your opinions into a chart or a spreadsheet assumption.'*

If there has been research conducted externally there is sometimes a debate as to whether it's better to give board members the originals or summaries produced by executives. A fair number of independent directors I know prefer the originals – suspicious lot. When asked why, they usually said that they were suspicious of the quality of consultants in general and felt that seeing the real work gave them a much better feel for the rigour and professionalism – thus giving them a feel also for how much weight these views should carry. My observation on this topic is that a huge amount depends upon the trust in which board members hold each other both in terms of honesty and competence. To try to generalise is dangerous. If you can't trust the executives to pick decent consultants then perhaps a deeper problem exists.

'Talk to a few peasants! You might learn something!'

This cartoon is not meant to be derogatory in any way or to show that a CEO is a modern day king or queen cocooned in their own little magic kingdom with boardroom colleagues. However, it is generally true that most board members live in a slightly different world to the majority of their customers and employees. Keeping a grip on the real world is tricky. The only way for many is to have regular doses of it. This doesn't just mean buying a tabloid newspaper every day, it means talking – and more importantly listening – to people at all levels and places inside and outside. In most of the really serious underperformers you tend to find a better idea of what the problems are and what needs doing to fix them from the most junior employees. Rule number one for most turnaround experts is firing the company prat. This is the person, usually fairly senior, who has no respect amongst customers or staff. Dizzy with their meteoric progress, they don't really know what they're doing and, what's worse, they can't stop doing it.

WHAT PRE-DISCUSSION SHOULD TAKE PLACE?

'So you would say your imminent failure is all down to the Finance Director you chose then'.

A thorny issue for chairmen is how far they should go in shaping discussions before the meeting. There is a broad consensus that chairmen should be extremely well prepared and they should sound out other directors before the meeting on contentious matters. They must, however, avoid 'putting the muscle on' or 'leading the witness'. Some chairmen pride themselves on the fact that they can and do write the minutes before the meeting and seldom have to change them. What, then, is the point of the meeting?

Sir Derek Birken, former Chairman of RTZ, had a clear view on this. He told me in his wonderfully direct and robust way that:

'I've no time for all this pre-meeting and sounding out stuff or for political boards. The chairman's job is to ensure there's an atmosphere of trust and cohesive team.'

Interestingly, Sir Christopher Hogg is of like mind:

'The board's overriding responsibility is to develop the company, which is far more about tough-minded discussion between executives and non-executives in an atmosphere of trust than it is about spinning endless webs of process around the executives on the assumption that evil will otherwise triumph.'

WHAT SHOULD BE ON THE AGENDA?

I guess this is the crunch topic once you've assembled the right people. Sir Christopher Hogg described this to me as 'really the most difficult bit'. Almost always the hardest part is obtaining the right balance between strategic and operational issues. For many debate tends to follow the classic curve shown in Figure 5 in terms of time and focus, with future issues receiving less attention.

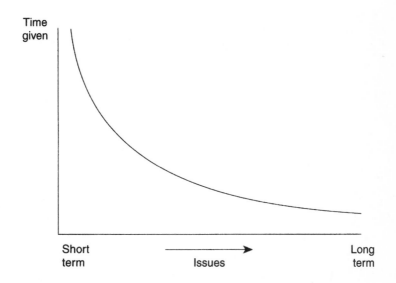

Figure 5   *Time/focus curve*

Most boards really have only six or seven key things to get right each year. Yet few of us really take the time to sit down in advance and decide what these are likely to be and then allocate the board's time accordingly. It can be very difficult to figure out what these six or seven things are in advance. There will inevitably be at least one major event during the year which alters the board's priorities. Hiding behind this excuse can be easy but there is considerable benefit to debating and gaining agreement as a board on what the critical issues are.

In underperforming companies you often find that one of these key items for the board to get right is strategy. At one board where I was asked along to see if they needed a non-executive it quickly became crystal clear that the company didn't have a strategy. They were really in three quite distinct businesses. Unfortunately they believed they were only in one. There was a strong belief that they had no competition because no one competitor spanned their complete product range. They did, however, have fierce competition in each segment.

At a suitable moment in the meeting the chairman turned to me and said: 'You've heard our debate this morning and met us all. Now tell us what on earth a non-exec could do for us.' My reply was that it would be arrogant on the basis of a couple of hours to give a detailed response but it did seem to me that someone objective might help develop the strategy. I was careful not to say 'get a strategy'. 'What the hell are you on about?' he said, obviously warming to me. 'The strategy is perfectly clear to all of us and we're in complete agreement on it, aren't we?' There was a rather helpful 'Um yes', 'Well kind of' response from the others, enabling me to suggest: 'An interesting experiment, perhaps when I'm gone, is to quickly go round the table and each say what you each believe the company's strategy to be.' A wry smile came from the finance director. Unfortunately the chairman noticed and pounced. 'Good idea. Let's do it now, Jim [the hapless Finance Director], you go first.' Sad but true, each of the six board members then gave a completely different strategy covering the whole range of possibilities.

Talking about strategy can be a lot more fun than ensuring the business is properly under control. So boards that spend too much time on strategy and not enough on ensuring operational policies are appropriate can easily become unstuck. Striking the balance is an art that excellent chairman develop and nurture. Sir Derek Birkin felt strongly that if:

'A board has the right strategy then you find that operational matters don't consume too much time at board meetings. This is because major capital expenditure approvals, policy matters and so on will just naturally fit. If they don't then you need to revisit the strategy.'

A minimalist gardener, Sir Denys Henderson, former chairman of ICI plc, notes:

'You don't pick a plant up and look at its roots every six months. Strategy is a bit the same. You have to take your time to get it right and then avoid tinkering with it unnecessarily.'

Spending your time on what matters will help you to avoid feeling like the chap signing above. Sadly what matters is not always what you enjoy so this can be difficult to achieve in practice, particularly for an expansionist board full of gusto.

So what does a typical outline agenda for a high performing company look like?

AGENDA

Approval of previous Minutes and
Matters Arising

Formal approvals of matters requiring limited
discussion

Executives' Reports
    Chief Executive
    Finance Director

Operational Policy Issues

Strategic Issues

Any Other Business

This order is typically chosen so that the operational, procedural and compliance type issues can be quickly dispensed with enabling ample time for the more important and enjoyable strategic items. However, if you adopt this approach and then go back and look at what time was actually allocated to the strategic issues you can easily get frustrated at what little time was really spent. An excellent chairman will of course minimise the time spent on subjects which can be dealt with by pre-reading and committees of the board. The really excellent chairman will also ensure that people have pre-read and do understand what is being approved.

One trick I have used is to jot down on the agenda before a board meeting how long each agenda item should take, then to the right how long I expect it to take, then to the right again how long it did take. If the chairman and I are getting on well I'll ask him how long he thought we spent. There is usually quite a difference between these four sets of times. The comparisons can be instructive.

If you having problems spending enough time on the strategic issues one technique to try is to switch the order of the operational and strategic issues for discussion to alternate board meetings, ie discuss the strategic issues before the operational at every other meeting. If you are having very severe problems, try skipping the executives' reports occasionally as well. When looking at the proportion of time taken by individual items the executives' reports are the ones which often take the longest and which people – especially the CEO – think takes much less time than they actually do. A technique used by John Foulds, former Chairman of the Halifax Building Society, to set expectations is simply to jot down the time anticipated for discussion beside each agenda item.

Another technique used by larger organisations where the nature of their business requires board approval of a high volume of operational items is to split the agenda in two. The first part, the 'summary' agenda, is for items requiring approval but no discussion. This is then followed by a 'discussion' agenda. The most sophisticated use of this I came across was at the Federal Reserve System which of course has the additional delight of holding a number of meetings open to the public. Only a tightly defined group of matters are allowed onto the summary agenda. A review process ensures that there is a relevant split between summary items and those brought to the board for discussion. This approach is found to be highly effective in large organisations and can easily be adopted in smaller companies.

For those fascinated by the subject of what might be the ideal number of items to have on an agenda, when the Top Pay Research Group and 3i did their 1999 poll of 1418 companies they found the range shown in Figure 6. I suspect little has changed since.

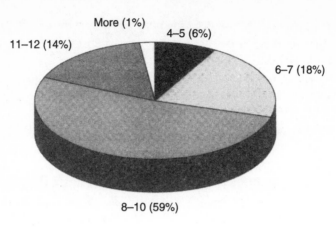

More (1%)

4–5 (6%)

11–12 (14%)

6–7 (18%)

8–10 (59%)

Figure 6   *How many items on the agenda?*

WHO SHOULD SET THE AGENDA?

Usually the chairman and the company secretary set the agenda. The company secretary focuses on the legal and compliance issues, the chairman on everything else. Most boards allow any board member to submit items for consideration by these two. In practice the chief executive will also have significant input and be shaping the chairman's thinking.

WHAT IS ALLOWABLE UNDER 'ANY OTHER BUSINESS'?

This was an issue of concern to several of the company secretaries I spoke to. One had a simple definition:

'Anything for which a board view or approval is essential, that can't wait until the next scheduled board meeting and only arose as an issue worthy of board attention since the board papers were dispatched. However, certainly not the approval of an acquisition that hasn't had discussion at a previous meeting.'

One other finance director whom I mentioned this to said:

'If only we'd had that rule there'd be at least ten dog companies we wouldn't have bought.'

AWAY DAYS

If there are approximately 1700 companies listed in the UK and on average they spend two days a year on board away days then that is 3400 days spent by each of the 5200 executive, 4600 non-executive and 1700 chairman taking part. Thirty-nine million days. And that's just listed companies.

So a lot of senior and expensive resource is committed to this form of meeting. But how effective is the away day format? I hear very mixed views. Some find them highly effective and absolutely essential in ensuring the company has the right strategy. Others find them an energy-sapping, expensive chore which has no positive effect on the company at all.

A few years ago when I was writing a play on strategy I tried to see if there was any best practice guidance published on running away days. To my surprise I couldn't find any. So I rang around the business schools to see if they had done anything on this. As many business school professors facilitate away days I thought they were bound to have something on it. Sadly, there was very little. Only my good friend Murray Steele at Cranfield had written something. Together we talked about this and then I informally canvassed the views of a wide group of directors to see what their experiences of away days were. In summary the response was 'mixed'.

What were the issues for those who felt their away days were ineffective? There were several:

- lack of clarity about the objectives for the away day;
- over-ambitious agendas;
- inadequate preparation;
- no follow-through post away day;
- poor choice of venue;
- weak external facilitation;
- over-dominant chairman or chief executive inhibiting real debate;
- over-dependence on finance director to do all the work beforehand;
- getting the executives out of functional or business line representative mode;
- personal agendas inhibiting open debate;
- poor experiences for non-board members attending;
- away days becoming ritualistic and too easy.

So Murray and I produced the list of tips below:

- Be clear on the purpose of the away day and your desired outcomes. (e.g. selection from a number of well-researched strategic options).
- Decide early enough whether to use an external facilitator and if so select one relevant to the issues being discussed who will do the necessary homework.
- The chairman or CEO should brief the facilitator about the team dynamics, politics and taboo subjects. (the facilitator will then have to interpret skillfully!).
- External facilitators, if used, need to be credible with executive and non-executive directors; they are not there to lecture but to facilitate. They must be prepared to challenge the chairman and chief executive in the same way as they are prepared to challenge other directors. They must be able to maintain an objective and neutral approach but also be engaged and have a clearly defined process for running the day which combines an element of flexibility. Finally they have to assist the chairman in generating the right atmosphere.
- Decide whether there will be non-board members present and if so brief them appropriately.
- Hold the away day offsite.
- Don't allow interruptions except in case of emergency.
- Don't start with an operational board meeting.
- Participants should be prepared to challenge each other, in particular to surface differences – a key to success is the quality of debate, both in content and challenge.
- No one has a monopoly on wisdom so no one should dominate the debate.
- Responsibility for implementing actions arising should be clear.
- Follow up and review the effectiveness of the day as part of your annual board review.
- Finally, the 'socialising' of the board is an important part of building a strong and cohesive board, so ensure that there is sufficient emphasis and time devoted to this.

BOARD CALENDARS

Historically the board calendar was just a list of dates, times and venues for the board meetings for the coming year. Increasingly companies large and small seem to be making much more sophisticated use of this simple planning tool. They seem to be used to:

■ ensure specific items are discussed at the appropriate time;
■ provide time for sufficient preparatory work to be performed;
■ make sure the less interesting, routine but essential items are not forgotten about;
■ remove clutter and avoid repetition of discussion.

Any calendar must be considered to be a plan and not something cast in tablets of stone. Issues will inevitably emerge during the year which are of significance to the board and which require considerable thought and discussion. It is sensible therefore not to overcrowd the calendar. Many Company Secretaries seem to have this off to a fine art and plan two years in advance which seems to balance rigour and flexibility.

An example of a calendar for a medium sized private company is provided with the CHEMCO case study in Appendix I.

The calendar overleaf is a fairly normal one for a plc.

January
29   11 AM   Remuneration Committee – Strategy Review
      2 PM   Board

February
26   10 AM   Environmental Committee

March
19   11 AM   Audit Committee – General View
      2 PM   Board

April
16   10 AM   Remuneration Committee – 1997 guidelines

May
4   2 PM   Regulatory Committee
20   6 PM   Board Cocktail function for key shareholders and customers
21   9 AM   Remuneration Committee – Review Executive Directors
      11 AM   Audit Committee – Annual Accounts
      2 PM   Board

June
2   6 PM   Accounts Board Committee
8   Preliminary Announcement of Results
16   Annual Accounts posted to shareholders

July
9   11 AM   Annual General Meeting
      2 PM   Board

October
1   9 AM   Audit Committee Annual Report
      2 PM   Board
13   *Evening* Strategy Away Day
14   *All Day*

November
3   2 PM   Environmental Committee
19   9 AM   Audit Committee – Half Yearly Accounts
24   2 PM   Board
25   6 PM   Accounts Board Committee – Half Yearly Accounts
26   Interim Statement

December
6   10 AM   Regulatory Committee
17   *Evening* Staff Christmas Party

HOW IS THE RIGHT ATMOSPHERE CREATED?

Let us suppose that you have managed to assemble the boardroom team of your dreams. You are also lucky enough to have the ideal room to hold your meeting in. Your agenda is perfectly pitched and there is a model set of accompanying board papers. What else can you do to maximise the chances of having an excellent board meeting?

Engendering an atmosphere of energy, purpose. seriousness and trust will be a natural objective for any thoughtful chairman. They will know they are getting it right because their boards enjoy and value the board meetings. The chairman's role during the board meeting is discussed in more detail later. But what can be done before a meeting takes place to ensure there is the right atmosphere?

Boosting the team spirit through extra curricular activities is an established method. Inviting the independent directors along to social events for customers, suppliers or staff is another. An independent director who is a real master of this art was Sir Max Williams. Sir Max, a former deputy chairman of 3i, has long been at the top of people's invitation list for such events. His perfect blend of charm, humility, brains and good humour have added much to the 3i board spirit over the period he was a director. Moreover, our customers and staff would come away from such events not only being impressed by him but with a feeling that we had genuine humans on the board. Showing humility can be difficult. It may not come naturally to all on a board. Having a seasoned campaigner like Sir Max around helps set the tone for the rest.

Board dinners on the eve of a meeting are popular especially amongst those who hold their meetings in locations where people will need to be there the night before. However, not everyone is smitten with this idea. Some I spoke to felt that this was the worst thing you could do with a bunch of workaholic fifty- or sixty-somethings. When I asked one of them why the reply was:

'Well, staying up way past your bedtime and having more to drink than normal after a long journey doesn't exactly make for a perky contribution the next morning does it?'

Another believed that the scheduled dinner the night before can inhibit some of the best independent directors taking appointments because of the logistics. He said that:

'The logistics can sometimes make a nice idea impossible. It is better to get the right people there for when it matters than to have some of the nicer refinements.'

The logistical challenges for board directors whatever the size of the company can be high but if you can arrange it so that you can travel together it can be productive. There is nothing quite like a long journey together to build on a good developing relationship or to crystallise your decision to end a poor one.

'The meeting is going to require great delicacy. Just between us, I'm glad we didn't bring Rayburn along.'

Having someone responsible for complacency avoidance is another essential role. As Raymond Seitz says:

'A bit of worrying does you good.'

One of the things he thinks that it is important for a new independent director to do is:

'To figure out what they do worry about and what they should worry about.'

'You must also avoid being frightened by your own shadows and becoming paranoiac.'

A board that can balance its sense of seriousness and purpose with a good sense of humour can enhance a business's performance considerably. Many of the masters of the art of chairmanship possess a keen sense of humour. Few of them are perceived as clowns or would tolerate court jester types for long.

Family companies have an atmosphere all of their own. The history of the family and those deeply personal interrelationships generated from the shared trauma and joy inevitably reach into the family company boardroom. When talking about succession in family companies at an event in Leeds one night I said:

'It must be terribly difficult to be objective about people you love.'

A classic Yorkshire tyke from the back was then heard to say:

'Aye, I know, it can be even harder if you hate them to death.'

One family company chairman I know who has been tremendously successful but plays his cards very close to his chest is wrestling with this issue of succession at the moment. He has two offspring both of whom are being groomed for potential succession. Both have been trained well, have had periods outside the business and are generally considered to be of high potential. The father very proudly told me recently that although he had absolutely no intention of retiring for years he had finally decided who would succeed him should he fall under a bus. 'Who?' I rather nosily enquired. 'I'm not telling a soul, not even Joan (his wife), and I'm certainly not putting it in the will. I don't want arguing over that.' 'So how will anyone know who it is?' 'Errrrr.'

Communication is always more difficult when emotional sensitivity is high.

'Your mother just called to remind you she owns controlling interest in this company'

SOME INTERNATIONAL COMPARISONS

I should say up front in this section that I don't believe in national stereotyping and that there is probably as much variability of board practice within any country as between different countries. However, there are cultural and legal differences between countries which do affect the way in which boards operate. Corporate history and the strength of a nation's capital markets also have an influence.

So how does the atmosphere differ?

USA

There are many things which make the way that boards operate in the USA different: the dominance of the President and Chief Executive officer role, the all-pervading influence of lawyers, the scale of ambition both personally and corporately and the culture of selling, to name just four.

In the USA the President and CEO role is effectively a combined Chairman and Chief Executive. Although there may be a chairman of the board they are very much the junior figure in terms of power and authority. It is the President who picks the Chairman, not the other way around. As one senior US headhunter once put it to me:

'No self-respecting CEO would want it any other way!'

A rules-based approach to company law has also had a big influence for good and bad, as I will describe later. When it comes to ambition there must be something in the water in the USA. The belief in what it might be possible to achieve is an endearing feature of the economy and has powered many of the world's great businesses and business leaders. Anyone who has read the biographies of the titans of the gilded age, Rockefeller, Carnegie, Ford, JP Morgan and others, knows this is not a product of the recent times but something deep in the pysche.

Perhaps the thing not much written about is what I describe as *'the culture of selling'*.

In order to explain this I need to indulge in a little political incorrectness and national stereotyping for a moment. It sometimes seems to many Europeans and Asians that Americans are genetically modified to sell. Taken positively, this is the much admired *'can do, get on with it'* attitude that has made the USA the number one economy and the superpower that it is today on so many fronts. Alternatively, it is sometimes hard for non-Americans to know where you are in the fog of bullshit. Personally I have a strong preference for *'can do'* people over *'analytical whingers'* but I have seen many occasions in the USA and outside where a team whipping itself up into a peak of *'team delusion'* could have done with a good old German or English cynic.

National traits would lead you to think that in the UK a board meeting would be a procedure-bound process and in the USA it would be a much more free-flowing 'Hi, Y'all, let's go for it' atmosphere. However, many feel that the reverse is true. Raymond Seitz, former US ambassador to the UK and an experienced board member on both sides of the Atlantic, once said:

'The English boards are much lighter and more fun. The US legal scene tends to sterilise a board and provides a tedious quality which it is hard to get away from.'

'Tom, I'd like you and your lawyer to meet my lawyer and my lawyer's lawyer.'

Viewing everything through the prism of potential litigation must inevitably reduce the level of risk-taking and entrepreneurial spirit for which the world admires America so much. This 'creeping legal fungus growing around a board' as Sir Christopher Hogg describes it, means that the atmosphere in the US may be much more about questioning judgements made than making them. No doubt everyone has their own favourite nutty US legal case: a popular one is the 'fast food chain sued for serving its coffee so hot you get burnt if you spill it'. My personal favourite was reported in an excellent article in the *Financial Times* entitled 'Trigger Happy Justice'. It involved a class action brought by a group of Northwest Airlines passengers for 'false imprisonment'. The basis of the claim was apparently that they were left stranded at Detroit Airport for several hours during a snow storm. Anyone seriously worried may like to feed their concern by buying a copy of *The Death of Common Sense: How the Law is Suffocating America* by Philip Howard.

Don't get too worried. I'm glad to report that there is still entertainment to be had at some US board meetings. Here are two slightly more unusual techniques for engendering a spirit of fun. The first is from the chairman of a rapidly growing technology business who:

> "Bangs a J Arthur Rank style gong during board meetings when there is something to celebrate.'

Amusingly his business is in mobile communications.

A slightly wackier method for which I can't imagine many takers in Europe:

> 'Before we start each meeting the President plays Aretha Franklin's 'R-E-S-P–E–C-T' on the compact disc player. Those who want to are encouraged to karaoke along.'

Formal board meetings in the US are generally more procedural than in Europe and I can't imagine that there is too much singing or banging of gongs. Yet they do use more frequent informal and social gatherings of the board as a way of building team spirit and knowledge.

No comparison of board life involving the USA could omit the impact of the collapse of the seventh biggest US listed company Enron Inc in 2001 and the subsequent Sarbanes – Oxley act in 2002. Other celebrated governance scandals such as Worldcom and the case of domestic goddess Martha Stewart's insider dealing followed, but Enron was the key event.

The shock waves are still reverberating not just for US business or businesses outside the USA with US listings. The accounting profession has been impacted worldwide and country by country governance practices have been reviewed and amended. As one might expect, these reviews have been significant in some countries and superficial in others.

Much has been written about the collapse of Enron, which also brought its auditors Arthur Andersen down with it. Enron had become an icon of capitalist success, its sophisticated management and financial techniques much admired and its management heroes. I was lucky enough to attend a course at Harvard Business School where the Enron Chairman Ken Lay gave a very impressive speech about the company, the value it had created, the wonderful careers it had made possible and its potential. No one present would have thought that just months later his company would be one of the best known in the world for the destruction of value to customers, suppliers, shareholders, staff and pensioners and for bringing down one of the world's most admired accounting practices. Still, the lawyers got to make a lot of money again!

The political reaction to Enron was swift and strong. The US government could not allow anything so visible to undermine the moral authority of capitalism. How could it preach the benefits of *'truth, justice and the American way'* without acting? Confidence in the New York Stock Exchange and the accounting profession could not be allowed to be challenged so significantly without response. So the result was the Sarbanes–Oxley act.

Sarbanes–Oxley certainly gained the attention of all CEOs of companies with US listings. Initial reactions to use a quote of President George W Bush for a different setting (the Iraq war), were chiefly ones of *'shock and awe'*.

Maryland senator Paul Sarbanes and Ohio congressman Michael Oxley were two lawyers who were both knowledgeable and credible. They were credible to business, the Senate and Congress and neither appeared to have vested interests

So what was in their act and why the *'shock and awe'*? The Act contained a great deal of detail, as one might expect, but here are the main points in summary:

■ A new 'Accounting Oversight Board' was formed under the oversight of the Securities and Exchange Commission (SEC) and accounting standards were brought under federal regulation.

■ The board was given the power to enforce the professional standards designed to provide independence of firms that audit public companies.

■ There were highly prescriptive new criteria for acceptable non-audit work.

■ Auditors were banned from doing audits where the CEO, CFO or Chief Accounting Officer had worked for the firm of auditors within a year of the audit.

- The audit committee would now be held clearly responsible for the audit, and audit committee members were no longer allowed to collect any fees from the company other than as a board and committee member.
- The company's principal officer and financial officers are required to certify the accuracy of the financial condition of the company as presented to the SEC. The Act also mandated forfeiture of executive compensation if there is non-compliance with the Act's procedures.
- A range of additional disclosure requirements relating to off balance sheet financing, conflicts of interests and executive share ownership.
- A range of requirements in relation to stock market analysts, their independence and the disclosure of their financial interests in companies.
- The Securities and Exchange Commission (SEC) was given the power of corporate governance oversight.

One other interesting aspect of Sarbanes–Oxley was the speed with which it took effect – many of its provisions took effect immediately, the rest within 30 days. This, combined with the power and conviction of the SEC, meant that things really did change very quickly.

So how did it go down? Deciding on the appropriate response was a challenge for boards and CEOs. Any hint of challenge to the Act might be taken by the press as if you had something to hide. However, immediate acceptance made it look like the titans were either weak or didn't realise the significant increase in personal risk and cost that they were agreeing to. In the end there was a bit of behind-the-scenes lobbying and they gritted their teeth and got on with it.

What will the long-term effect be? Sarbanes–Oxley will have raised the standards of governance. It must have put some people off being outside directors and forced some high calibre managers into the arms of the willing and able private equity industry. Inevitably it will deter some companies from other countries from having US listings. And of course it has been an absolute jamboree for lawyers.

The debate stirred up by Sarbanes–Oxley also led to some challenge around the absolute power of the combined role of President and CEO and the effectiveness of many Chairmen. This, I think, will be a healthy debate long term.

France

In France the equivalent of the UK plc, the German AG or US Inc is the SA. This stands for *Société Anonyme*. Private companies are normally a Société à Responsabilité (SARL). The two main components of a French board are the PDG (*président directeur général*) and the *conseil d'administration* (the board).

A PDG is supposed to be elected by a board who have been appointed by the shareholders. In practice the PDG is king. He chooses the board and the shareholders agree. His power and authority are much wider and greater than the CEO in an equivalent UK or US business. French corporate culture remains an elitist one in which the king – sorry, PDG – and his inner circle dominate. Management styles vary but many treat their boards with complete disdain and effectively as a rubber stamp. It is a sin of course for a royal subject to put the king in a position where he has to reveal ignorance on a subject or a weakness. Loyal subjects are expected to be in position for the king's arrival, which is customarily ten to 15 minutes after the scheduled start. Their king seldom feels the need to warm up his audience with a few jokes or other pleasantries. So the start and bulk of French board meetings are serious and formal in nature.

In spite of the law requiring all companies to have a formal board and hold board meetings, many smaller and private companies, the SARLs, don't have either in practice. Because the law requires it, they tend to have board meetings which never take place. At these so-called paper meetings members of the board are just asked to vote a certain way without any previous discussion or information on the issues involved. The individual head of the company, particularly a family one, is so dominant that the function of a board has never been very important. All members of the board usually come from the same family and they are joined by the family lawyer or some other 'right hand' closely associated with the family. Communication is informal and does not usually take place in what could be considered to be a boardroom.

Le conseil d'administration for the larger businesses tends to meet less frequently than an equivalently sized UK, US or German board. Normal form is for quarterly meetings. The board must have between three and 12 members. No more than a third can be executive. PDGs have a penchant for powerful bankers on their boards. There is also a limit on the number of directorships any individual can hold. No one can sit on more than eight boards. Usually these boards are fairly passive in successful companies. Research by 3i in France showed that in smaller businesses half have less than four people on the board.

Things may be changing in the public arena in France. A series of high profile difficulties, including Vivendi, combined with institutions, politicians and journalists jumping on the worldwide corporate governance bandwagon, will undoubtedly have an impact. Combine this with the natural French love of elegance and elaboration, the domination of the state, so many proud kings and the emergence of a few queens and you can expect an interesting time ahead.

Germany

Germany has a two-tier board system. These tiers are a management board known as *der Vorstand*, which runs the company, and a supervisory board known as *der Ausfsichtsrat* in the larger businesses and the *Beirat* for smaller, private companies. Supervisory boards monitor the performance of the management board. Germany's equivalent of the managing director, president, chief executive or *président directeur général* is the *Geschäftsführer*.

There are various rules for how boards should be organised and composed depending on their position and scale. The key rules are that:

- Every AG (*Aktiengesellschaft*), ie 'share company' must have a *Vorstand*.
- A small GmbH (*Gesellschaft mit beschränkter Haftung*), ie limited liability company of less than 500 employees, may have a single-tier board with shareholder elected directors only.
- In larger AG and GmbGH seats on the *Aufsichtsrat* are shared between shareholders and employees, two-thirds for shareholders and one third for employees. These companies must have a *Vorstand*.
- Major AGs with more than 2000 employees have a similar structure to the above, but the composition of their *Aufsichtsrat* is different. Half of the directors are shareholder representatives, the others represent the employees. The chairman is always a shareholder representative.

Unlike in the UK or the USA most public companies have a dominant shareholder with a least 25 per cent of the equity. These are generally not banks as is commonly thought.

Many *Vorstände* meet once a week and sometimes for a whole day. The *Vorstand* therefore is somewhat similar to the executive committees which operate in US and English businesses. The *Aufsichstrat* tends to meet three or four times a year. These meetings tend to be highly formal affairs largely focused on compliance and legal issues with little emphasis on the strategic aspects. A cultural tendency only to speak on something if you are qualified to do so tends also to lead to statements and opinions rather than debate. The lower level of merger and acquisition activity may also reduce the need to discuss shareholder issues at the board.

The debate over whether a two-tier system is better or not hasn't really been well developed. Much of the debate has been driven by 'the grass is greener on the other side' feelings. The reality is that a dominant chairman can rule equally well under either system. Indeed if you look at the *Mittelstand,* the medium to large private German companies which are the power house of the German economy, there is no doubt that in most of them the paternalistic owner calls the shots. Moreover, a number of high-profile scandals have led to increased public questioning over whether the two-tier approach really has been as effective as it has been made out. A lack of openness combined with that natural and endearing confidence of German businessmen to have absolute faith that their way is correct has tended in the past to allow them to win discussions. It has also inhibited the self-doubting Anglo-Saxons from questioning two-tier board effectiveness.

Another feature which clearly influences the style and behaviour of German boards is that cross shareholdings between companies and between companies and banks are more common. There has therefore been a greater mutual dependency than in many other countries – a healthy state of affairs in that good relations with shareholders have been more important. Considerable help has been available when required. However, some suggest that this has inhibited change and led to a lack of clarity of purpose for many businesses. It has also meant that the bankers have been able to quietly sort difficult situations out and persuade another client to absorb a business going under before it might formally fail.

The influence of German bankers has been much written about, partly because it has been more common for the banker to sit on the board. Whilst many believe this practice is a means of bankers supplementing their income I think it has far more to do with status. A local German banker is generally more highly regarded than his English equivalent so the business is delighted to have such a prominent figure on board. The banker is equally delighted to increase his influence.

From his point of view, however, the situation has become more risky. Seeing some of your most highly regarded colleagues in the newspapers and in court over recent major collapses has clearly put personal risk on the agenda.

Other issues which will affect the way German boards are conducted in the near future are the tensions created by the need to update working practices to remain cost competitive and the obvious tensions arising from the absorption of the former East Germany. The increasing globalisation of business and the accelerating pace of merger and acquisition activity as evidenced by the watershed deals of Daimler and Chrysler merging and Deutsche Bank's difficult acquisition of Bankers Trust have had a major influence. The high profile departure of the Chairman of BMW in 1999 also added to this cultural shift and heralded an era of greater openness. For many *Mittelstand* companies there are also succession issues which, as this is often a root cause of board disharmony, should make for an interesting time ahead.

TRAINING

'Watch me doing it badly, son, and you'll learn a lot.'

This is frankly how many learn the art of the boardroom. We learn by watching and partaking with the masters and at the expense of those not so adept. We are happy to pay handsomely to invest in training for most functional and management positions. However, our willingness to invest often stops the moment people join the board. Poor differentiation between management training and director training is another frequently heard complaint. Of course the cynics believe that the majority of money spent on training is wasted and misguided.

Raymond Seitz, the former US ambassador to London, is particularly interesting to talk to on boardroom training. In making his transition from the world of government to the world of commerce and in taking up his board appointment at Lehmans he was lucky enough to have a tailored programme to ensure that not only was he well prepared for his role as a director but that he also had a good grounding in what Lehmans was all about. Lehmans organised 15 three-hour sessions on what they did and the markets in which they operate. Additional general governance and financial training was provided by Price Waterhouse.

The Institute of Directors' courses on becoming directors and the differences between being a manager and a director are generally deemed to be good value. They are also well attended by real people – an important characteristic of any useful training course.

One other aspect of training and learning naturally inhibited by the process of a board meeting is experimentation. We seem reluctant to experiment in board meetings. Having got to the board there is a natural fear of being seen to be learning or getting it wrong. The stakes are considered to be too high. This is a shame, as we might develop more as board members and as a board as a whole if we were prepared to let go and try out different approaches. Done sensibly, not only can you learn a lot by experimenting a bit, you can also have more fun and are more likely to end up more effective as a result. Just thinking about it helps enormously. Asking others how they do it is equally instructive. At 3i we have found the case study sessions for directors to be the most useful activity in this area and to be the events which have most impact, ie people develop their approach as a result.

Another easy way to develop the board is to link the review of how the board is doing with trying to give everyone on the board some educational input relating to their board role each year. One heavyweight chairman with whom I discussed this point told me that he thought this an excellent idea:

'But don't get too clever about it. Try and mix the basic skills such as listening with something a bit more broadening like sending your most dour FD on a one-day American-style sales skills course.'

A ROUGH GUIDE TO HIGGS

What was 'Higgs'?

Early in 2002, in the aftermath of the Enron collapse in the USA, Marconi in the UK and other high profile corporate failures around the world, the UK Government asked Derek Higgs, a prominent city figure, to conduct a review of the role and effectiveness of non-executive directors. His report went to two cabinet ministers Patricia Hewitt (Department of Trade and Industry) and Gordon Brown (Chancellor of the Exchequer). Almost all of its recommendations were incorporated into the combined code for listed companies.

Although the review focused on larger corporate businesses, as with the earlier Hampel and Cadbury reviews, Higgs was asked to consider how any changes he recommended would impact on smaller companies.

Higgs' overall conclusion was that essentially the UK model of corporate governance was sound but there was an opportunity to improve through greater consistency of *'best practice'*. He summarized what was *'best practice'* in his report.

There was a very positive initial reaction on publication of the report in January 2003. Well, at least for the first few days. This, however, was then followed by a considerable and heated debate, especially over the role of the Senior Independent Director. Some of this debate was helpful and well informed and some of it was quite the opposite.

Sir Adrian Cadbury's well-accepted *'Comply or Explain'* principle, which Higgs adopted, was also challenged. The principle was that there may be specific circumstances where a company can justify not complying with the code; if this is the case then the company ought to be able to clearly explain why and others can then judge whether the specific non-compliance makes sense. However, many chairmen and companies felt that the approach of the institutional shareholders, their governance officers, the voting advisory groups and the press would lead to *'Comply or breach'* if they couldn't *'tick all their little boxes'*. In their view the reality was that they wouldn't be given the opportunity to explain and if they didn't adhere to the combined code in its entirety they would get hassle.

Interestingly, after a period of hot debate things settled down, most of the recommendations were or are being implemented without trauma and Derek became Sir Derek.

How was the review conducted?

In a fairly straightforward and pragmatic way. In line with the Labour Government's general approach to such reviews, but unlike the preceding Cadbury, Greenbury and Hampel reviews, no formal committee was established. A small team drawn from the DTI and the Treasury was provided and Higgs could then enlist support and elicit views from a wide range of other interested parties.

His process comprised:

- Extensive research
- Formal and informal consultation
- Analysis
- Formulation of proposals
- Testing of proposals
- Presentation to Government
- Publication
- Refinement and effecting change.

The poll conducted by MORI early on in the review of 650 directors, and the census taken of UK boards, were essential building blocks in the research. The census proved especially interesting in revealing the exact demographics of UK listed company boards.

The formal consultation process elicited over two hundred formal responses. As with any consultation process, the views provided included those from the blatantly self-serving to the cunningly disguised self-serving. Happily they also included many well-balanced and helpful responses as well.

What were the main conclusions?

As has been said earlier, Higgs concluded that the basic model in the UK was sound. He found great support for the principle of the unitary board and no demand to move to a continental European style two-tier system. The same degree of consensus occurred when it came to the benefit of separating the roles of Chairman and Chief Executive.

It was no surprise that he found widespread recognition that the role of the non-executive had become more challenging and that their risks had increased ahead of their rewards. Higgs did, however, find a divergence of view on whether there was a shortage of the right people to fill these roles. Yet he did say that there may be a shortage of people willing and able to take on the role of Chairman.

He felt strongly that appointment processes could become more rigorous and transparent and that the current supply was being drawn from too narrow a pool.

Challenging the popular view that there were a large number of people holding multiple directorships, he pointed to the evidence. Only a quarter of non-executives amongst his census held more than one listed appointment.

When it came to the diversity issue he simply stated the obvious, that we have some way to go in the UK. The review by Laura Tyson from London Business School picked up this point. Yet there has been little real progress since.

On board reviews and evaluating board performance he acknowledged that this was a developing art and that there was a need to avoid a triumph of form over substance. He avoided being too prescriptive but did say that the board should state in its annual report whether such performance evaluation is taking place and how it is undertaken. So I guess we can look forward to lots of reports saying that *'The board has put in place a rigorous annual review of its performance and is supported by XX, leading firm of consultants, in the process'*.

I have made reference to many of the more detailed points arising out of Higgs in the relevant places elsewhere in this book but here is a quick summary.

Higgs' recommendations

Nothing earth shattering. In summary, 'clarity'. Clarity, with respect to the role of the board and the roles of its members, clarity, with respect to appointments and processes and, finally, clarity in terms of communications between the board and shareholders.

The full review can be obtained from the DTI and the recommendations are described in considerable detail in another book by the author, *Tolley's Non-Executive Directors' Handbook*.

The main area of controversy was over the articulation of the role of the Senior Independent Director('SID') and in particular the interaction the SID would have with institutional shareholders. This and the early reporting of it got the backs of many chairmen up; who felt he was challenging their power and undermining their role, so challenged the whole thing. Further fuel was added to the fire by the suggestion that chairmen should not chair nominations committees. Once things settled down, this latter point was revised and people realised that all he was saying was that there ought to be a clearly designated senior independent director to whom institutions could go if they had a problem with the chairman.

A rough guide to the 1998 Hampel committee's report is contained in Appendix IV for reference.

What happened to his recommendations?

They were incorporated into the combined code for listed companies and to date there have been few implementation issues for companies.

During ...

'Managing the Meeting'

'The meeting will come to order.'

Responsibility for managing the process of the meeting is usually shared between the chairman and the company secretary with the latter focusing on the detailed preparations, corporate governance, compliance issues and minutes, while the chairman concentrates on the conduct of the meeting itself. My research on this subject revealed that the role of the company secretary is much underrated and there are several acting as quasi chairmen.

WHAT'S THE ROLE OF THE CHAIRMAN?

There are numerous books and papers on this subject, some of which you will find listed in the bibliography, including Sir Adrian Cadbury's excellent *Corporate Governance and Chairmanship*. I won't make any attempt to regurgitate or plagiarise them here. A few years ago I developed a menu-style appointment letter from a company to its new chairman or independent director (Appendix III). In this letter the following is proposed with regard to the role of the chairman:

- to organise the composition, business and efficiency of the board;
- to lead the board in the determination of its strategy and in the achievement of its objectives;
- to ensure the board has accurate and clear visibility of results achieved and likely future trends;
- to ensure board committees are properly established, composed and operated;
- to ensure effective relationships are maintained with all major stakeholders in the business – customers, shareholders, employees, suppliers, government, local community, industry, etc;
- to enhance the company's public standing and image overall;
- to develop a strong working relationship with the chief executive/managing director and ensure there is a clear definition and agreement of the division of responsibility.

In a private equity or venture capital context the owners would also require the chairman to:

- implement the investment and exit strategy;
- judge the executive team on their operational and financial performance;
- be responsible for management change.

SO WHAT ABOUT THE CHAIRMAN'S ROLE AT THE BOARD MEETINGS THEMSELVES?

Probably the best way to answer this question is through some observations and anecdotes on easy traps to fall into. Most of these spring out of experiences with the over-dominant. These naturally are the

most memorable. However, the under-dominant or over-consensual chairman is often worse for the business.

Responsibility for the quality of the debate rests with the chairman. According to Sir Denys Henderson the chairman's role at the meeting is 'to synthesise the optimum decision from the various experts around the table'. It is not always easy for a chairman, especially one who was the builder or saviour of the business, to avoid 'being the meeting'. Despite the best of intentions it is all too easy to give out the wrong signals. The separation of Chairman's and CEO's roles is now perceived wisdom in the UK and enshrined in the combined code for listed companies. It does, however, remain a minority sport in the USA.

Sam Goldwyn's legendary quip makes the point:

'I want you all to tell me what you think, even if it costs you your jobs.'

Another dramatic signal from a board that all was obviously not well between a chairman and a finance director came with the words:

'If I want your view, Jim, I'll ask for it.'

Even this is better than what I heard one chairman say: 'If I want your view, I'll tell you what it is.' Generating a real debate and involving all in the discussion is quite an art.

Lord Alexander, a former barrister and therefore expert on the subject of leading witnesses, believes the best way to avoid this trap is

'Millicent, send in a fly.'

for the chairman to introduce an item briefly and with no indication of his own position. They should then set out the background, concluding with 'it seems to me this raises the following issues ...' An executive or non-executive is then chosen to present the issues more fully and lead the discussion. Only at the end of this discussion will he give his view.

Alan Greenspan at the Federal Reserve System adopts a similar approach by stating the item and asking each board member in turn to ask questions and express views. Only when everyone has had the opportunity to hear from the others are they then asked to state their position on the subject. These two are lucky not to have shrinking violets on their boards but what do you do if you have an annoyingly quiet dissenter or silent seether? How do you draw them out? I suppose you could 'just ask them what they think'. They still may be diplomatically and unhelpfully brief in response.

Highly tuned antennae and a powerful sense of intuition are handy assets for a chairman. A lovely example of this was given to me by one of the masters who wished to remain anonymous. He told me of another chairman's pivotal remark:

'I feel Martin throbbing beside me desperate to express a view.'

Once someone's discomfort with a position is picked up the wise chairman then employs additional devices to draw out the overly shy.

'Would you please elaborate on "then something bad happened".'

Many telephone all of their board members following each board meeting to check they were comfortable with the outcomes and the discussion. Non-executive directors have to feel that this is done in a non-manipulative way. One popular variant of this approach has been described to me by one of what I call the Old Toughies as the 'behind the bike shed afterwards' approach, perhaps expressing disappointment that a board member didn't contribute at a vital moment and sending a clear signal that they will be expected to next time. Of course it can be risky to rely upon someone at a vital moment if you haven't supported them in their moment of need. Beating someone up who is already starting to introvert generally makes them retreat into their shells even further as many a bully has found out before. Really smart chairmen note the silence and have a sensible one to one later.

Another trap for those who would say 'never go in without an idea about what you want out' is either to give the impression – or worse, make it the reality – that the other participants are playing out the chairman's dream meeting. To do so is to treat them like clowns in a side show. Being a ringmaster is fun and I guess you must have a bit of that in you to want to be a chairman in the first place but if it is too orchestrated 'Why have them there?' The best example I came across of the power of a real debate came from Jon Foulds who described one of his most pleasing moments as chairman:

'Miss Howell, send in the clowns.'

'When we arrived for the meeting the night before we were all unanimous in the view not to proceed with a particular proposal. The debate at the board the following morning, however, came out a different way. Everyone was happy with the decision to proceed with the proposal. Even better, we were right to do so.'

I guess it might have been easy not to have had the discussion at the board.

For any successful team with an inspiring leader the development of an air of invincibility is an obvious danger. A team that is very well welded together might also suffer from an increasing homogeneity of thought. The feeling of being able to complete your colleagues' sentences, know exactly how they will react and so on provides some with a considerable degree of comfort. Thankfully it fills others with horror. You have to have someone who 'is prepared to water down your treacle' when things are a bit too sweet. It is always handy to have at least one person who can make things a little less cosy or perhaps even a bit uncomfortable.

Anglo-Saxon board members feel better for making a decision. There is an expectation by those putting proposals to the board that a decision will be made. Not to do so can easily be taken as a sign of weakness. In comparison, Japanese boards seem adept at delaying the decision until it is the right time to decide. Their sense of the right time is the time when the decision can be properly implemented. Allowing a decision to be made when a bit more debate or perhaps the seeking of an external view might produce a better result is an easy trap to fall into. This is not to encourage that other Anglo-Saxon trait, procrastination. A chairman's instinct and gut feel is the critical thing here. There are

Decisions, decisions

occasions where decisions are made which stack up logically, having well prepared and well argued papers to support them, but are just plain wrong. Discussions about acquisitions emphasise this point best. Sir Denys Henderson reinforced this point for me by saying:

'I've only used my chairman's casting vote twice. Both were gut-feel points against the run of the meeting and logic. In both cases I'm very glad I did.'

'I don't need this aggravation!'

'He don't need this aggravation!'

'I realise, gentlemen, that thirty million dollars is a lot of money to spend. However, it is not real money and, of course, it's not our money either.'

That this is an American cartoon is ironic in some ways. One of the differences between US and British boards is supposed to be the greater emphasis in the US on shareholder issues and the greater sense, as Norton Reamer puts it:

> *'... that this isn't any old company, it's theirs.'*

Robert Monks, the shareholder activist who is somewhat cynical on the subject of US board behaviour, observes that:

'So we are agreed. Honesty is the best policy. Okay. Let's label that Option A.'

'US boards talk much more about shareholder value but in practice they aren't any better.'

Setting the tone is a vital duty for any chairman. Alan Greenspan is recognised as a master of this. A tone of 'serious integrity and professionalism' runs throughout his board meetings as well as his organisation. People expect an orderly consistency from the Fed. They have to feel it's under tight control. Other organisations may want the mood to be different but a chairman of any board has to generate an environment and atmosphere of trust as well as engender a sense of seriousness. A company's sense of integrity is easily lost by a bad example set by the board. As a lawyer friend of mine always says:

'If in doubt fall back on the truth.'

The subject of integrity and the natural flow of dilemmas which emerges for all directors is something I've covered in another book, *Directors' Dilemmas*.

If you do have a chairman and a chief executive clarity between their respective roles is crucial. Beware of the many over-prescriptive pieces written on this subject. Gaining clarity and it working almost intuitively because of the skill sets and styles of the individuals concerned is far more important than what each person actually does. There is a body of opinion which feels that having a full-time chairman makes this potential difficulty inherently more likely to occur. Having the former chief executive as a chairman is also likely to lead to potential conflict.

'But to make a long story short ...'

Naturally a good chairman will finish on time without people feeling it's rushed or too rigid. As one football fan who also happens to be a chairman of a FTSE 100 company put it:

> *'A good chairman finishes on time, occasionally needing a bit of extra time to get a result in a big match. A bad one has to resort to penalty shoot-outs to get a conclusion. It's never a satisfying game for the players or the crowd if you only ever get through on penalties.'*

Being a chairman is a tricky job requiring many skills. Fundamentally he or she has to command respect through former achievements. A clear mind and considerable determination will need to be matched by a keen sensitivity and openness to the ideas of others. They also need to regularly think about the process of their board and its composition. Developing the other directors is a further key responsibility. The good news is that there are many people who are first class at this and love to do it. One observation from meeting these masters in companies big and small is that they all, despite their busy schedules, have time to talk to people. When I asked how, they almost universally replied:

> *'Oh I'm really lucky, we have an excellent chief executive and my secretary is superb.'*

WHAT ABOUT THE CHIEF EXECUTIVE OR THE MANAGING DIRECTOR?

Let's make the assumption that there is a separate and non-executive chairman of the board. There are a whole set of other issues if they aren't separate. Most people have found it very hard to make the executive chairman and chief executive combination work. Even harder, as Barclays bank found in the late nineteen nineties, to make the combination of an executive chairman, an executive deputy chairman and a chief executive work, no matter how good they may or may not be individually.

Making the clear distinction that the chairman runs the board and the chief executive or managing director runs the company is helpful. The lack of this distinction, which may exist because the chairman is weak, is often what leads to trouble. This is especially true if the chairman is weak and happy for the chief executive to run the meetings and simply feed him his lines. When the chairman is weak and unhappy for this to happen this will lead to stress for the entire board as agenda setting becomes an increasingly over-political exercise.

Before moving on we ought to address an obvious question:

'What's the difference between a chief executive and a managing director?'

I know there's been some clever stuff written about this but to an unsophisticated mind like mine it appears to be mostly semantic in nature. My own favourite definition of the distinction is: 'About fifty thousand'.

So often it really does seem to be more to do with the size of the company than the job description. Another simple distinction is that the chief executive is the executive leader of a group of companies each of which, or smaller groups of which, may have their own managing directors. In the United Kingdom the chief executive title has largely replaced the group managing director one. What remains is the variability in roles from company to company.

When I originally wrote this chapter, five FTSE 100 companies didn't have a chief executive, mostly as a result of boardroom bust-ups. The average time in their role for the top group is around four years. I wonder what you do after being chief executive of a FTSE 100?

The chief executive role has become increasingly demanding and the spotlight increasingly intense. The press have become far more interested, influential and involved in removing chief executives of high-profile companies. This means that chief executives today must pay far more attention to their relationships with non-executive than perhaps they used to. Non-executives could and have in some situations been used as the ideal conduit to a hostile press when it comes to sacking a public company chief executive. 'He no longer has the confidence of the non-executives' is becoming as popular a choice as, 'he no longer has the confidence of the institutional shareholders'.

A vicious circle can then easily develop in which the non-execs leak this to the press and then fire the chief executive because 'he no longer has the confidence of the press'. So what should the chief executive do in a board meeting given this background? Should he or she think positively and 'come to receive the endorsement and encouragement of the board and to gain useful input to their plans as well as a rigorous testing of them'? Even more so can they expect 'to be motivated by the experience'? Whatever the case they ought to feel that 'board meetings are an opportunity not a chore and that they are much, much more than an expert witness.'

Despite the appearances they may give and what they say, strong chief executives are seldom motivated by the regular show-event for the non-executives. Feeling that you made it through the meeting without much of a testing or without gaining any new input to your ideas is likely to be an unfulfilling experience. Coming away with an even-better decision or an interesting new angle and with the enthusiastic support of a bunch of tough-minded and impressive people will feel much better.

The skilful chief executive will pick up those really useful comments from the non-executives and not only incorporate them but do so enthusiastically rather than grudgingly. These are the ones that recognise that non-executives like their contributions to be recognised and acted upon just like anyone else. They avoid the trap of appearing defensive in defending a good plan. Defensiveness can easily be interpreted as an inability to listen or a reluctance to change.

How the chief executive relates to other executive board members in the meeting is another interesting topic. A chief executive who answers for the rest of his executive directors looks much weaker than the one who is very comfortable letting them join the debate without fear of loss of face. The greeting of a top chimp in a chimpanzee pack – 'Hi would you like to pick around in my hair?' – sums this up well for me. If you have decided that the purpose of your board is to get something additional from the stimulus of the debate then having others pick around the scalp of the idea might result in a better-groomed result. It also makes 'the groomers' in the pack feel closer and a lot more involved and committed to your appearance. A bunch of quiet executives throughout the meeting are as worrying as those who, leaving their strident stance at the door, have to look to the chief executive for approval to speak.

In my experience, chief executives generally have a high need for control. The time of the month when they are not in control inherently leads to tension, before, during and after the meeting. If this is combined with a chairman they fear, they are irritated by, or they simply just don't rate, then this frustration will generally find it's way into the meeting. It then becomes hard to avoid this frustration becoming destructive.

One handy tip for the chief executive who has a chairman who becomes over involved is to get the chairman busy on other things. An easy solution is to recommend them as a non-executive elsewhere. I have seen many examples of this tactic working very well for all concerned, particularly the chairman who was formerly chief executive.

It seems perfectly natural for the chairman, chief executive and company secretary to sit down together and plan how involved the chief executive should be in setting the agenda. A chairman who leaves it to the chief executive or a chief executive who isn't involved in the process is for me a clear sign that something is wrong.

The chief executive's job is the one that many people aspire to and few attain. Most chief executives I know enjoy the job and the pressure it brings and are not disappointed by it. Disappointed leaders are not leaders for long and find it hard to motivate the rest of their team.

WHAT'S THE ROLE OF THE FINANCE DIRECTOR?

Every board is fundamentally dependent upon the quality of their finance director and every board member knows how much harder the job is to do without a high quality FD. Yet how do you know you've got a good one? This is especially important to know before you join a board.

Many years ago I felt that this was an issue not being given enough prominence and so set up a series of workshops for independent directors and 3i's own investment executives. We called them 'How do you know a good FD when you see one?' and they turned out to be very popular right across Europe. This was especially the case in countries such as Germany where historically the FD role has not had the prominence it has in the UK or the USA.

Of course, before you can determine whether you have someone who is appropriate for the role and the situation you need to be clear what the role is. So we spent some of the time establishing what the role of an FD was. There was a great deal of consistency right across Europe that the role was a combination of 'ensuring' and 'adding value'.

Ensuring that:

- financial controls and systems are effective;
- financial resources are appropriate to meet the company's short- and long-term needs;
- the board is made fully aware of the company's financial position and performance and has good visibility of future financial performance;
- the company has good relationships with providers of finance; and
- the financial team is appropriate and highly motivated.

Adding value by:

- being an active and contributing member of the board on issues other than finance;
- communicating well internally on financial matters so that staff had a good appreciation of the company's financial position and the impact on the company's finances of their actions;
- having a high reputation externally; and
- providing the board with insightful analysis from which to make key decisions.

What a tough job, no wonder good FDs are like gold dust.

Within the context of a board meeting the FD will frequently be the major supplier of information to the board. They are also often the major recipient of actions arising. It can sometimes therefore be hard for them to find airspace on subjects other than those relating to finance, as they will have used considerable airspace on the subject of their expertise. The best, however, overcome this and don't find it a challenge. They are also very good at both supporting the CEO and providing sufficient challenge. It is almost impossible to achieve this unless they are high calibre and high integrity.

WHAT'S THE ROLE OF THE COMPANY SECRETARY?

'As the great ones depart, and are eating their dinner
The secretary sits, getting thinner and thinner
Racking his brains as he tries to report
What he thinks that they think that they ought to have thought.'

There is much debate amongst company secretaries as to what their role is. For many, apart from the obvious formalities to attend to, 'It's what they want it to be plus the bits that the FD doesn't want to do.' Many company secretaries have greater responsibility than their title or salary indicates and have branched out into the risk management business largely through having dealt with the administration of the company's insurance policies. Some are ideally suited and well trained to deal with this new role but many sadly aren't. With regard to board meetings most of the company secretaries I spoke to suggested that their role was:

'to make the process as smooth as possible for the directors and to be their independent conscience.'

Company secretary handbooks and training materials suggest this means the following.

Before the meeting

- To notify directors of the time, date and place of the meeting.
- To prepare agenda with the chairman and then circulate it with associated papers.
- To be responsible for all the housekeeping arrangements, room bookings and preparation (including checking the clock, booking refreshments, etc).
- To advise all other relevant people (those preparing papers, information, advisers, etc).
- To organise advisers to the board. This can be particularly important especially in a flotation or bid process.
- If listed, to make appropriate Stock Exchange notifications.
- To prepare a briefing note for the chairman before each meeting, two pages in bullet point form. For formal resolutions such as share issues and so on it's normal for these to be prepared in minute form to avoid separate detailed agendas.
- On day of meeting to check again all items are covered, all papers have been made available, etc.
- To ensure any documents which might be referred to are to hand (accounts, memorandum and articles of association, etc).

During the meeting

- To be prepared to resist the temptation to speak on anything other than procedural matters. The company secretary should not be part of the discussion unless it's a procedural issue.
- To record the names of directors present at the beginning of the meeting and those that arrive or depart during.
- To check that a quorum is present and maintained, and, importantly, if one or more of the directors has an interest in an item, to check that an independent disinterested quorum is available.
- To report any apologies for absence and note them for recording in the minutes.
- During the course of the meeting, to take notes of the proceedings and of the instructions given and decisions reached. Many feel that the sense of the meeting cannot in practice be fully grasped by a person who takes shorthand notes.

- To be prepared to advise on any point of procedure. Without invitation or request to inform the chairman if any action proposed to be taken by the board is unlawful or contrary to the memorandum and articles of association or a trust deed.
- To make the precise arrangements for entry for those attendees only present for part of the meeting.
- To ensure the removal of any confidential reports or letters from the boardroom.

After the meeting

- For a listed company, to make appropriate notifications to the Stock Exchange, eg regarding dividends.
- To notify any departments or individuals of any decisions affecting them or on which they need to take action.
- To note items deferred.
- To prepare and circulate draft minutes then issue final approved minutes.

All the above sounds like a lot of hassle – why do people do it?

Some people have a natural affinity for hassle and detail and just love to organise things. They usually also have a strong belief in what they are doing and don't necessarily require the high profile and wide recognition of other board roles. Given it takes 16 exams to qualify as a company secretary in the UK these days and most qualify through part-time correspondence courses you really do have to want to do it. One company secretary told me that the job is ideal for nosey people who are good at keeping confidences. She added that the job is well worth doing for the view you get of the participants. There seems to be low mobility amongst this group and one told me that they seemed to provide another useful service – 'the continuity man and link with the past'.

It is also noticeable that whilst the proportion of women involved in most board roles is still low there is a high proportion of female company secretaries. Why is this? Of course there is ample opportunity at this point to fall into every sexist trap possible. I'll attempt to avoid this by giving you the views of some of the female company secretaries I talked to:

'Most women like to see their offspring kept out of jail.'

'Why? Because we naturally take a lot upon ourselves.'

'It is a natural role for someone with a strong maternal instinct to want to see everything in order.'

'There is a greater acceptance by middle aged men of professional women than those who rise up the ranks in a functional position.'

'A company secretary's position is an easier position to take a career break from than sales and marketing.'

THE SILENT SEETHER AND OTHER PERSONAE

The character, style and performance of any board is really established by the individuals who are on it. You may find some of the cameos below familiar. This was the part of the book most of the press picked up on when it was first published. Amusingly, I received a call from a secretary in another FTSE 100 who told me that all the board secretaries had been playing 'spot the boss'!

The silent seether

'After 34 years of marriage you thought you knew me, didn't you?
Well, welcome to the real world!'

Amongst a lot of boards you will find a silent seether. These are usually very clever, very shrewd people who sadly lack either confidence or arrogance enough to get themselves heard. Instead they sit there seething whilst others do all the talking and make the wrong decisions. Their attempts at interjecting are often too late and the momentum of the debate too great to take their view on board. Later, amongst their colleagues or at home, they vent their spleen, often threatening to resign if it happens again. Of course they never do. They just continue to sit and seethe. Until they snap.

The seether

A close relation to the silent seether, only neither as quiet or bright. Often the over-promoted insecure type they can also be known as a 'chippy' – they always seem to have a chip on their shoulder or something unnecessary to prove. A skilful chairman can use seethers to great effect. By getting them to provide an extreme version of what he wants said the chairman can get the required result with a 'That's a bit strong, Tom,' or a 'I don't feel we can go quite that far yet, Sarah.' More often than not, though, seethers just turn out to be a pain.

The key influencer

Not necessarily the chairman or managing director, perhaps a powerful family member, heir apparent, non-executive, key shareholder representative or adviser.

Mr or Mrs Wonderful

They do exist. Ideal board member material: strong views but will listen to others; questions rather than states but you know damn well where they are coming from; motivated by what is best for the board rather than their own personal position; never a slave to political correctness or to the convenient, expedient but flawed compromise; shares responsibility for a problem even when they counselled against the course of action causing all the trouble.

The quiet floater

A diplomat who never does much so has never done much wrong. A master at letting others do all the fighting and emerging the winner by making a small compromising contribution at the end, thus providing the chairman's summary and the company secretary's minute.

The dangerous ones with nothing more to offer than their silken tongues

A source of great irritation in life are those who have a wonderful capacity to sound good but aren't. Whenever they speak it sounds so convincing, so right. It's only when you stop to think, perhaps when the oozing charm has ceased and you set about trying to convert their eloquent words into action, that you realise it's complete and utter claptrap.

The really useful old hand

Always handy to have one of these sage guys around. They have seen many swings of the economic and industry cycle, survived numerous crises and had the joy of as many triumphs. They seem to possess an innate sense of when to be optimistic and encouraging and when to sound the cautionary note. Their store of general and specific industry knowledge is usually undervalued by the board. Their fierce loyalty to the inherently successful values of the business is matched by their keen sense of when it's time to change. A role for the classic coach and mentor, someone you would love to have as an uncle or aunt.

The really useless or dead hand

These sad cases have little to offer. They are usually masters from the school of decision avoidance and are fearful of anything that involves too much change or disturbance of their cosy little world. Others only tolerate them because of their shareholding or some other accident of history. They tend not to be the brightest of people and so in their desire to procrastinate they love having more explanatory information and papers to hand. Someone once said that as we get older our eccentricities become exaggerated. This lot start with a full set to begin with.

The great debater

Some people just like to talk. This group approach every issue with an open mouth and will joyfully race past the boundary of exploring the options and move out to explore the world. Board meetings tend to be much longer and as a result the other board members' attention wanes. Unfortunately this can be at precisely the wrong moment. A great appetite for the decision may then have more to do with a desire to finish the meeting than any real confidence in it.

The young pretender or heir apparent

A difficult position to get right when you are ready to assume control, it is accepted that you will be the successor but you haven't reached the formal position yet. Many an heir apparent has come to grief on the rocks of arrogance and jealousy. It is so tempting to flex your muscles and exercise that power when it isn't really yours. Others knowing it soon will be may be suitably compliant. Beware, though, because your 'Top Chimp', the person you are succeeding, may change his mind about you if you usurp his power and don't show him sufficient respect. Any heir apparent needs a mentor and a constructive critic to keep them balanced.

The pulse

This is that person who, whatever is going on, has an innate sense of what people think both inside and outside the company and how they feel. They will help the board spot the wonderfully logical decision that no one will carry out or when it is time for the mood to change. Tremendously helpful at calibrating the divisional managing director's – or baron's – presentations. Also pretty useful at dealing with the seethers.

Rosey

No matter what the issue Rosey finds a positive interpretation. Whilst they may be useful in cheering up the rest, they are typically an over-promoted super salesman unsuited to a board role.

Badvisor

This is the over-involved professional advisor who persuades the chairman that he or she should attend a board meeting as an expert on a particular issue. The board is initially delighted to have him or her come along. He or she fulfils the observer role well, contributing only on his or her area of expertise and when his or her views are sought. However, at subsequent meetings he or she becomes a complete pain.

Flushed with his or her early success, he or she starts to make uninvited contributions and talks with great force on subjects he or she knows nothing about. This person becomes known as the badvisor because of his or her capacity to cloud vision and get everyone steamed up.

All of the above explains why getting, as Lord Cuckney says, 'the right people on board' matters more than anything else. This doesn't simply mean the individuals but it also means the mix and the collective style. Get the wrong mix and watch your problems grow.

PRESENTATIONS TO THE BOARD

Presentations by non-members of the board typically fit into two categories:

'to inform, present or communicate';

or:

'to seek approval or stimulate a debate'.

You have to be clear to presenters and board members what the purpose is.

One company that is reputed to be a master of the art of making sure that presenters go away highly motivated is Mars. It seems able to do this even when those presenting get a thorough going over. Reasons given by the presenters for this are that:

'There is clear evidence that the board acts on a good proposal well presented.'

'Board members have read their papers and take you to task on all the right points. That is the most vulnerable ones or the ones you didn't even think of.'

'It scares me silly beforehand but I love it when I'm there.'

It is clear that these events fit with the rest of the Mars culture. They are therefore seen as natural and understandable. However, not every multi-national gets its logistics right, as evidenced by one horror story I was told by a company secretary of a company that claims:

'Our people are our most important asset.'

The MD of the South African subsidiary of a major UK plc was asked if he might come and give a presentation to the board. A huge effort was put into the preparation for his visit. Understandably he viewed the request as a great honour and a signal that he was destined for higher things. All his family, friends, colleagues, key customers and suppliers had been told as well. He dutifully arrived the day before the meeting to get himself settled, comfortable and further prepared. Customary practice in this company, presumably to make people feel really relaxed before they did their presentations, was to ensure all presentees were sitting outside the boardroom in an ante room at least an hour before they were due to perform. This was just in case the board arrived at the agenda item early. Our South African was due to perform at three o'clock so dutifully arrived at five minutes before two. Three o'clock passed by but at three thirty the company secretary popped out to say: 'We're terribly sorry but something's cropped up and we're a bit behind. Hang on here and I'll try to squeeze you in later.' Four, five and six o'clock came and went. At six thirty the chairman emerged and said: 'I really am most terribly sorry. We just didn't get time for you today. Something really important arose that we simply had to deal with. I hope you have a good flight back.' I wonder what impression of the board he was about to convey to his friends back home?

People understandably get very worked up about presentations to boards. For rising stars or those under threat it may be a make-or-break presentation. For external advisers, a possible opportunity to generate more from an existing client relationship or perhaps to lose it makes it a serious business.

The masters of the art were broadly unanimous on this subject and all appeared to put quite a lot of thought and effort into putting presenters at their ease. Not leaving them hanging about can be difficult if they are not invited to the whole of the meeting. One tip on avoiding this was:

'To dispense with the normal ritual of having presenters on just before or after lunch so that they can join it. Have them on first so you know they'll be presenting on time. In this way they have less time that morning to get worked up. An added benefit is that board members' attentions are usually strongest earlier in the meeting anyway.'

Another chairman always rings presenters the day before to check they are okay and that they have everything they need. He takes the opportunity to wish them well and assure them that the board is looking forward to it. He will have also given the presenter a feel for the depth of knowledge each of the independent directors has on the particular topic. A few hours after the meeting he rings the presenter to congratulate or otherwise. The same chairman is also very skilful in sheltering them a little from the more aggressive members of his board.

How well a chief executive prepares the presenter came up as an issue with most of the presenters I talked to. Other than the overconfident they all welcomed the guidance from their CEO or chairman. However, you also have to end up with something that is in the speaker's language and that they are comfortable presenting. The presenters urged 'control freak' chief executives to exercise great self-control in this area and focus on the likely discussion points arising.

DE BONO'S HATS

Sir Edward de Bono, the most celebrated and entrepreneurial of lateral thinkers, is naturally of the view that:

'Thinking is the ultimate human resource.'

However, never to be accused of being complacent, he believes that:

'most people, convinced they are competent at thinking (like humour and sex), make no efforts to improve.'

In his book Six Thinking Hats he proposed a way for any group to improve the quality of its thinking. All you need to do is to give each member of the meeting six different coloured hats. White, red, black, yellow, green and blue are the colours. Obvious isn't it?

Sir Edward recommends that you confine each stage of a discussion to thinking only from the perspective of a single colour. Each colour's perspective is as follows:

- *White.* White is neutral and objective. The white hat is concerned with objective facts and figures.
- *Red.* Red suggests anger, rage and emotions. The red hat gives the emotional view.
- *Black.* Black is gloomy and negative. The black hat covers the negative aspects – why it cannot be done.
- *Yellow.* Yellow is sunny and positive. The yellow hat is optimistic and covers hope and positive thinking.
- *Green.* Green is grass, vegetation and abundant fertile growth. The green hat indicates creativity and new ideas.
- *Blue.* Blue is cool, and it is also the colour of the sky, which is above everything else. The blue hat is concerned with control and the organisation of the thinking process, and also the use of the other hats.

The hats are supposed to allow you to think, say things you otherwise wouldn't and focus on one thing at a time. Imagine an ever-optimistic sales director doing a little black hat thinking or perhaps the gloomiest of finance directors doing a little yellow hat musing. The power is obvious and not just confined to generating a more rounded debate. Looking at things from a different perspective might actually improve the cohesiveness of the group and force the fierce defenders and promoters of their patch to be broader in their thinking.

One problem with all of this is the fact that a typical board director might feel a little silly with a bright yellow hat on. You obviously don't need to wear the hats to adopt this approach. One chairman from Scotland taken with the concept had little flags on cocktail sticks made for his board. Many of course have always tried to segment the debate at the board in a cruder 'let's look at the upside ...', 'Now what about the downside' fashion. (Those I've met who use it usually do so for the away day sessions on strategy.)

Whatever the style of your board, an experimental six-hat session would be fun and may stimulate broader debate.

SUBCOMMITTEES – THE COMMON ONES, THE RELEVANT ONES

Subcommittees of boards of larger companies enjoyed a proliferation in the 1990s. These subcommittees usually consist of three to five members of the board who meet three to four times a year normally immediately before or after a full board meeting. They can save time by being delegated the detailed discussion of technical, time-consuming, complex or less strategic but vital issues. They also allow for more considered discussion with external advisers. The balance of what is discussed at board meetings and what is delegated to these committees must be thought through carefully. Some directors see the proliferation of these committees as a potentially dangerous abdication of responsibility. Care in the drawing up of terms of reference and scope of responsibility is therefore important. As is the avoidance of stifling bureaucracy. It is all too easy to get carried away.

Many boards have established audit and remuneration committees but there are usually other ones specific to each business which can be useful. A review of the most time-consuming operational items for the board will often reveal them. For example, in 3i where our business is investing there are two subcommittees which are highly specific to our business. These are our Investment Committee and the Valuations Committee. The Investment Committee approves all investments above a certain size leaving the main board only very large investments or those which present a major policy issue to approve. A critical determinant of 3i's performance and market capitalisation is the value we ascribe to our more than three thousand investments. A special subcommittee of the board monitors both the valuation policies used and their application.

Whatever the nature of your business there are likely to be a couple of areas which can be treated in this way. Professor Jay Light from Harvard, a seasoned outside director, believes 'every board, no matter what size, should have a new products committee.' You may, if you are in oil, gas or chemicals or any other environmentally sensitive industry, need an environmental committee. In the US there has been a growing trend towards the 'strategy subcommittee of the board'.

In smaller companies with small boards and perhaps only one independent director it might seem difficult to adopt this approach. However, any smaller companies have adopted and adapted the underlying principles of delegation, specialism and planning to their own requirements and situation. An advisory board is a common technique for the smaller company to gain access to a wider pool of committed knowledge on an affordable basis. This has been especially popular in early-stage scientific businesses. Businesses making their first significant international moves may well have an international advisory board. Capturing the knowledge of people who have successfully operated in the area of interest and who are aware of the pitfalls has been the key to success for many an international foray.

Who should you pick to be on the subcommittee?

'The ones who don't volunteer.'

Clearly you must have people who ultimately do want to do it. There is value to be had by having at least one member, though, who is not an enthusiast in that area and can therefore bring some balance. For example, I think an essential member of any remuneration committee is a highly skilled communicator. Problems companies have had in this highly charged area have often not been about the levels of remuneration paid but their communication and timing.

A few remarks on the most popular subcommittees now follow.

Audit committees

The main terms of reference for an audit committee are generally to:

- review the financial statements before publication;
- consult with external and internal auditors (if there are any) regarding any matters arising in the course of the audit which should be brought to the board's attention;
- report to the board on the adequacy of internal systems and financial controls;
- report to the board on the scope of the external audit;
- recommend to the board the appointment and remuneration of the external auditors.

Another useful thing for an audit committee to do is to educate. It might be shocking to say it and no doubt many will want to lynch me for doing so, but my guess is that there is a high proportion of company directors who don't really know the basis on which their business recognises profit. A useful job for any audit committee is to make this understandable to the non-accountants amongst us. Explaining accounting policies is not easy, particularly in international businesses, but it is important. Apart from profit recognition other obvious areas for education might include stock valuation, valuation policies with regard to other assets and the level and nature of the financial risk in the business.

The management letter from the auditor always make interesting reading for a potential independent director. All too often these are confined to the finance director's file and not aired.

Understanding the real quality of the audit is much easier if you have something to compare it with. Whilst changing auditors is a hassle for a business, getting others to regularly pitch is not. Many good ideas flow from these beauty parades and if you are serious about changing, if there is good reason to, the existing auditors are more likely to provide a keener service. Internationalisation has meant that there is growing investment by a company in its auditors.

One other critical point to make in respect of audit committees is to make sure you are happy you have an effective one. Having a committee doesn't absolve you of responsibility!

Although the Higgs report stole the limelight in early 2003, another report, published on the same day and with the catchy title of 'Audit Committees: combined code guidance' was significant.

What was the Smith report all about?

Inspired by the Financial Reporting Council and led by the hugely popular and respected Sir Robert Smith, it didn't attract anything like the same debate as the Higgs review. However it was obviously less threatening to many and the attention focused on Higgs meant it received a lot less attention.

Sir Robert did an excellent job of updating best practice and the report is very clear. A very detailed analysis of it is contained in another of the author's titles *Tolley's Non-executive Directors' Handbook*. The main points the report concerned itself with were:

- constitution;
- membership;
- attendance at meetings;
- frequency of meetings;

■ authority;
■ responsibilities;
■ reporting procedures

It was, however, disappointing to me that amongst the many skills and attributes required of chairmen and members of audit committees there was no mention of the ability to add up.

Remuneration committees

Few issues are more emotive than 'remuneration'. Potentially the most entertaining and high hassle committee to take part in on a public company board these days is the remuneration committee ('Remco'). Non-executive directors are generally keener to serve on the Remco than the audit committee because the balance of power, work and risk is more attractive.

Whether we like it or not, other people's pay is inherently fascinating to humans. Some would also say that the envy of journalists and politicians has also fuelled interest. The regular occurrence of high profile gaps between reward and performance has also ensured a regular supply of stories to feed that fascination. Journalists who cover this increasingly complex subject have become ever more sophisticated. The technical proficiency of many of them on this subject is now well ahead of the average director.

For some quoted companies the annual general meeting has become a *'remuneration issue fest'* with the preparation involved becoming enormous, much to the delight of the many remuneration consultancies and shareholder voting advisory groups now in business. There is a considerable amount of technical detail on this subject in another of the author's titles, *Tolley's Non-Executive Directors' Handbook*; however, some headline issues are covered below.

The combined code for listed companies sets out three principles on the setting and make up of directors' pay and these are:

1. Have a Remco to make recommendations to the main board on remuneration policy and to determine the remuneration of each individual director.
2. Remcos should have at least three members, all of whom should be independent non-executives.
3. The Chairman and the Chief Executive should attend the meetings by invitation only.

So if you are listed you have to have one and it is about making it as effective as possible. If you aren't, should you bother? In private equity or venture capital backed businesses the investors will normally require them. However, the constitution of decisions relating to remuneration issues is normally set out in investment agreements between management and investors. The Remco in these situations is principally concerned with benchmarking and issues relating to new joiners or exiting directors.

In owner-managed businesses there may seem little point; the owners are simply deciding whether to take their financial gain as income or capital and there is no one outside who could be disadvantaged in the process. In family businesses the same circumstances may apply but a Remco can prove to be a very helpful mechanism to satisfy non-management shareholders.

The combined code also sets out three principles for determining the remuneration of directors:

1.   Pay enough to attract relevant talent but don't overpay.
2.   Link some element of pay to corporate and individual performance.
3.   Have a formal and transparent process and don't let anyone set their own pay.

Before getting into any detail on process issues relating to remuneration a board needs to step back and have a few simple objectives. For me these are:

■   The overarching objective is to build shareholder value. Never forget that or allow anything to cloud it.
■   Remuneration policy and process should align rewards with the performance objectives of the company.

In order to achieve these objectives you will have to have schemes which attract and retain the most appropriate talent, which are market driven, are commercial and fair, comply with legal and accounting standards, avoid unnecessary complexity and finally are tax efficient for the company and the director.

A series of remuneration case studies is included in another of the author's books, *Directors' Dilemmas*. In many situations confusion arises over what is reward for a job done and what is an incentive for a job to be done. In others the confusion is around what is remuneration for a role fulfilled, and what is really a distribution to share-holders.

Terms of reference for a Remco will typically involve some or all of the following:

- Determining remuneration policy.
- Targets for performance related remuneration.
- Pension arrangements.
- Remuneration arrangements for new directors.
- Termination and compensation arrangements for departing directors.
- The individual remuneration package for each individual director.
- The preparation of the remuneration report for the annual report.
- Where remuneration consultants are used, the selection, management and remuneration of them.
- Ensuring relevant linkage with the nominations committee.

A couple of other points are worth making.

Firstly, when using remuneration consultants, never, ever choose from a choice of one; pitch it like any other supplier, manage them tightly and ensure you get a relevant firm who understands your remuneration world. The benchmarking game can easily get out of hand.

It is also important to consider the *'remuneration cycle'* to ensure you have the right linkage with financial reporting. All of this takes time to plan and whoever is chairman of the remuneration committee will need to work closely with the company secretary and finance director to make this work.

The Remco chairmanship is now a serious job requiring a serious time commitment, a high degree of awareness of current best practice and a very high level of communication skills and patience. They also need, with the relevant executives, to ensure that all decisions can be communicated clearly within and outside the company, including the many lobbying and voting advisory groups which exist. Most of these bodies are highly trained, highly professional and very sensible. However, there are still many that aren't, have never been near a board-room and frankly haven't got a clue what they are doing.

A final point of commercial importance is that coming up with the right performance measures is always tricky. Worry it through, spend the time but recognise that we live in an imperfect world.

Nominations committees

The remuneration committee might be the headline grabber and membership of it may bring useful power but it is the nominations committee (Nomco) that has risen most in terms of real power over the last few years. This is largely because it was starting from almost a zero base.

If you are a listed company then the combined code says you have to have a nominations committee to lead the process for board appointments and make recommendations to the board.

In the Higgs report reference is made to the analysis and census of UK listed boards. According to this analysis almost all FTSE 100 companies in 2002 had Nomcos whereas only 30 per cent of those outside the FTSE 350 have them. He went further in his report and said that:

'Where nomination committees do exist they are the least developed of the board's committees, usually meeting irregularly and often without a clear understanding of its role in the appointment process.'

So what's the point of having one and do the big listed companies only have them because they have to?

The reality is that many listed companies do only have Nomcos because they have to. However, I believe strongly that a well-constituted and composed Nomco which has the respect of the board as a whole can add a lot of value, especially if it is advised by a high quality search firm. By high quality I don't mean that they have to be a top tier firm in the search industry. High quality in this context means highly professional, relevant and independently minded.

To have a rigorous and efficient process for picking the best people for your board that is highly defensible if challenged ought to add value. Nomcos which are a triumph of form over substance or simply rubber-stamping exercises for chairman or chief executives are a waste of effort and not worth the bother.

There has been much debate about the pros and cons of the Chairman being the Chairman of the nominations committee, and this is covered in the Rough Guide to Higgs on page 57. In my view, if the Chairman is the leader of the board team then they absolutely should chair the Nomco for everything other than the selection of their own successor. When it comes to their own successor they will obviously have significant input.

Sir Adrian Cadbury, a highly thoughtful and pragmatic man and the wise elder of corporate governance in the UK is clear what he thinks on this issue. In his excellent book *Corporate Governance and Chairmanship* he says:

'I believe that the Chairman of the board should wherever possible chair this committee, since it is chairmen who are responsible for the workings of their boards and who should therefore play a leading part in selecting their team.'

The value of an effective Nomco really does come to the fore when it is dealing with the two key appointments of Chairman and Chief Executive. Most boards have a succession plan and will charge the Nomco with the responsibility of ensuring that an effective plan is in place. In order to do this they will have to have a good idea of the strengths of the existing board as well as good visibility on executives beneath the board. Today there is also the pressure from institutions, no matter how good the internal candidates are, to benchmark them against external candidates.

What about non-listed companies and smaller businesses with a small number of non-execs? In their case it is usually the major shareholder who decides, but many are now seeking external input to their decisions.

The recruitment of non-executives has become a much more developed art than a decade ago. The demands of the job are much greater, as are the risks and the time commitment required to fulfil the role effectively. In public companies the nominations committee will need to plan the rotation of non-executives and in many there tends to be an appointment of a new non-executive almost every year.

In summary the role of the Nomco is changing, membership is becoming more influential but the art still has some way to go.

DEALING WITH DISHARMONY

A certain amount of creative tension and a challenging environment are healthy. Lots of companies thrive because just such an environment exists at all levels generated by the board. But sometimes there seems to be a thin line between creative tension and a right good scrap. Or worse, a whole board of silent seethers, who emerge occasionally for a sporadic outburst of violence. Why does it matter? Well, running a company looks tricky enough when the board is at the peak of its harmonious powers. Running it when it's enjoying a period of open hostility must be downright impossible. Just look at the damage to companies such as Lonrho or Cable & Wireless during their periods of painful and highly public disharmony. So it seems well worth looking at how disharmony can arise and how it might be dealt with.

Janet Morgan, a fascinating lady with extensive non-executive experience and an engagingly keen observational eye, gives a delightful talk on some aspects of board disharmony. She commences by comparing human behaviour to that of chimpanzees. After all, she says, we apparently have 98 per cent of our genes in common. Anyone who doubts this should have a look at an excellent children's book called *How to speak Chimpanzee*.

The process of a top chimp's or, sorry, chairman's succession usually provides an ideal climate for considerable disharmony to emerge. Chimps handle this in a number of different ways. An easy method avoiding any difficulty is to prepare a 'chosen one' who is demonstrably the most able of the pack and, more importantly, has their respect. In which case, apart from the tensions and sadness caused by the parting of a dearly beloved elder statesman who is wandering off to his field to die, it's reasonably harmonious.

A slightly less easy but sometimes manageable process is the warmongering 'waving of a big stick or baring of fangs' by a powerful youngster who frightens the elder in a moment of weakness. The elder quickly reaches the conclusion that it's not worth the bother fighting and quickly goes, though with not quite as much dignity as his friend who adopted the 'chosen one' strategy. Others will usually let it appear that it was the retiring chairman's idea all along. Sadly this approach may result in considerable regret a short while later. If the youngster has moved too soon or is just simply not up to the job, disharmony emerges.

Another situation arises when the elder decides to teach the young whipper-snapper a lesson on the occasion when he's cheeky enough to come along again and bare his fangs. The result this time is far more bloody. A quick resolution is all that can be hoped for but it can sometimes takes ages for a victor to emerge. When one does he and his opponent are so weakened and everybody else so fed up with the battle that the victor will only have grudging support to go with his permanent scars. It's generally not too long before someone else will take advantage of his weakened state and the inevitable mistakes made in the heat of the previous battle to effect another change.

A more abrupt but effective method chosen by aspirant successors is known as the 'coconut routine'. Here the ambitious one simply chooses his moment to lull the incumbent into a lovely and relaxing little glade.

Once he's been in there a while and the youngster has pandered to his every whim and he's become over-relaxed, the cheeky chimp suddenly leaps out from behind a tree and bonks him on the head with a coconut. A sudden and triumphant victory.

I think Janet is right that considerable disharmony arises around the time of any succession. Why? Because it's a deeply personal thing and most people who get to be on boards are almost by definition highly ambitious. This is not just about the succession of the top chimp either. The prospect of replacing any member of the team can cause similar problems. Few boards regularly do a thorough survey of top talent within and without. Understandably shareholders and others outside the business will focus their attention and thinking on the top chimp. They believe that if they get the top chimp right the rest of the pack will also be right. This is not always the case.

Another circumstance where disharmony occurs frequently is where there are joint ventures or consortium companies. These arrangements, usually born triumphantly, seldom last the course without some measure of disharmony. Neatly aligned objectives at the outset can quickly diverge. The characters thrown together are usually chosen for their technical competence or their current position, not their ability to fit with the people from the other party or parties. Hence the probability that they'll get on swimmingly in such a highly charged situation is naturally low.

Well, let's imagine you are in a tricky spot on your board, everybody seems to be fighting over the bananas and the board hasn't had the wonderful benefit of hindsight to see it coming and avoid it. Or perhaps worse, you're the one that's causing all the trouble. What can you do about it?

During a series of events on this subject I made heavy use of the advice of the Suzy Lamplugh Trust. This trust was established following the disappearance without trace of a young estate agent. Her situation touched the nation's hearts. The trust in her name was set up 'to empower all people to live safer lives'. It has done some tremendous work in raising awareness and training people to deal with the consequences of aggression. You might think this seems a bit extreme – a little bit of board disharmony is in no way comparable – but how about these little snippets taken directly from some of the Trust's excellent short guides:

- 'A person on the brink of physical aggression has three possible choices: to attack, retreat or compromise [back to the chimps]. You need to guide them to the second or third.'

- 'Offer a compromise such as talking through the problem, or divert the aggression into such actions as banging the table or tearing up paper.'
- 'Try to talk things through as reasonable adults. Stay calm, speak gently, slowly and clearly.'
- 'Always respect other people's personal territory and never hide behind your authority, status or jargon.'
- 'Keep your distance and avoid looking down on your aggressor.'
- 'Avoid an aggressive stance – crossed arms, hands on hips, a wagging finger or a raised arm will challenge and confront.'
- 'Keep your eye on potential escape routes. Keep yourself between the aggressor and the door. If the threat of violence is imminent avoid potentially dangerous locations such as the tops of stairs.'
- 'Never put a hand on someone who is angry.'
- 'If you manage to calm the situation down, gradually re-establish contact. A cup of tea for each of you may cushion the aftershock.'

And my favourite:

'Don't get in a lift with anyone who makes you feel uneasy.'

All excellent advice whenever there's any boardroom disharmony about. If this fails many of us fall back on Robert Kennedy's old adage:

'Don't get mad, get even.'

Thinking of the USA I recently found a very interesting book on a related subject. It is called *The Paranoid Corporation*. The authors William and Nurit Cohen look back at some of the highest profile major corporate crises to see what with the wonderful benefit of hindsight could have indicated that all was not well beforehand. They come from the psychologist's perspective!

They believe that problems are almost always due to two types of organisational illnesses which are easily cured once recognised:

● *psychoses:* 'illnesses in which contact with reality is lost';

● *neuroses:* 'disabling emotional disorders'.

The symptoms to look out for are some or all of the following:

- Psychoses:
  - manic behaviour;

- manic depression;
- schizophrenia;
- paranoia.

■ Neuroses:
  - neurotic behaviour;
  - depression;
  - intoxication;
  - obsessive compulsion;
  - post trauma syndrome.

I think most of us in the venture capital world would admit to not investing in someone unless at least some of the above are present!

From my own experiences manic behaviour is the one which strikes a chord in the post-disaster review. It is also often due to excessive enthusiasm following on from a string of successes. Someone, obviously a reader of the Cohens' book, once told me rather cruelly that the easiest way to spot manic behaviour is to think of a venture capitalist. The medical symptoms are:

'expansive moods, grandiosity, excessive excitement, low attention to detail and few hard plans.'

So what's the best way to deal with serious disharmony? The collective wisdom of the masters of the art on this subject seems to be:

■ At the outset observe rather than participate.
■ Find a catalyst and a galvaniser.
■ Establish what the reality of the situation is.
■ Get the participants to accept reality.
■ Gain clarity and unity of purpose.
■ Jettison those who don't share it!
■ Use strict 'rules of the game'.
■ Try a little impact therapy.
■ Recognise progress.
■ Participate like crazy!

This, I think, recognises that in a really difficult case consensus management is unlikely to work. You can't always arrange it so everyone is a winner. There are usually a significant number of losers in the process. In my experience, first-class change managers recognise this and deal with those likely to lose with considerable humanity.

Trying to act like an observer rather than as a participant is a marvellous first step. This is why people often deal with external shocks better than the slow malingering developing internal one. It is also I think a major reason why introducing someone new boosts the chances of turning a business around Someone new, no matter how rampant a doer they may be, has to look and think first before acting. It is also very difficult for most human beings to admit failure. Ditching the things they have valued or sold so highly before can be too traumatic. The emotional investment is sometimes too great. Finding and installing a galvaniser is also key. You have to have someone people will follow, particularly if it is a painful period. Those in pain and those most uncertain have to believe it will get better and that the person in charge has it under control. Many of the best galvanisers I have seen in operation also go in for what I can only describe as impact therapy.

'Catherine, have everyone stop whatever they're doing.'

If you want to make a significant change you have to get people's attention and send them very clear signals as to how serious the situation is and what new standards you want to set. In many cases this needs to be done rapidly. In such cases it is the highly visible emotive things which grab attention. These are not necessarily the most significant in cost terms but set the tone superbly.

Good examples I have heard of in severe turnarounds are:

'A new turnaround MD who ordered a car transporter for his first day and had each of the directors ceremoniously drive their new BMWs up on to it. They were replaced with much lower status cars that afternoon. In cost terms the benefit to the company was not huge. However, in the meetings later that week painful sacrifices were called for from the rest of the workforce and there was very little opposition.'

'In a company with a history of appalling cash management the new chairman demanded a fax each morning from each subsidiary managing director of their cash balance. It was easy for him to get it himself from the bank but the impact this received did focus attention on a critical feature.'

'A good way for a new CEO in a hierarchical organisation which needs a dramatic change in behaviour is to communicate directly at all levels of the organisation. Just look at what Archie Norman achieved at Asda with his "Tell Archie" campaign.'

'When I go into a company that has a history of minor improprieties which undermine the culture I fire the first person I hear of doing anything untoward. It has more impact if it is over something fairly minor. I find this quickly stops the rot.'

'Often in these situations you get a crisis of confidence. It is just as important to praise and congratulate at the same time you are beating others up. Small gestures and rewards which show your appreciation have big impact. There is nothing wrong with celebrating success even if the company overall is still in a precarious spot.'

'I get the directors to ceremoniously destroy some symbol of the past. Usually a symbol of excess. This could be anything from the fountain in the atrium to the chairman's private toilet.'

'You have to promote a junior hero as quickly as possible. Doing so emphasises that you share people's values and that there is as much opportunity as downside for people. It also helps shake up the middle rankers.'

'Get simple rules established on what it is and is not all right to spend money on. If you have made it clear and people are doing what you want, encourage them. If they are not, then fire them. The word gets around.'

'Most people grab the chequebook as soon as they get in. Of course I do that as well but it is just as important to grab the order book. No orders for anything without my say so. This also helps you to find out pretty quickly what people are committing to.'

A more in-depth treatment of conflict resolution techniques, as well as a series of case studies to practise with, is contained in *Directors' Dilemmas*, also published by Kogan Page.

After ...

'The Follow-up'

The legendary management guru Warren Bennis once said that real power was the ability to convert vision into reality. A board's real power then should be judged by its ability to convert its decisions successfully into actions. Yet when researching this book for the first time, few people talked about this aspect. The follow-up receives less attention. This chapter covers some of the issues involved.

WHAT SHOULD BE IN THE MINUTES?

Whether to record a summary of the discussion and the debate or just the decisions taken by the board seems to be a common dilemma. In the horribly litigious climate of the United States people seem to oscillate between these two positions. On the one hand the more sterile the minute the less for a lawyer to have a go at; on the other the easier a negligence suit might be. There are strongly held and differing views on both sides of the Atlantic and no clear consensus. Some adopt a traditionally neat, English, compromise and use the following style of words:

- The board took the following factors into account in reaching the decision to continue to manufacture the XYZ product following the recent leak at the ABC plant.
- The safety inspectorate confirmed the plant was made safe on DD/MM/YY. In their view the reason for the leak had been clearly identified and a number of minor procedural changes were recommended.
- A paper from the company's technical director highlighted a number of procedural enhancements which the board immediately approved.
- Workforce representatives were comfortable with the proposal to continue manufacture.
- The board also noted the positive press reporting about the company's major incident plan.
- The board wished to thank the human resources team for the way in which they provided support for the individuals injured and their families.
- The XYZ product is a long-established and significant profit earner for the group.

One of the questions I have asked chairmen and independent directors is how often they refer to previous board minutes. 'Never' was a more common response than I had envisaged. Not too surprisingly, for companies undergoing crisis 'always' was a popular response. The reasons many gave for not referring to previous minutes were twofold. Firstly their company secretary would usually circulate draft minutes for comment immediately following the board meeting. 'Immediately' typically meant within a fortnight. They would always read these and ensure that their recollection was the same as in the minutes, although the company secretaries often said:

'Few people question them and if anyone does it is always Bloggs.'

For subsequent board meetings the company secretary would normally ensure that in the preparation of papers relevant minutes from previous meetings would be noted. Most company secretaries bring relevant and recent board meetings with them to all board meetings. A number of company secretaries in larger businesses are now taking advantage of sophisticated document scanning and searching systems. For smaller companies and those less technically minded a good old fashioned indexing system seems to do the trick.

Minutes are usually written by the company secretary or in a larger business their assistant. Many now avoid shorthand for minute taking on the grounds that it encourages them to write too much. Most will circulate the minutes to all board members and those affected by a decision of the board who need to take action or be aware.

Sometimes people interpret what has been said as something quite different and the language of board minutes is an art form in itself. Here are some examples:

- 'The board concluded that the acquisition of ABC company made an excellent strategic fit.'

or put another way:

- *'We couldn't find any financial justification for this deal whatsoever.'*
- 'The board had a healthy discussion over the proposed expansion of the company's plant in North Carolina.'
- *'We had a right good punch up and no one could find North Carolina on the map.'*

■ 'The board was saddened by the resignation of Mr Andrew Smith and thanked him for his service to the company through a difficult period.'

■ *'Thank God he resigned before we had to fire him.'*

■ 'The board approved the £100 million acquisition/buy-back of shares in the company from the market.'

■ *'We've run out of ideas and leaving us with the money could be dangerous.'*

■ 'After a long and far-reaching discussion to which all board members contributed it was agreed to accept the managing director's original proposal.'

■ *'As the company secretary I dozed off during this debate and I knew you would do what the MD said in any event.'*

■ 'Mr Zap, the marketing director, reported that the company was entering into a paradigm shift in the market-place.'

■ *'There is a new product out there and we don't know what the hell is happening.'*

■ 'After careful consideration the matter was deferred to the next meeting.'

■ *'Too difficult to get our minds around. If we leave it for a bit it might go away.'*

■ 'There was a long debate about the proposed information technology strategy. It was agreed that the auditors be asked to prepare a report verifying the proposals and commenting on the cost implications.'

■ *'We couldn't understand a word of it and we'd better get someone else to give it the OK.'*

■ 'The board considered the position statement from the auditors and decided that on balance taking all things into account the company met the solvency criteria.'

■ *'We're hopelessly bust but we might just get saved by that big potential new order.'*

■ 'Having regard to the duties imposed upon them as directors under the Companies Act and, in particular, having carefully considered the implications of the Insolvency Act, the directors unanimously agreed, in the light of the encouraging discussions held between the chairman, finance director and messrs Nat Lloyds Bank, that the company should continue to trade until such time as these discussions had inter alia been drawn to a mutually satisfactory conclusion.'

■ *'The company is more or less bust and the minutes are being prepared by our lawyers in case the receivers get nasty.'*

- The chairman suggested that the board strategy away day would be more effective if held in more informal and relaxed surroundings away from the office.'
- *'Three days golf at Gleneagles – yippeeeee!'*
- 'The chairman reminded the board of the importance of receiving board papers in good time.'
- *'I don't want to see another motorcycle courier on my doorstep at 9.30 pm on a Sunday night ever again.'*
- 'In reply to the independent director's question the finance director drew attention to page 2 of the financial report and said that there had been no change from the previous occasion.'
- *'The FD wondered whether he ever read any of the board papers and indeed why he asked the same bloody stupid question every month.'*
- 'The sales director explained that the period two sales budget shortfall was due to seasonal factors.'
- *'That should hold them for a bit.'*
- 'The sales director explained that the cumulative shortfall in sales at period six masked a very encouraging picture on potential new orders for the following six months.'
- *'He's praying very hard.'*
- 'In reporting the continued budget shortfall in period nine the sales director explained that this followed the worst:

(a) Weather

(b) Market conditions

(c) Levels of consumer confidence

(d) Dumping by foreigners

(e) Strength of the currency

(f) Lack of government spending he could remember for thirty years.'

- *'Aaargh!'*
- 'The chairman welcomed the new sales director to the board and congratulated him on his proposals to totally reorganise the salesforce and distribution network.'
- *'Spotted at last.'*

HOW SHOULD THE BOARD COMMUNICATE ITS DECISIONS?

"You're fired, Donaldson!"   "I'm sorry, I don't get
                                    your drift, sir."

During my research it quickly became apparent that many boards were unaware of the impressions they were giving to other members of the business through the process of the board meetings. Put simply, well organised and highly effective meetings give all those who are involved in the preparation, the meeting itself or the follow-up an impression of a well organised and highly effective board. The opposite is obviously also true. A board's image is important but often only thought of in the context of its members' images.

There is no point having a board meeting which felt great, was intellectually stimulating and from which some inspired decisions emerged if you can't then put them into action because of poor communication. Sir Denys Henderson, who considers this one of the most important aspects of board meetings, uses a simple mnemonic to help him. He calls it 'The Four Cs':

Conviction: that a major course of action is right.

Commitment: from the key players in the drama is high.

Communication: about the decisions which have to be implemented.

Cooperation: from those needed to carry the decision out will be forthcoming.

Strong conviction may be displayed in all sorts of ways. The great historic leaders and business heroes have always been able to communicate a spirit of determination to achieve the desired aim no matter what the challenges or practical difficulties were at the time. This devout belief that what they are trying to achieve is 'the right thing' runs right throughout the team and is a virus which spreads like wildfire. Disbelievers tend to go quickly and quietly. Just remember the way Kennedy told the American people that they would have a man on the moon. It seems pretty clear he didn't really know whether it could be done, and there certainly wasn't unanimity over it either.

Generating and then demonstrating a sense of strong conviction from a group rather than an individual is more demanding. After all, it will often be the case that a decision to proceed with a proposal may not be unanimous whether there is a vote or not. Some chairmen will choose not to proceed if it might threaten the unity of the board. Those with strong conviction are normally very good at letting you know where they stand. They are sometimes less comfortable at letting others know where they stand.

Appropriate consultation is critical. How irritating it can be when you have had a proposal from the best performer in the business who looks to have researched it superbly before a lively and deep debate at the board approves it only to find some area of research no one thought of shows quite quickly that it's a non-flyer. There is an old chemical industry saying handy for situations when you feel things are being ill considered:

■ *'You can't build the plant and then think about the safety.'*

Consultation is important from at least two points of view. Firstly the more people you listen to who have useful knowledge on the subject the more likely you are to have covered all the angles. Secondly you are much more likely to gain the commitment and cooperation required for your chosen plan if people have been involved in helping to form it. This is perhaps why the methods used by Japanese companies to commission new plants are traditionally compared with those of Europeans. In Europe we take only two months to decide to build a new plant and then three years to build it. In Japan it takes a year to gain consensus and to reach the decision to build it, but only then a year for construction.

Commitment from the key players is much easier when there is a unity of purpose. You need to avoid the prospect of anyone leaving the board meeting and saying 'they decided'. Several chief executives I know do this by example. In a recent situation a board decided, following pressure from some of its employees, to 'get more green'. It decided to introduce several 'paper reduction strategies' immediately. This might have sounded trivial but a board is much more likely to get the commitment of others in the organisation if it too is committed to doing what matters to them.

Cooperation from your champions is achieved when they are thrilled at the prospect of carrying out the board's decision. All the other people who will get extra work or be affected need to be told in an appropriate way too. You have to get them motivated, directly or otherwise. Many boards now circulate the chief executive's report to the rest of the organisation.

A striking example of the dangers of not giving enough attention to consultation and communication with stakeholders was what happened to Shell in 2004. Failure to communicate effectively cost the chairman Sir Philip Watts his job.

BOARD REVIEW

When I wrote the first edition of this book in 1997 I wrote:

Few of us do this even though we analyse the hell out of everything else in the business in our search for higher standards and more profit. Surprising that the business process re-engineers haven't got to it yet. Or perhaps they and we think that a board meeting is such a special, mystical and inviolate thing that we shouldn't?

You get an interesting reaction when you ask people about reviewing agendas, minutes and the process of a board meeting. There's pretty well universal agreement that it's a good idea. Most people will then go on to tell you that they do it but informally and are pretty vague as to how. 'I think about it a lot on long aeroplane flights and in the bath,' one chairman told me. Another said that he wished he had the nerve 'to invite the most awkward arrogant sod in the company to review the board's process!' Amusingly when I asked him who he thought this might be he said: 'Second thoughts, not such a good idea, it's me.'

Although it would be easy to put together a Cosmopolitan magazine style 'How was it for you, dear?' questionnaire in order to get feedback, this may not be the natural medium for board members. Imagine trying to rate your partners out of ten for compatibility, the effectiveness of their boardroom foreplay, their ability to respect you in the morning or their willingness to think about safety when excited!

A more straightforward list of things to review and do might be:

- composition of the board;
- frequency of meetings;
- allocation of time;
- the boardroom;
- what six or seven key things do we need to get right this coming year?
- are they allowed for in the board agenda?
- try and get to visit some other board meetings – ask them what they have on their agendas at the moment.

Pretty unsophisticated heh!

Since then the consultants have certainly moved in, much hot air has been blown on the subject, but many have recognised that there is value in conducting pragmatic reviews and the Higgs review has provided a stimulus. Overall the art of board review has moved on to a higher level and the debate has been healthy.

Two key issues for a chairman to decide when establishing a board review process are obviously what aspects will be reviewed and secondly where you want to be on what I call the *'formality spectrum'*.

The way in which reviews are conducted is as important as what is being reviewed. I have seen a very wide range of approaches adopted. At the informal end of the *'formality spectrum'* lies the traditional lunch with a board member where the chairman waits for the right mood and then gives a bit of feedback. If there is any negative feedback to give, it is given in coded language. At the other end of the *'formality spectrum'* is a hugely bureaucratic, sterile and inefficient process involving considerable external support and cost and which somehow, despite the process, ducks the real issues.

When it comes to what to review I would tend to go back to my little triangle.

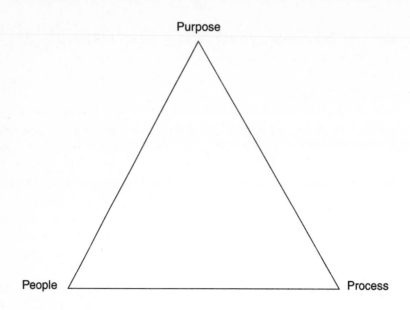

It is fairly straightforward using this to list the things you want to do under each of the headings. It should be a very quick job to review the purpose and one wouldn't expect this to change much. Most reviews will therefore tend to focus on the people and the process issues.

Many chairman have decided to take a step-by-step approach to board reviews, striking a balance between the informal and formal, and this seems to me to be the right way.

The Higgs report recommended the following with respect to board reviews:

- performance evaluation of the board, its committees and its individual directors should be undertaken at least once a year.
- the chairman should act on the results of this evaluation by recognising the strengths and weaknesses of the board and, where appropriate, appointing new board members or seeking the resignation of directors; and
- the board should state in the annual report whether such performance evaluation is taking place and how it is conducted.

In summary, 'just do it', 'act upon the result' and 'tell your shareholders how you are doing it'. No surprise then that almost 90 per cent of the 762 directors surveyed in Independent Remuneration Solutions 2005 report said that they would be conducting a review. The majority of them were on public company boards. Most of them thought that the process would take about a day for each board member time and cost more than £25,000 if they used a consultant to support the process.

As boards have experimented with different approaches a range of issues have emerged.

The quality and effectiveness of consultants in this area is highly variable. It is after all a new market and one which has attracted not just those with the requisite skills but also a bunch of people ill qualified to do the job, just looking for a fast buck. As with any consultancy supplier, the customer has to be clear what the job is, what they are prepared to pay, how they are going to manage the supplier and to conduct a proper pitch to select the right firm or individual. Many boards have used consultants simply to assist in exploring the range of approaches available, with the aim of helping them make the right selection.

For a process to be effective it must be led by the chairman, the leader of the board team. The chairman also must subject him or herself to the same depth of feedback as the rest of the team. Most turkeys don't vote for Christmas, so some chairman will inevitably feel very threatened by the idea of a board review process. The mere suggestion to some might be taken as an insult. But reviews are hard to argue against if they start in a very basic way, so in these circumstances they tend to begin with reviewing board process and duck the people issues. However, it usually doesn't take too long for the people issues to emerge. For example, common agreement that board meetings are hopelessly ineffective is giving the Chairman feedback.

On the subject of feedback I personally have a strong preference for conversation rather than questionnaire. You tend to get so much more this way. However, if the relationships aren't robust or developed, there is a place for either using a consultant to gather the feedback and play it back or for a straightforward questionnaire to be used as a first step.

There has been so much written on the art and science of 360 degree feedback processes that I won't cover it here. However, I think it is worth making the point that it is hard for someone to meet expectations if there isn't any clarity about what those expectations are. It is still the case that many non-executives don't have clear objectives. It is no surprise then that a common complaint from those departing is that *'The first time you told me what you wanted me to do was when you told me I hadn't done it'*. In my view the responsibility for establishing some good sensible objectives lies both with the chairman and the individual director.

As many listed companies are now reporting on the processes that they are using to conduct board reviews, I expect there will, like in so many other areas, be a 'norming' process that will take place over the next few years. What I hope is that board reviews will not become a chore, will not become a triumph of form over substance and will genuinely turn out to be useful things to do to add value for shareholders. Otherwise what's the point!

Conclusion

Every musician or sportsman knows that whenever they think about their technique they improve their performance. Whatever the size of your company, whether you are an experienced practitioner or aspirant, I hope that there has been something in this book that has struck a chord and provoked thought.

Appendix I:

The **CHEMCO** Case Study

THE SITUATION

You are the chairman of a north-west based chemicals company, CHEMCO, which has a £30 million turnover and £1.5 million profits before tax.

A regular monthly board meeting has been scheduled for 10.00 am today. Unfortunately yesterday there was an explosion at one of the company's plants. Three people were killed and a cloud of toxic gas was released causing the evacuation of local buildings within a one mile radius.

CHEMCO was established in the 1950s and has had an excellent safety record. Like many similar companies, there have been minor leakages over the years, but this is the first serious incident. There are 150 employees and the company is owned by its management (60 per cent), an institutional investor (30 per cent) and former employees (10 per cent). Of the £30 million turnover £10 million relates to a Dutch subsidiary and there is an ambitious European expansion plan.

Rather than call an emergency board meeting last night, you chose to focus on ensuring the plant was made safe, dealing with the media and personally visiting the families of those killed. You managed to speak to all the executive directors face to face and your two independent non-executive directors by telephone. The experience has been traumatic for you, your management and the employees. As yet, no obvious cause has been identified.

There are seven topics for discussion:

1. What should the agenda for this meeting be now and how long should it last?
2. What did you think of the original agenda and of the company's board calendar (see below)? What do you think an ideal board agenda should consist of?
3. Do you think the supporting information provided is adequate for this meeting? If not, what else might you reasonably require as a director of the company?
4. Describe what you think the chairman's role should be at this meeting. Who else other than the board members should attend?
5. What impression do you think the board should give to the various interest groups – employees, customers, suppliers, the media, the families involved and others?
6. Role play the meeting for 30 minutes on the attached revised agenda and then decide what you would record as minutes.
7. What subcommittees should you expect the board of a company like this to have as a matter of course and what would be their remits? Should the board establish any new subcommittees to deal with its new circumstances? If so, what and with what remits?

SUPPORTING INFORMATION

- Original agenda
- Profiles of board and key players
- MD's initial report on accident
- Sales director's report
- Technical director's report
- Board calendar
- Revised agenda (topic 6 only!)

Original agenda

AGENDA
CHEMCO Board Meeting
at 10.00 am on today's date
CHEMCO offices

1. Previous Minutes
2. Managing Director's Report
3. Finance Director's Report
4. Pricing Strategy for Next Quarter
5. Potential Acquisition for £4m of Small CHEMCO
6. Company Car Policy
7. Annual Insurance Review
8. Presentation by our Dutch MD
9. Any Other Business

12.30 pm   Lunch
           Guests: Rudi Van den Dam (Dutch MD)
           Mike Smith (Small CHEMCO MD)

Profiles of the board

Chairman   (53)   Experienced chemical manufacturing man. Early career with ICI. Joined CHEMCO ten years ago as MD when the turnover was £5 million and profits £300,000. Led a management buy-out ten years ago and became chairman. A consensus style of leader with strong communication and marketing skills.

Managing Director   (47)   Another ex-ICI man. Joined two years before the buyout as production director, became MD when the buy-out took place. A traditional, highly professional attender to detail. Very well regarded in the industry and a leading light on safety issues. Slightly autocratic and intolerant, but commands considerable respect within the business.

Finance Director   (39)   Formerly manager of the CHEMCO audit. Joined at the same time as the MD. Known within the company as Mr 'Scenario'. Always presents the options available and is a perfect judge of their outcome, but not a natural decision-taker!

Technical Director   (39)   Promoted to the board last year. Known as 'brains' throughout the company. Very bright. Has in-depth knowledge of the company's plants and processes. Less commercially adept, though wonderful with customers when explaining company's technical merits. Not generally confident when dealing with the outside world. Recently nominated as technical advisor to the Industry Safety Council.

Sales Director*   (44)   Home-grown, natural salesman. Strong
                                       on motivating the sales-force. Slightly
                                       difficult relationship with production,
                                       but wins their respect through perfor-
                                       mance rather than attitude. Particularly
                                       sensitive to the company's image and
                                       reputation.

Independent Director 1 (52)   Nominee   of   institutional   investor.
                                       Seasoned campaigner for chemical in-
                                       dustry who has been successful in an
                                       earlier MBO.

Independent Director 2 (54)   Previously European MD of a multina-
                                       tional engineering company. He is
                                       highly numerate and marketing led and
                                       is on the Board for his international
                                       management experience.

*Not on main board, but usually attends.

MD's initial report of accident

■ At approximately 10.00 am a pipe in section 16 of the main plant burst, showering a team of ten who were performing maintenance in the area with high temperature, toxic gas. Debris from this explosion also burst a nearby storage tank causing leakage of product X producing an orange, pungent cloud which, although not life threatening, caused major eye and skin irritation. The blast in section 16 could be heard throughout the plant and in our adjacent head office.

■ Buildings were evacuated (as per the regular safety training) and a bewildered and frightened staff assembled in the car park.

■ The injured were attended by first-aiders, again in accordance with procedure and training.

■ Side-effects of the leaking gas (eg severe eye and skin irritation and coughing) exaggerated the fear of a further explosion.

■ Emergency services were on the scene in minutes.

■ All mains power and services were isolated.

■ Of the ten in the area, the initial report was that the two nearest were dead, three others unconscious and the rest suffering severe shock and blast damage.

■ Gas and power officials arrived within ten minutes to assist the fire service and make safe the plant.

■ The company's lawyers provided a solicitor on site within an hour to help with employee's statements and to advise the company generally.

■ The media arrived in force with some fairly intrusive camera crews and aggressive questioning of employees: 'Whose fault is it?' 'Was this an accident waiting to happen?' etc. Distressed employees became angry at the intrusion, leading to further difficulties.

■ Two hours after the blast, the first factory inspector arrived on the scene.

Sales Director's Report

You asked me for a clear and concise assessment and some suggested actions.

- This is a major blow to our credibility because quality has been a major USP of ours and we have been able to command a high price because of our record.
- Our competitors will have a field day. We will need to cut prices to respond.
- Hopefully, the cause will be due to the maintenance contractor and we can rightly say it was their responsibility. We should change contracts immediately to reinforce this message.
- We will need the chairman to visit our top ten customers as soon as possible (ie this week) to reassure them.
- The more active PR campaign discussed at our May board meeting should be activated immediately. The best form of defence is attack.
- We must do something immediately to restore the morale of the salesforce. I suggest that the increased delegated authority proposals we discussed at the last board meeting are implemented immediately.

Technical Director's Report

- We have followed the emergency procedures to the letter and I am convinced we could not be faulted on compliance grounds.
- There must always be the possibility that the maintenance was not carried out in accordance with the procedures manual, although given the incapacity of those actually present, we just can't say at this point.
- The contractor has been used by us for the last four years. All of the contractor's staff performing maintenance yesterday were trained on this type of plant and accredited as per the contract. However, all were new to our plant. Our own trainee who was joining them as a formal part of his key programme is still in his six-month probationary period and the supervisor who was scheduled to join him was absent with flu. The stand-in supervisor decided to continue as the maintenance was classified as essential and was a routine item. I was not notified of the supervisor's absence.
- In order to help the company I feel I should resign with immediate effect and also stand down from the Industry Safety Council role. I must accept responsibility.

CHEMCO board calendar

CHEMCO Board Calendar 200*			
All meetings held in boardroom at Mills Road unless otherwise indicated.			
January 26th (Tuesday)	11.30 am	**REMUNERATION and APPOINTMENTS COMMITTEE**	
	1.00 pm	**LUNCH**	
	2.00 pm	**BOARD**	
February 23rd (Tuesday)	1.00 pm	**LUNCH**	
	2.00 pm	**BOARD** – followed by	
	c. 4.30 pm	**AUDIT COMMITTEE**	
March 30th (Tuesday)	11.00 am	**REMUNERATION and APPOINTMENTS COMMITTEE**	
	1.00 pm	**LUNCH**	
	2.00 pm	**BOARD**	
April 27th (Tuesday)	1.00 pm	**LUNCH**	
	2.00 pm	**BOARD** – Environmental Review	
May 11th (Tuesday)	10.00 am	**ANNUAL ACCOUNTS REVIEW**	
	11.00 am	**ANNUAL BONUS/PROFIT SHARE APPROVAL**	
18th (Tuesday)	1.00 pm	**LUNCH**	
	2.00 pm	**BOARD** – Approval of Dividend/Accounts	
25th (Tuesday)		**CUSTOMER EVENT** – Paris	

June		
1st (Tuesday)		**AUDIT COMMITTEE**
29th (Tuesday	1.00 pm	**LUNCH**
	2.00 pm	**BOARD**
July		
27th (Tuesday)		**ANNUAL GENERAL MEETING**
September		
28th (Tuesday)	11.00 am	**AUDIT COMMITTEE**
	1.00 pm	**LUNCH**
	2.00 pm	**BOARD**
October		
25th (evening) –		
26th (Tuesday)		**AWAY DAY CONFERENCE** Castle Howard
27th (Wednesday)	1.00 pm	**LUNCH**
	2.00 pm	**BOARD**
November		
16th (Tuesday)		**ANNUAL CONFERENCE** London
30th (Tuesday)	1.00 pm	**LUNCH**
	2.00 pm	**BOARD**
December		
14th (Tuesday)	1.00 pm	**LUNCH**
	2.00 pm	**BOARD**
	7.00 pm	**STAFF CHRISTMAS PARTY**

200*
Timetable of Calendar Items at Board Meetings

January   Insurance

February   Pensions

March   Environmental
                   Capital Expenditure Approvals

April   Information Systems

May   Safety
                   Balance Sheet Structure

June   Car Policy
                   Capital Expenditure Approvals

July   Marketing

August   Human Resources

September   Litigation
                   Capital Expenditure Approvals

October   Technology

November   Training

December   Capital Expenditure Approvals

Revised Agenda

CHEMCO Board Meeting
at 10.00 am on today's date
CHEMCO offices

- Communications:
  - employees
  - customers
  - suppliers
  - media

- Accident Investigations

- Likely Financial Impact

- Plant Re-start
  - when

- Stock Shortages/Customer Reaction

- Small CHEMCO Acquisition
  - press ahead or call a halt?

- Rudi Van den Dam's Presentation

- Any Other Business

Appendix II:

The Convo Case Study

Convo is a South Coast food manufacturing business. It was founded by its Chairman and Chief Executive, Archie Cresswell. Archie is an infectiously enthusiastic and effervescent process engineer who, over a ten year period, has grown Convo from nothing into a business with a forty million pound turnover. In the process he has been awarded a CBE and developed a profile for the business far in excess of its size. Convo has also won a Queen's Technology Award together with a string of industry prizes for innovation.

The business manufactures a mix of own label and branded products for the major UK multiple Supermarkets. It wins customers on the strength of its highly innovative way of processing, preparing and presenting its products. Three customers account for seventy per cent of sales; the balance are smaller retailers and an exciting but somewhat volatile French agent.

Archie's former employer, BigFood Co, supply most of the processing plant. They also own forty per cent of Convo through their initial support of Archie. Archie, his Finance Director, Paul Tate and the other two executive directors own fifteen per cent. Five per cent has been granted in employee shares. The remaining forty per cent is held by an institutional syndicate who invested five years ago to fund the building of a new plant. They did so in anticipation of a float three years ago.

The business has a public aura of success but the institutions are clearly becoming concerned, hence your recent appointment to the board as a non-executive director. You can understand some of their increased anxiety and have decided to jot down the following analysis:

1. The company's strategic direction is making it increasingly reliant on its few key customers. This factor also seems to be moving it closer to competing head-on with global players, such as Unilever and Nestlé.

2. Cash generative growth years fuelled by a high-margin environment are over. Surplus cash has been invested in developing new brands and building plant capacity. Recent construction of a new head office/warehouse complex has exacerbated the problem through cost overruns and disruption to deliveries. The retailers have been unsympathetic, so have the institutions with regard to deferring dividend payments. Convo is up to its overdraft limit of £8m.

3. You feel that the business has outgrown its management, which is largely inbred. Financial controls are poor, management information is over-elaborate and tends to cloud rather than highlight key issues. You are not convinced about the profitability of two of the eight key product groups. Management is demoralised by constant changes in strategic direction by the mercurial but much loved Archie.

4. The relationship with BigFood Co has become strained and less productive for Convo. Convo had to become far too involved in the detailed design of the latest machines and in fixing the considerable number of teething problems on installation. BigFood Co's new Chief Executive has allegedly been questioning the strategic sense in holding minority investments. Having said that, you are suspicious that they might be interested in acquiring control on the cheap. The Convo Board is divided into two (if not three) camps and there is much gathering of interest groups pre board meetings. BigFood Co's board representative has become evermore vocal and disparaging in his remarks.

5. This and next year will probably be loss-making given the margin squeeze from the retailers and the fact that the latest equipment is still producing at costs much higher than budgeted. There is no possibility of a claim on BigFood Co.

6. Despite all of the above, this fundamentally remains a business with enormous potential in its market and has a deeply committed and talented workforce.

Profiles of the Board members are given below. As the only independent board member, all partners (other than BigFood Co) seem to be looking to you to take the lead and catalyse the situation. You need to consider the following questions:

- What are the issues?
- How could the current situation have been avoided?
- What are the options?

Note

The articles of association for the company give BigFood Co two board votes, the institutions two board votes and management one vote. There is no casting vote for the chair. There are no compulsory purchase shareholder leaver provisions except in the termination for cause as stipulated in the service agreement of the individual director concerned. In this instance an executive shareholding may be compulsorily purchased at valuation.

Board Profiles

Archie Cresswell (45) Chairman and Chief Executive

An extreme workaholic. He loves the company – it's his baby and he knows every single employee on a first-name basis. Over the years, despite his ego, he has never paid himself adequately. Eighteen months ago the board insisted on awarding him a one hundred per cent salary increase and forced a three-year rolling contract on him. He seems a straightforward, open chap who can see that all is not well. He dominates the company, is strongly defensive of his own position and feels let down by his team. Beneath a seemingly naive and homespun exterior he can prove wonderfully adept at playing off the two shareholding factions (BigFood Co and the institutions). Domestically he is supported by a strong family who think the world of him and his achievements even though he neglects them.

Paul Tate FCA (42) Finance Director

A local man who qualified with a minor firm in the next town but got bored with auditing. Two years after qualifying he moved into broader commercial management, mostly in trading and commodity businesses. When Archie set up Convo and asked him to be Finance Director he was flattered and thrilled and considered the prospect a hugely exciting one. He did, however, have to gear up and borrow from his father-in-law to invest at the start and in subsequent rounds. A natural overcomplicator who will often miss the central point, like Archie Paul is a workaholic and is having severe problems at home. He and his wife enjoy the reflected glory of being part of the Convo success story and, despite a relatively low income, are big spenders.

Terence Foster PhD (38) Technical Director

A brilliant food technologist who pioneered the first, and still most successful, Convo product. He has always worked with Archie and has an undying loyalty to him despite growing frustration at the difficulty in finding cash to enhance the plant. Terence is financially and commercial unaware and very much the brains of the team. He hates formal presentations to investors but is always thrilled at the prospect of showing visiting buyers and the local University round the plant. He dislikes any general management activity.

Heather Brigland MBA (41) Commercial Director

Joined only two years ago from Unilever after an earlier spell at Bain and a career break. Brought in to bring more rigour to strategic thinking and planning. Sadly she has has never been able to break in to the core team of Archie, Paul and Terence and is considered and treated very much as an outsider with no influence over the board. This is a shame as intellectually she makes excellent points and if she were listened to would add a great deal. However she often tends to blow it by missing trivial practical points. She also seems to be perpetually trying to alienate Réne by scoring points.

Réne Faux (45) BigFood Co representative

Joined BigFood Co in France as a graduate the same year as Archie, although they didn't meet until they both got their first general managers jobs. Initially they got on well but once sat on the same project group and fell out violently over a redundancy programme. Réne's career faltered and he has been deeply envious of Archie's independence and very visible success. However, recently he feels he has been gaining ground and, with two highly successful acquisitions behind him, has risen to prominence within BigFood Co. He only got the board representation job at Convo when his predecessor, a former mentor of Archie's, retired. There is nothing more he would like than to put Archie in the position of having to report to him or give up his business. Archie dislikes Réne with a surprising intensity.

Angelique Beaulie (32) BigFood Co's second representative

Réne's associate. She tends to be quiet but demonstrates remarkable insight and presence when she does join in the conversation. Réne is slightly irritated by Angelique's ability to say in a few well-chosen and charming words what needs saying.

Clive Maxwell (37)

The board representative from the lead venture capital investor. Convo is his star investment and he's done much trumpeting of it inside the institution. He's becoming increasingly uncomfortable as he is out fund-raising himself and it isn't going that well. His boss has made it clear to him that if the fund-raising falls through because of problems at Convo, he won't have a job.

You – The Independent Director

A seasoned campaigner with experience of five appointments in young food companies, all of whom have experienced growing pains. You love a problem. That's handy!

Convo Subsequent challenges

Challenge one

Having stabilised the position, you decide that management has to be regrouped, and that Archie has to go. You have obtained the attached summary of his service contract. The institutions are behind you but you haven't discussed it with BigFood Co. yet.

What board process do you need to go through and what difficulties do you foresee in implementation?

Challenge two

Instead of removing Archie you decide to adopt a gradual approach and persuade Archie to bring in a new Managing Director beneath him together with a new Finance Director to replace Paul Tate. After eighteen months, Archie falls out with both of them. You remain impressed with the changes they have made.

What would you do now and what board process do you need to go through to implement your decisions?

Challenge three

The financial position deteriorates significantly and the business needs five million pounds injected. The institutional investors have been asked and they have resolved that they will only put up this money if there are management changes. BigFood Co is prepared to provide the money without changing management but insists on acquiring control at a depressed rights issue price. Archie refuses to open up the bidding to outside parties.

What would you do now?

Service Agreement

ARCHIBALD CRESSWELL (the 'Executive')
and
CONVO LTD (the 'Company')

Summary Points

Position:	Managing Director or in such other capacity as the Board of Directors of the Company ('the Board') may determine.
Period:	For three years from 31 March 200* until 31 March 200* and thereafter unless and until determined by either party giving to the other not less than twelve months prior written notice.
Remuneration:	Salary £150,000 per annum inclusive of all directors fees subject to an annual review on 31st March in each year. The Executive and his family are to be entitled to private medical insurance. In addition ten per cent of salary will be paid annually into a private pension fund. The Company will also pay for life assurance cover equal to four times salary.

Expenses:	All reasonable expenses incurred by the Executive in the discharge of his duties will be reimbursed.
Motor Car:	BMW 730i fully expensed.
Restrictions:	For so long as the Executive owns shares or is employed by the Company he will not compete with any food businesses of the Company or its subsidiaries, solicit customers or entice away employees.
	If his employment is terminated the above restrictions apply for twelve months following the date of termination.
Termination:	The Company can terminate, without notice, if guilty of material or persistent dishonesty, misconduct or serious breach of obligation, if incapacitated by illness or mental disorder or subject to bankruptcy. In such an event the Executive can make no claim for compensation.
Suspension:	If allegations arise out of serious breach of obligations, the Board can decide to suspend the Executive.
Board Appointments:	Upon termination of this agreement, the Executive resigns his directorships.

Appendix III:

The Menu Style Appointment Letter for an Independent Director

Objective: To align the expectations of the company and the independent director (ID) from the outset and set the tone of the relationship.

Method: A brief punchy letter between the company and the ID. Where the ID is a nominee there will also need to be a nomination letter from the shareholder concerned.

POINTS TO COVER

- Background to appointment
- Formality of appointment
- Basis of ID role
- If chairman, additional description of chairman's role
- How the ID will gain familiarity with the business
- Information flow
- Membership of board committees
- Meeting with auditors
- Intended term/rotation, termination process
- Time commitment

- Notification of other appointments
- Fees and how payable
- Insurance arrangements
- Independent professional advice
- Review process
- Security

BACKGROUND TO APPOINTMENT

For example: 'Following our recent MBO/MBI/raising of investment capital/acquisition of/decision to move into the German market etc the board has decided it could benefit from the appointment of an/additional independent director/chairman.'

FORMALITY OF APPOINTMENT

The board has/will approved/approve a resolution appointing you as a director; as from 1 January 200* the terms of your appointment as an independent director of this company are set out in the following paragraphs. I understand that the nominating institution has set out the terms of your nomination in a separate letter.

BASIS OF THE INDEPENDENT DIRECTOR ROLE

Independent directors have the same responsibilities to the company as any other director.

Your primary role is to:

- bring an independent and broad view to the board;
- be involved in the creation of a robust strategy;
- review and monitor the detailed plans and budgets needed to make it work.

We expect you to provide practical guidance in a wide variety of other areas including:

- being a confidential sounding board for the directors;
- enabling the board to make best use of time so that sufficient consideration is given to the development of strategy and the management structure;
- objective assessment of the company's performance and guidance on the principles of corporate legislation and compliance;
- financing;
- communication with customers, suppliers, government authorities and, most importantly, employees;
- ensuring the board has adequate systems to safeguard the interests of the company where these may conflict with the personal interests of individual directors; eg to exercise a duty to the company in such areas as board remuneration;
- ensuring that all shareholders are being provided with sufficient and timely information with which to monitor the performance of the company;
- to help ensure that the company maintains a high standard of executive leadership;
- to help ensure that the company makes and implements proper and timely plans for management successions.

CHAIRMAN'S ROLE

(ie if an independent chairman is being appointed)

- To lead the board in the determination of its strategy and in the achievement of its objectives.
- To take responsibility for organising the composition, business and efficiency of the board.
- To ensure the board has accurate and clear visibility of results achieved and likely future trends.
- To ensure board committees are established and adequately composed.
- To take responsibility for ensuring effective relationships are maintained with all major stakeholders in the business: shareholders, employees, customers, suppliers, government, industry, etc.
- To take overall responsibility for enhancing the company's public standing.
- To take responsibility for developing a strong working relationship with the chief executive/managing director and ensure there is a clear definition and agreement of the division of responsibilities.

HOW THE INDEPENDENT DIRECTOR WILL GAIN FAMILIARITY WITH THE BUSINESS

Obviously the ID will have had extensive information (written and verbal) in getting to this point so the list below is over-comprehensive.

■ We are delighted to provide you with the attached information pack containing:

 – Copies of the last five years' audited accounts, together with the management letters from our auditors

 – Management accounts for the year to date

 – A sample of our promotional literature

 – General information about the company

 – Our latest strategy (four-page business plan exec summary)

 – An organisational chart/CVs of board members

 – Our 'Who's Where' telephone guide

 – Shareholding analysis

 – Memorandum and Articles of Association

 – A summary list of our current banking covenants and the terms of investment by X

 – Papers and agenda for our last board meeting

 – List of key dates

 – Latest company newsletter.

■ During your first three months of office we would like you to visit each of our three sites and spend one day working in the business at a front-line level.

- As a first project we would like your informed views on how effective our current contract review process is.
- We would like you to take part in our Board Away Day at Noggings Hotel on 10 January 200* (papers attached).
- We would like very much, if you agree, to do a profile of you for the next edition of our newsletter. Jane Banks will be in touch to discuss this with you.

TIME COMMITMENT

Overall we anticipate two days/month after the induction phase. This will include:

- our monthly board meetings, one of which will be on the same day as the AGM. Board meetings are held at our three sites in rotation;
- our annual Board Awayday;
- half a day at our annual customer exhibition;
- the staff Christmas party!

Any time commitment above and beyond that currently envisaged will be paid for as described below.

INFORMATION FLOW

On a regular basis we would expect to provide you with:

- monthly management accounts;
- board discussion papers;
- information on any other matters material to the board.

Board agendas and related papers are sent one week in advance of each board meeting.

NOTIFICATION OF OTHER APPOINTMENTS

We will expect you to discuss potential new appointments with our chairman and keep us informed of any changes.

MEMBERSHIP OF BOARD COMMITTEES

We would very much like you to become a member of our audit/remuneration/appointments committee/s. The composition, terms of reference and recent papers of this/these committee/s are attached.

MEETINGS WITH AUDITORS

We would expect you to have an annual meeting with our auditors to discuss relevant matters. Our current audit partner is R Moxill of Grabit and Run (tel no).

INTENDED TERM/ROTATION/TERMINATION PROCESS

We are appointing you with the intention of the appointment lasting for a three-year period subject to annual review and termination by either side on a month's notice. There is to be no compensation due for loss of office.

REVIEW PROCESS

We think it would be a good idea for you and (the Chairman) to have a discussion as to how the appointment is working out after the initial three-month induction phase. Thereafter it would be good practice for us to sit down annually and discuss effectiveness. I would hope and expect in the interim if there were any matters which caused you concern about the role you would discuss them with me as soon as is appropriate for you.

FEES AND HOW PAYABLE

- The fee payable to you will be £20,000 per annum payable monthly in arrears. I understand you would like this paid to your company IND Ltd. You should submit your invoice before the 21st of each month to ensure you meet our payment run.
- Reasonable out-of-pocket expenses incurred by you in carrying out your duties will be reimbursed. To obtain payment please submit one of the attached expense claim forms.
- If you have incurred unforeseen, but agreed, extra time on our behalf over the anticipated 24 days pa, we will make an additional payment of £1000 per day.

INSURANCE OBLIGATIONS

- We expect you to make our own arrangements with regard to directors' and officers' liability insurance.
- The company purchases and maintains directors' and officers' liability insurance for all of the directors with a current indemnity limit of £10 million. Our Finance Director, John Honest, will be in touch with you to arrange details.

INDEPENDENT PROFESSIONAL ADVICE

Occasions may arise when you need to seek legal or financial advice in the furtherance of your duties. If this arises and you wish the company to pay for it you must give prior written notice to the Chairman of the subject of such advice and an estimate of the level of expenditure to be incurred.

SECURITY

Our three sites have a card security system to control entry. We would like you to have free access to the business. Could you contact our Personnel Manager, John Henry, to arrange your card?

Appendix IV:

A Rough Guide to Hampel

When was the Hampel Report?

The Hampel Committee was established through the initiative of Sir Sidney Lipworth the Chairman of the Financial Reporting council. It produced a final report in January 1998.

> 'In the wake of Greenbury's report on remuneration and at a time when the press were making serious merry over high-profile remuneration situations, the UK's Tory government was engulfed in sleaze accusations and close to breathing its last and the Labour opposition was baying for legislation.'

What were they asked to do?

To review the findings of the Cadbury committee on Corporate Governance and the Greenbury committee on Remuneration. Then to concentrate on how these findings might be implemented. Their work was aimed at publicly listed companies.

> 'Pull all the previous stuff together, recommend a code of conduct and save the government legislating.'

Who was on the committee?

The sponsors were the London Stock Exchange, The Confederation of British Industry, The Institute of Directors, The Consultative Committee of Accountancy bodies, The National Association of Pension Funds and the Association of British Insurers. Sir Ronald Hampel, the Chairman of ICI, a FTSE 100 business that although strategically challenged was known for doing things properly, led the committee. Sir Ronnie was widely considered to be a sensible man, balanced politically, effective behind the bike sheds and a good chairman. He was joined by: Sir Nigel Mobbs and Sir Clive Thomson to give the views of big business; Michael Coppel, Chairman of a small plc, to act as the voice of smaller businesses; Giles Henderson, Senior Partner of leading city law firm Slaughter and May, and Peter Smith, Chairman of accountants Coopers and Lybrand, Tony Richards from Henderson Crossthwaite and David Thomas from Equitable Life to give the shareholders perspective; and Tom Ross from Aon to provide expert remuneration input.

'That should keep everybody happy.'

What did the final report say?

In summary nothing much new and certainly nothing controversial. It simply pulled it all together quite nicely. Correctly it started by reminding us that, 'the primary purpose of business is to create wealth', a point which was in danger of being lost as the corporate governance bandwagon rolled on. Another excellent point, which did get a little lost, was that there was strong support for the unitary board in preference to a two-tier system. The report raised the shareholder responsibility issue that the institutions should stop whingeing and start acting by voting.

It reinforced the view that disclosure was more powerful than legislation and that principles were more important than guidelines. I suppose one way of expressing this is to say that what boards did was more important than what they said they did. As the report only costs £10 (see bibliography) I will only comment on the principles here.

So what were these Principles of good corporate governance?

These related to Directors, Directors' remuneration, Shareholders and Accountability and Audit.

Directors

The board. Every listed company should be headed by an effective board which should lead and control the company.

'Better start with a safe statement of the bleeding obvious.'

Chairman and chief executive. There are two key tasks at the top of every public company – the running of the board and the executive responsibility for running the company's business. A decision to combine these roles in one individual should be publicly explained.

'We don't think it's a good idea to have a combined Chairman and Chief Executive but we've got a few mates or clients who seem to do it rather well.'

As less and less PLC's combine the role this is dying as an issue in the UK.

Board balance. The board should include a balance of executive directors and non-executive directors (including independent non-executives) so that no individual or small group of individuals can dominate the board's decision taking.

'We found this one tricky. We're not sure whether the non-execs should be in the majority so we copped out. Wonder what the definition of dominate is?'

Supply of information. The board should be supplied in a timely fashion with information in a form and of a quality appropriate to enable it to discharge its duties.

'Wow!'

Appointments to the board. There should be a formal and transparent procedure for the appointment of new directors to the board.

'The Chairman or Chief Executive decide between themselves. There should be a proper selection process. We all know that whatever formal process is put in place, a Chairman who wants his mates appointed will get them through it, thus ending up with a board that will continue to let him do what he likes.'

Re-election. All directors should be required to submit themselves for re-election regularly and at least every three years.

'We all know that if you want to get rid of someone the re-election process isn't the way.'

Directors' Remuneration

The level and make-up of remuneration. Levels of remuneration should be sufficient to attract and retain the directors needed to run the company successfully. The component parts of remuneration should be structured so as to link rewards to corporate and individual performance.

'Look, we know most reward schemes reward strong performances in good businesses if they join and cash in at the right times in the cycles of their industries and economies. We also know that the lucky weak guys get rewarded for being there at the right time as well. It isn't so bad either for the unlucky weak guys who get found out. They command a premium to go. We really wish it wasn't like this but we can't come up with anything better.'

I write the above as the Chief Executive of a well-known group in the UK is reportedly being paid almost £1.5m as a pay-off. The value of his group is the same as when he joined over five years ago.

Disclosure. The company's annual report should contain a statement of remuneration policy and details of the remuneration of each director.

'Wish we were remuneration consultants or printers.'

Shareholders

Shareholder voting. Institutional shareholders have a responsibility to make considered use of their votes.

'Stop whingeing and start voting but don't give the gun to the trigger-happy people who don't have the competence.'

This is an area where surprising progress has been made, most notably in the celebrated case of Lucas Varity. Here was a case where a company's dominant Chief Executive was soundly beaten in his objective to move the domicile of the business from the UK to the USA, the cynic would say to be closer to his main house.

The dilemma was that his record was strong but what he wanted to do looked wrong. Large- and small-shareholders, who I'm sure a few years earlier wouldn't have bothered, rejected the proposal. Don't feel for the guy too much though, the outcome was that the company was put into play, an auction proceeded and he made a small fortune from his options.

Dialogue between companies and investors. Companies and institutional shareholders should each be ready, where practicable, to enter into a dialogue based on the mutual understanding of objectives.

'An index investor is an index investor. A FTSE 100 company is a FTSE 100 company.'

Evaluation of governance disclosures. When evaluating companies' governance arrangements, particularly those relating to board structure and composition, institutional investors and their advisers should give due weight to all relevant factors drawn to their attention.

'Committee-speak worthy of an EEC communiqué.'

The AGM. Companies should use the AGM to communicate with private investors and encourage their participation.

'We know the institutions find analyst meetings more helpful. Yet the rigour of having to prepare for the eclectic and often spot-on questions the private shareholders ask is, we believe, worth hanging on to. This is despite the fact that for some companies the cost of mounting the AGM is greater than the combined value of the shares of those attending.'

Accountability and Audit

Financial reporting. The board should present a balanced and understandable assessment of the company's position and prospects.

'We haven't anything new to say to this.'

Internal control. The board should maintain a sound system of internal control to safeguard shareholders' investment and the company's assets.

'Or this.'

Relationship with auditors. The board should establish formal and transparent arrangements for maintaining an appropriate relationship with the company's auditors.

'We're nearly finished now.'

External auditors. The external auditors should independently report to the shareholders in accordance with statutory and professional requirements and independently assure the board on the discharge of its responsibilities under financial reporting and internal control above in accordance with professional guidance.

'Hooray we've done it.'

What was the reaction?

Big business: *'Sounds sensible. We won't be hampered by Hampel.'*

Politicians: *'Boring issue now we've got more interesting things to think about.'*

Press: *'Not a lot to have fun with.'*

Smaller businesses: *'Not much in here for us, this is for the big boys.'*

Advisors: *'Yippeeee, more fees for helping people to read it and to show that they are complying.'*

Appendix V:

A Rough Guide to Greenbury

The main thrust of the Greenbury report in 1995 was concerned with disclosure and accountability. Emphasising fairness and balance is inherently difficult in these documents. They did, however, state:

> 'UK companies mostly deal with directors' remuneration in a sensible and responsible way.'

> *'Keep this in perspective – most of us are good guys.'*

Another quote from the Introduction:

> 'The detailed provisions have been prepared with large companies mainly in mind, but the principles apply equally to smaller companies.'

> *'Our brief is to look at the big boys. We don't know too much about the little guys anyway. However, most of what we've come up with seems like common sense to us so it probably applies. In private companies the executive directors are probably the shareholders as well, so if the shareholders are being ripped off they are ripping off themselves.'*

The code itself contains nine key points on the remuneration committee:

1. To avoid potential conflicts of interest, boards of directors should set up RCs of non-executive directors to determine on their behalf, and on behalf of the shareholders, within agreed terms of reference, the company's policy on executive remuneration and specific remuneration packages for each of the executive directors, including pension rights and any compensation payments.

    'Self-regulation by executive directors on pay doesn't look to have worked so let's leave it to the non-executives. All right, the executives have traditionally picked the non-executives and there are many cross-directorships. We are, however, placing the responsibility and the spotlight on the non-execs who have more to lose than to gain by getting it wrong. We've also spotted that selective disclosure has hidden the level of true benefits.'

2. RC chairmen should account directly to the shareholders through the means specified in this code for the decisions their committees reach.

    'If there is the possibility that they may have to stand up at the AGM and defend their decisions they'll take it seriously. All right, we know that only a small proportion of shareholders turn up at AGMs. However, institutional shareholders are becoming sporadically more interested and active on these issues with varying degrees of ability and common sense.'

3. Where necessary companies' articles of association should be amended to enable RCs to discharge these functions on behalf of the board.

    'Better make sure they've really got the legal power to act.'

4. RCs should consist exclusively of non-execs with no personal financial interest other than as shareholders in the matters to be decided, no potential conflicts of interest arising from cross-directorships and no day-to-day involvement in running the business.

    'Just to make it clear, we mean the real non-execs.'

5. The members of the RC should be listed each year in the committee's report to the shareholders. When they stand for re-election the proxy cards should indicate their membership of the committee.

'Don't try shooting them quietly or sticking poodles up.'

6. The board itself should determine the remuneration of the non-executive directors including members of the RC within the limits set out in the articles of association.

    'This should avoid the executives getting their own back.'

7. RCs should consult the company chairman and/or CEO about their proposals and have access to professional advice inside and outside the company.

    'This is not just emotive, it's technical and tricky and you do need some calibration with what everyone else is doing etc. You don't want to dream it up in a short meeting half an hour before a full board meeting begins.'

8. The RC chairman should attend the company's annual general meeting to answer shareholders' questions about directors' remuneration and should ensure that the company maintains contact as required with its principal shareholders about remuneration in the same way as for other matters.

    'We'd better repeat point 2 just to make it clear!'

9. The committee's annual report to shareholders should not be a standard item of agenda for AGMs. But the committee should consider each year whether the circumstances are such that the AGM should be invited to approve the policy set out in their report and should minute their conclusions.

    'Some of us wanted to go even further.'

The proposed terms of reference of a remuneration committee in the Greenbury report are fairly broad and therefore easily adapted to any size if it is appropriate to have a remuneration committee in the first place. They are:

- To determine on behalf of the board and the shareholders the company's broad policy for executive remuneration and the entire individual remuneration packages for each of the executive directors and, as appropriate, other senior executives.
- In doing so, to give the executive directors every encouragement to

enhance the company's performance and to ensure that they are fairly but responsibly rewarded for their individual contributions.

■ To comply with our code of best practice!

■ To report and account directly to the shareholders, on the board's behalf, for their decisions.

Bibliography

Brassey, Richard (1995) *How to Speak Chimpanzee*, Orion Publishing Group Ltd, London

Cadbury, Sir Adrian (1990) *The Company Chairman*, Director Books, Fitzwilliam Publishing, Cambridge

Cadbury, Sir Adrian (1992) *Report of the Committee on the Financial Aspects of Corporate Governance*, Gee Publishing Ltd, London

Cadbury, Sir Adrian (2002) *Corporate Governance and Chairmanship*, Oxford University Press Ltd, Oxford

Charkham, John (1994) *Keeping Good Company*, Oxford University Press Ltd, Oxford

Cohen, William and Cohen, Nurit (1993) *The Paranoid Corporation*, Amacom, New York

De Bono, Sir Edward (1990) *Six Thinking Hats*, Penguin Books Ltd, London

De Vries, Manfred Kets (1995) *Life and Death in the Executive Fast Lane*, Jossey-Bass Publishers, San Francisco

Dunne, Patrick (1992) *Increasing Calls on Independent Directors: A 3i Analysis*, 3i plc, London

Dunne, Patrick (1994) *Angel Investors: A 3i Analysis*, 3 plc, London

Dunne, Patrick (1995) *Running Board Meetings: A 3i Analysis*, 3i plc, London

Greenbury, Sir Richard (Chairman) (1995) *Directors' Remuneration: A Report of a Study Group* (The Greenbury Report), Gee Publishing Ltd, London

Hampel, Sir Ronald (Chairman) (1998) Committee on Corporate Governance, Final Report

Higgs, Sir Derek (2002) review of the role and effectiveness of non-executive directors

Hodgson, Phil and Hodgson, Jane (1992) *Effective Meetings*, Century Business Publishing, London

Howard, Philip (1996) *The Death of Common Sense: How the Law Is Suffocating America*, Warner Books

Independent Remunerations Solutions (2005) *The Independent Chairman and Non-Executive Director Survey*. Independent Remuneration Solutions, 9 Savoy Street, London WC2R 0BA. Tel: 020 7836 5831

Jack, Andrew (1993) *Audit Committees: A Guide for Non-Executive Directors*, Accountancy Books in association with The Board for Chartered Accountants in Business

Lorsch, Professor Jay (1989) *Pawns or Potentates?*, Harvard Business School Press, Boston

Semler, Ricardo (1993) *Maverick*, Century Publishing, London

Stuart, Spencer (1995) *Board Trends and Practices at Major American Corporations*, 277 Park Avenue, New York NY 10172

Suzy Lamplugh Trust (1995), *Personal Safety at Work for You*, The Suzy Lamplugh Trust, London

Top Pay Research Group (3i Independent Directors Programme) (1999) *The Independent Chairman and Non-Executive Survey*

Index

The
Complete Book
of
Corporate Legal Forms

Daniel Sitarz
Attorney-at-Law

Nova Publishing Company
Legal Publications Divison
Boulder, Colorado

Cover design by Christine Jacquot of Spectrum Graphics, Pomona, IL

Manufactured in the United States.

Library of Congress Catalog Card Number 92-061937
ISBN 0-935755-08-X

Library of Congress Cataloging-in-Publication Data
     Sitarz, Dan, 1948-
     The Complete Book of Corporate Legal Forms / Daniel Sitarz
     248 p. (Legal Self-Help Series) includes index;
     ISBN 0-935755-08-X : $18.95
     1. Corporations--Law and Legislation--United States--Forms. 2. Forms (Law)--
     United States--Popular Works. I. Title. II. Series.
     KF   1993   346.   LC92-061937

Nova Publishing Company is dedicated to providing up-to-date and accurate legal information to the public. All Nova publications are periodically revised to contain the latest available legal information.

1st Edition; 1st Printing: April, 1993

This publication is designed to provide accurate and authoritative information in regard to the subject matter covered. It is sold with the understanding that the publisher and author are not engaged in rendering legal, accounting, or other professional services. If legal advice or other expert assistance is required, the services of a competent professional person should be sought.

From a Declaration of Principles jointly adopted by a Committee of the American Bar Association and a Committee of Publishers

DISCLAIMER

Because of possible unanticipated changes in governing statutes and case law relating to the application of any information contained in this book, the author, publisher, and any and all persons or entities involved in any way in the preparation, publication, sale, or distribution of this book disclaim all responsibility for the legal effects or consequences of any document prepared or action taken in reliance upon information contained in this book. No representations, either express or implied, are made or given regarding the legal consequences of the use of any information contained in this book. Purchasers and persons intending to use this book for the preparation of any legal documents are advised to check specifically on the current applicable laws in any jurisdiction in which they intend the documents to be effective.

NOVA PUBLISHING COMPANY
Legal Publications Division
4882 Kellogg Circle
Boulder CO 80303

Distributed to the trade by:
National Book Network
4720 Boston Way
Lanham MD 20706
1(800)462-6420

Table of Contents

Chapter 5:
Articles of Incorporation 45

Chapter 6:
Corporate By-Laws 58

Chapter 7:
Corporate Directors Meetings 78

Chapter 8:
Corporate Shareholders Meetings 100

Chapter 9:
Corporate Resolutions

Chapter 10:
Corporate Stock 158

Chapter 11:
Corporate Shareholder Agreement 165

Chapter 12:
"S" Corporation Status 172

Preface

This book is part of Nova Publishing Company's continuing series on Legal Self-Help. The various self-help legal guides in this series are prepared by licensed attorneys who feel that public access to the American legal system is long overdue.

With the proper information, the average person in today's world can easily understand and apply many areas of law. However, historically, there have been concerted efforts on the part of the organized Bar and other lawyer organizations to prevent "self-help" legal information from reaching the general public. These efforts have gone hand-in-hand with an attempt to leave the law cloaked in antiquated and unnecessary legal language; language which, of course, one must pay a lawyer to translate.

Law in American society is far more pervasive than ever before. There are legal consequences to virtually every public and most private actions in today's world. Leaving knowledge of the law within the hands of only the lawyers in such a society is not only foolish, but dangerous as well. A free society depends, in large part, on an informed citizenry. This book and others in Nova's Legal Self-Help series are intended to provide the necessary information to those members of the public who wish to use and understand the law for themselves.

However, in an area as complex as corporate law, it is not always prudent to attempt to handle every legal situation which arises without the aid of a competent attorney. Although the information presented in this book will give readers a basic understanding of the areas of law covered, it is not intended that this text entirely substitute for experienced legal assistance in all situations. Throughout this book there are references to those particular situations in which the aid of a lawyer or other professional is strongly recommended.

Regardless of whether or not a lawyer is ultimately retained in certain situations, the legal information in this handbook will enable the reader to understand the framework of corporate law in this country and how to effectively use legal forms in the operation of their business corporation.

To try and make that task as easy as possible, technical legal jargon has been eliminated whenever possible and plain English used instead. Naturally, plain and easily-understood English is not only perfectly proper for use in all legal documents but, in most cases, leads to far less confusion on the part of later readers. When it is necessary in this book to use a legal term which may be unfamiliar to most people, the word will be shown in *italics* and defined when first used. A glossary of legal terms most often encountered in corporate legal documents is included at the end of this book.

Chapter 1

Choosing to Form a Corporation

One of the first decisions that a potential business owner must confront is how the business should be structured and operated. This crucial decision must be made even before the business has actually begun operations. The legal documents which will generally accompany the formation of a business can follow many different patterns, depending on the particular situation and the type of business to be undertaken.

Initially, the type of business entity to be used must be selected. There are many basic forms of business operating entities. The five most common forms are:

- Sole proprietorship,
- Standard partnership,
- Limited partnership,
- Standard corporation,
- "S" corporation.

The choice of entity for a particular business depends on many factors. Which of these forms of business organization is chosen can have a great impact on the success of the business. The structure chosen will have an effect on how easy it is to obtain financing, how taxes are paid, how accounting records are kept, whether personal assets are at risk in the venture, the amount of control the "owner" has over the business, and many other aspects of the business. Keep in mind that the initial choice of business organization need not be the final choice. It is often wise to begin with the most simple form, the sole proprietorship, until the business progresses to a point where another form is clearly indicated. This allows the business to begin in the least complicated manner and allows the owner to retain total control in the important formative period of the business. As the business grows and the potential for liability and tax burdens increase, circumstances may dictate a re-examination of the business structure. The advantages and disadvantages of the five choices of business operation are detailed below.

The Sole Proprietorship

A sole proprietorship is both the simplest and the most prevalent form of business organization. An important reason for this is that it is the least regulated of all types of business structures. Technically, the *sole proprietorship* is the traditional unincorporated one-person business. For legal and tax purposes, the business is the owner. It has no existence outside the owner. The liabilities of the business are personal to the owner and the business ends when the owner dies. On the other hand, all of the profits are also personal to the owner and the sole owner has full control of the business.

• *Disadvantages*

Perhaps the most important factor to consider before choosing this type of business structure is that all of the personal and business assets of the sole owner are at risk in the sole proprietorship. If the demands of the creditors of the business exceed those assets which were formally placed in the name of the business, the creditors may reach the personal assets of the owner of the sole proprietorship. Legal judgements for damages arising from the operation of the business may also be enforced against the owner's personal assets. This unlimited liability is probably the greatest drawback to this type of business form. Of course, insurance coverage of various types can lessen the dangers inherent in having one's personal assets at risk in a business. However, as liability insurance premiums continue to skyrocket, it is unlikely that a fledgling small business can afford to insure against all manner of contingencies and at the maximum coverage levels necessary to guard against all risk to personal assets.

A second major disadvantage to the sole proprietorship as a form of business structure is the potential difficulty in obtaining business loans. Often in starting a small business, there is insufficient collateral to obtain a loan and the sole owner must mortgage his or her own house or other personal assets to obtain the loan. This, of course, puts the sole proprietor's personal assets in a direct position of risk should the business fail. Banks and other lending institutions are often reluctant to loan money for initial small business start-ups due to the high risk of failure for small businesses. Without a proven track record, it is quite difficult for a small business owner to adequately present a loan proposal based on a sufficiently stable cash flow to satisfy most banks.

A further disadvantage to a sole proprietorship is the lack of continuity which is inherent in the business form. If the owner dies, the business ceases to exist. Of course, the assets and liabilities of the business will pass to the heirs of the owner, but the expertise and knowledge of how the business was successfully carried on will often die with the owner. Small sole proprietorships are seldom carried on profitably after the death of the owner.

• *Advantages*

The most appealing advantage of the sole proprietorship as a business structure is the total control the owner has over the business. Subject only to economic considerations and certain legal restrictions, there is total freedom to operate the business however one chooses. Many people feel that this factor alone is enough to overcome the inherent disadvantages in this form of business.

Related to this is the simplicity of organization of the sole proprietorship. Other than maintenance of sufficient records for tax purposes, there are no legal requirements on how the business is operated. Of course, the prudent business-person will keep adequate records and sufficiently organize the business for its most efficient operation. But there are no outside forces dictating how such internal decisions are made in the sole proprietorship. The sole owner makes all decisions in this type of business.

As was mentioned earlier, the sole proprietorship is the least regulated of all businesses. Normally, the only license necessary is a local business license, usually obtained by simply paying a fee to a local registration authority. In addition, it may be necessary to file an affidavit with local authorities and publish a notice in a local newspaper if the business is operated under an assumed or fictitious name. This is necessary to allow creditors to have access to the actual identity of the true owner of the business, since it is the owner who will be personally liable for the debts and obligations of the business.

Finally, it may be necessary to register with local, state, and federal tax bodies for I.D. numbers and for the purpose of collection of sales and other taxes. Other than these few simple registrations, from a legal standpoint little else is required to start up a business as a sole proprietorship.

A final and important advantage to the sole proprietorship is the various tax benefits available to an individual. The losses or profits of the sole proprietorship are considered personal to the owner. The losses are directly deductible against any other income the owner may have and the profits are taxed only once at the marginal rate of the owner. In many instances, this may have distinct advantages over the method by which partnerships are taxed or the double taxation of corporations, particularly in the early stages of the business.

The Partnership

A *partnership* is a relationship existing between two or more persons who join together to carry on a trade or business. Each partner contributes money, property, labor, or skill to the partnership and, in return, expects to share in the profits or losses of the business. A partnership is usually based on a partnership agreement of some type, although the agreement need not be a formal document. It may even simply be an oral understanding between the partners, although this is not recommended.

A simple joint undertaking to share expenses is not considered a partnership, nor is a mere co-ownership of property that is maintained and leased or rented. To be considered a partnership for legal and tax purposes, the following factors are usually considered:

- The partners conduct in carrying out the provisions of the partnership agreement;
- The relationship of the parties;
- The abilities and contributions of each party to the partnership;
- The control each partner has over the partnership income and the purposes for which the income is used.

• Disadvantages

The disadvantages to the partnership form of business begin with the potential for conflict between the partners. Of all forms of business organization, the partnership has spawned more disagreements than any other. This is generally traceable to the lack of a decisive initial partner-

14

ship agreement which clearly outlines the rights and duties of the partners. This disadvantage can be partially overcome with a comprehensive partnership agreement. However, there is still the seemingly inherent difficulty that many people have in working within the framework of a partnership, regardless of the initial agreement between the partners.

A further disadvantage to the partnership structure is that each partner is subject to unlimited personal liability for the debts of the partnership. The potential liability in a partnership is even greater than that encountered in a sole proprietorship. This is due to the fact that in a partnership the personal risk for which one may be liable is partially out of one's direct control and may be accrued due to actions on the part of another person. Each partner is liable for all of the debts of the partnership, regardless of which of the partners may have been responsible for their accumulation.

Related to the business risks of personal financial liability is the potential personal legal liability for the negligence of another partner. In addition, each partner may even be liable for the negligence of an employee of the partnership if such negligence takes place during the usual course of business of the partnership. Again, the attendant risks are broadened by the potential for liability based on the acts of other persons. Of course, general liability insurance can counteract this drawback to some extent to protect the personal and partnership assets of each partner.

Again, as with the sole proprietorship, the partnership lacks the advantage of continuity. A partnership is usually automatically terminated upon the death of any partner. A final accounting and a division of assets and liabilities is generally necessary in such an instance unless specific methods under which the partnership may be continued have been outlined in the partnership agreement.

Finally, certain benefits of corporate organization are not available to a partnership. Since a partnership can not obtain financing through public stock offerings, large infusions of capital are more difficult for a partnership to raise than for a corporation. In addition, many of the fringe benefit programs that are available to corporations (such as certain pension and profit-sharing arrangements) are not available to partnerships.

• *Advantages*

A partnership, by virtue of combining the credit potential of the various partners, has an inherently greater opportunity for business credit than is generally available to a sole proprietorship. In addition, the assets which are placed in the name of the partnership may often be used directly as collateral for business loans. The pooling of the personal capital of the partners generally provides the partnership with an advantage over the sole-proprietorship in the area of cash availability. However, as noted above, the partnership does not have as great a potential for financing as does a corporation.

As with the sole proprietorship, there may be certain tax advantages to operation of a business as a partnership, as opposed to a corporation. The profits generated by a partnership may be distributed directly to the partners without incurring any "double" tax liability, as is the case with the distribution of corporate profits in the form of dividends to the share-holders. Income from a partnership is taxed at personal income tax rates. Note, however, that depending on the individual tax situation of each partner, this aspect could prove to be a disadvantage.

For a business in which two or more people desire to share in the work and in the profits, a partnership is often the structure chosen. It is, potentially, a much simpler form of business organization than the corporate form. Less start-up costs are necessary and there is limited regulation of partnerships. However, the simplicity of this form of business can be deceiving. A sole proprietor knows that his or her actions will determine how the business will prosper, and that he or she is, ultimately, personally responsible for the success or failure of the enterprise. In a partnership, however, the duties, obligations and commitments of each partner are often ill-defined. This lack of definition of the status of each partner can lead to serious difficulties and disagreements. In order to clarify the rights and responsibilities of each partner and to be certain of the tax status of the partnership, it is good business procedure to have a written partnership agreement. All states have adopted a version of the Uniform Partnership Act. Although state law will supply the general boundaries of partnerships and even specific partnership agreement terms if they are not addressed by a written partnership agreement, it is more conducive to a clear understanding of the business structure if the partner's agreements are put in writing.

The Limited Partnership

The *limited partnership* is a hybrid type of business structure. It contains elements of both a traditional partnership and a corporation. The limited partnership form of business structure may be used when some interested parties desire to invest in a partnership but also desire to have limited liability and exercise no control over the partnership management. Limited partnerships are, generally, a more complex form of business operation than either the sole proprietorship or the standard partnership.

Limited partnerships are also subject to far more state regulations regarding both their formation and operation. All states have adopted a version of the Uniform Limited Partnership Act. If the limited partnership form of business is chosen, the services of a competent business attorney should be used for drawing up the proper documents.

A limited partnership consists of one or more general partners who actively manage the business of the partnership and one or more limited partners who are mere investors in the partnership and who have no active role in the management of the partnership. A general partner is treated much as a partner in a traditional partnership, while a limited partner is treated much as a shareholder in a corporation. The general partners are at personal risk in a limited partnership. The limited partners enjoy a limited liability equal to their investment as long as they do not actively engage in any management of the partnership.

• *Disadvantages*

In as much as the business form is still a partnership, there is still a potential for conflict among the partners. This potential is somewhat mitigated in the limited partnership by the distancing of the limited partners from the actual management of the partnership. If the passive limited partners engage in any efforts to exert control over the management, they risk losing the benefits of limited liability that they enjoy.

Limited partnerships are formed according to individual state law, generally by filing formal Articles of Limited Partnership with the proper state authorities in the state of formation. They are subject to more paperwork requirements than a simple partnership.

Similar to traditional partnerships, the limited partnership has an inherent lack of continuity. This may, however, be overcome in the case of the retirement or death of a general partner by providing in the Articles of Limited Partnership for an immediate reorganization of the limited partnership with the retired partner eliminated or the deceased partner's heirs or estate becoming a limited partner.

• *Advantages*

The limited partners in such a business enjoy a limited liability, similar to that of a shareholder in a corporation. Their risk is limited to the amount of their investment in the limited partnership. The general partners remain at full personal risk, the same as a partner in a traditional partnership.

Since the limited partners will have no personal liability and will not be required to personally perform any tasks of management, it is easier to attract investors to the limited partnership form of business than to a traditional partnership. The limited partner will share in the potential profits and in the tax deductions of the limited partnership, but in fewer of the financial risks involved.

The Corporation

Corporations are the focus of this book. A corporation is a creation of law. It is governed by the laws of the state of incorporation and of the state or states in which it does business. In recent years it has become the business structure of choice for many small businesses. Corporations are, generally, a more complex form of business operation than either a sole proprietorship or partnership. They are also subject to far more state regulations regarding both their formation and operation. The following discussion is provided in order to allow the potential business owner an understanding of this type of business operation.

The *corporation* is an artificial entity. It is created by filing *Articles of Incorporation* with the proper state authorities. This gives the corporation its legal existence and the right to carry on business. The Articles of Incorporation act as a public record of certain formalities of corporate existence. Preparation of Articles of Incorporation is explained in detail in Chapter 5. Adoption of corporate *By-Laws*, or internal rules of operation, is often the first business of the corporation, after it has been given the authority to conduct business by the state. The By-Laws of the corporation outline the actual mechanics of the operation and management of the corporation. The preparation of corporate By-Laws is explained in Chapter 6.

In its simplest form, the corporate organizational structure consists of the following levels:

- Shareholders: who own shares of the business but do not contribute to the direct management of the corporation, other than by electing the directors of the corporation, and voting on major corporate issues.

- Directors: who may be shareholders, but as directors do not own any of the business. They are responsible, jointly as members of the *board of directors* of the corporation, for making the major business decisions of the corporation, including appointing the officers of the corporation.

- Officers: who may be shareholders and/or directors, but, as officers, do not own any of the business. The officers (generally the president, vice president, secretary, and treasurer) are responsible for the day-to-day operation of the corporate business.

• *Disadvantages*

Due to the nature of the organizational structure in a corporation, a certain degree of individual control is necessarily lost by incorporation. The officers, as appointees of the board of directors, are answerable to the board for management decisions. The board of directors, on the other hand, is not entirely free from restraint, since they are responsible to the shareholders for the prudent business management of the corporation.

The technical formalities of corporation formation and operation must be strictly observed in order for a business to reap the benefits of corporate existence. For this reason, there is an additional burden and expense to the corporation of detailed record keeping that is seldom present in other forms of business organization. Corporate decisions are, in general, more complicated due to the various levels of control and all such decisions must be carefully documented. Corporate meetings, both at the shareholder and director levels, are more formal and more frequent. In addition, the actual formation of the corporation is more expensive than the formation of either a sole proprietorship or partnership. The initial state fees that must be paid for registration of a corporation with a state can run as high as $900.00 for a minimally-capitalized corporation. Corporations are also subject to a greater level of governmental regulation than any other type of business entity. These complications have the potential to overburden a small business struggling to survive. The forms and instructions in this book are all designed to lessen the burden and expense of operating a business corporation.

Finally, the profits of a corporation, when distributed to the shareholders in the form of dividends, are subject to being taxed twice. The first tax comes at the corporate level. The distribution of any corporate profits to the investors in the form of dividends is not a deductible business expense for the corporation. Thus, any dividends which are distributed to shareholders have already been subject to corporate income tax. The second level of tax is imposed at the personal level. The receipt of corporate dividends is considered income to the individual shareholder and is taxed as such. This potential for higher taxes due to a corporate business structure can be moderated by many factors however. Forms dealing with taxation of corporations are contained in Chapter 14.

• *Advantages*

One of the most important advantages to the corporate form of business structure is the potential limited liability of the founders of and investors in the corporation. The liability for corporate debts is limited, in general, to the amount of money each owner has contributed to the corporation. Unless the corporation is essentially a shell for a one-person business or unless the corporation is grossly under-capitalized or under-insured, the personal assets of the owners are not at risk if the corporation fails. The shareholders stand to lose only what they invested. This factor is very important in attracting investors as the business grows.

A corporation can have a perpetual existence. Theoretically, a corporation can last forever. This may be a great advantage if there are potential future changes in ownership of the business in the offing. Changes that would cause a partnership to be dissolved or terminated often will not affect the corporation. This continuity can be an important factor in establishing a stable business image and a permanent relationship with others in the industry.

Unlike a partnership, in which no one may become a partner without the consent of the other partners, a shareholder of corporate stock may freely sell, trade, or give away their stock unless this right is formally restricted by reasonable corporate decisions. The new owner of such stock is then a new owner of the business in the proportionate share of stock obtained. This freedom offers potential investors a liquidity to shift assets that is not present in the partnership form of business. The sale of shares by the corporation is also an attractive method by which to raise needed capital. The sale of shares of a corporation, however, is subject to many governmental regulations, on both the state and federal levels.

Taxation is listed both as an advantage and as a disadvantage for the corporation. Depending on many factors, the use of a corporation can increase or decrease the actual income tax paid in operating a corporate business. In addition, corporations may set aside surplus earnings (up to certain levels) without any negative tax consequences. Finally, corporations are able to offer a much greater variety of fringe benefit programs to employees and officers than any other type of business entity. Various retirement, stock option, and profit-sharing plans are only open to corporate participation.

The "S" Corporation

The *"S" corporation* is a certain type of corporation that is available for specific tax purposes. It is a creature of the Internal Revenue Service. "S" corporation status is not relevant to state corporation laws. Its purpose is to allow small corporations to choose to be taxed, at the federal level, like a partnership, but to also enjoy many of the benefits of a corporation. The details of obtaining "S" corporation status are contained in Chapter 12.

In general, to qualify as an "S" corporation under current IRS rules, a corporation meet certain requirements:

- It must not have over 35 shareholders;
- All of the shareholders must be individuals;
- It must only have one class of stock;
- Shareholders must consent to "S" corporation status; and
- An election of "S" corporation status must be filed with the IRS.

The "S" corporation retains all of the advantages and disadvantages of the traditional corporation except in the area of taxation. For tax purposes, "S" corporation shareholders are treated similarly to partners in a partnership. The income, losses, and deductions generated by an "S" corporation are "passed through" the corporate entity to the individual shareholders. Thus, there is no "double" taxation of an "S"-type corporation. In addition, unlike a standard corporation, shareholders of "S" corporations can personally deduct any corporate losses.

The decision of which business entity to choose depends upon many factors and should be carefully studied. If the choice is to operate a business as a corporation or "S" corporation, this book will provide an array of easy-to-use legal forms which will, in most cases, allow the business owner to operate the corporation with minimal difficulty while meeting all of the legal paperwork requirements.

Chapter 2

Corporate Record-Keeping

The business arena in America operates on a daily assortment of legal forms. There are more legal forms in use in American business than are used in the operations and government of many foreign countries. The business corporation is not immune to this flood of legal forms. Indeed the operation of a corporation, in general, requires more legal documents than does any other form of business. While large corporations are able to obtain and pay expensive lawyers to deal with their legal problems and paperwork, most small businesses can not afford such a course of action. The small business corporation must deal with a variety of legal documents, usually without the aid of an attorney.

Unfortunately, many business people who are confronted with such forms do not understand the legal ramifications of the use of these forms. They simply sign them with the expectation that it is a fairly standard document, without any unusual legal provisions. They trust that the details of the particular document will fall within what is generally accepted within the industry or trade. In most cases, this may be true. In many situations, however, it is not. Our court system is clogged with cases in which two businesses are battling over what was really intended by the incomprehensible legal language in a certain legal document.

Much of the confusion over corporate paperwork comes from two areas: First, there is a general lack of understanding among many in business regarding the framework of law. Second, many corporate documents are written in antiquated legal jargon that is difficult for even most lawyers to understand and nearly impossible for a lay person to comprehend.

The various legal documents that are used in this book are, however, written in plain English. Standard legal jargon, as used in most lawyer-prepared documents, is, for most people, totally incomprehensible. Despite the lofty arguments by attorneys regarding the need for such strained and difficult language, the vast majority of legalese is absolutely unnecessary. As with any form of communication, clarity, simplicity, and readability should be the goal in legal documents.

Unfortunately, in some specific instances, certain obscure legal terms are the only words that accurately and precisely describe some things in certain legal contexts. In those few cases, the unfamiliar legal term will be defined when first used. Generally, however, simple terms are used throughout this book.

All of the legal documents contained in this book have been prepared in essentially the same manner by which attorneys create legal forms. Many people believe that lawyers prepare each legal document that they compose entirely from scratch. Nothing could be further from the truth. Invariably, lawyers begin their preparation of a legal document with a standardized legal form book. Every law library has multi-volume sets of these encyclopedic texts which contain blank forms for virtually every conceivable legal situation. Armed with these pre-prepared legal forms, lawyers, in many cases, simply fill in the blanks and have their secretaries re-type the form for the client. Of course, the client is generally unaware of this process. As the lawyers begin to specialize in a certain area of legal expertise, they compile their own files containing such blank forms.

This book provides the owners of corporations with a set of legal forms which has been prepared with the problems and normal legal requirements of the small business corporation in mind. They are intended to be used in those situations that are clearly described by their terms. Of course, while most corporate document use will fall within the bounds of standard business practices, some legal circumstances will present non-standard situations. The forms in this book are designed to be readily adaptable to most usual business situations. They may be carefully altered to conform to the particular transaction that confronts your business. However, if you are faced with a complex or tangled business situation, the advice of a competent lawyer is highly-recommended. If you wish, you may also create forms for certain standard situations for your corporation and have your lawyer check them for any local legal circumstances.

The proper and cautious use of the forms provided in this book will allow the typical corporation to save considerable money on legal costs over the course of the life of the business, while enabling the business to comply with legal and governmental regulations. Perhaps more importantly, these forms will provide a method by which the business-person can avoid costly misunderstandings about what exactly was intended in a particular situation. By using the forms provided to clearly document the proceedings of everyday corporate operations, disputes over what was really meant can be avoided. This protection will allow the business to avoid many potential lawsuits and operate more efficiently in compliance with the law.

The Importance of Corporate Record-Keeping

The amount of paperwork and record-keeping required by the use of the corporate form of business may often seem overwhelming. Sometimes, it may even seem senseless. However, there are some very important reasons why detailed records of corporate operations are necessary. A corporation is a fiction. It is a creation of the government to enable businesses to have a flexibility to function in a complex national and even international marketplace. This form of enterprise provides the most adaptable type of business entity in today's world. Through the use of a corporate entity, a business may respond quickly to the changing nature of modern business. Of course, the limited liability of corporate investors is also a great advantage over other forms of business organization.

A corporation is, in many cases, afforded the legal status of a person. It may sue or be sued in its own name. A corporation may own property in its own name. In most situations, a corporation is treated as if it has a life of its own. In a legal sense, it does have a life of its own. It was born by filing the Articles of Incorporation with a state and it may die upon filing Articles of Dissolution with the state. While a corporation is *alive*, it is said to exist. During its existence, it can operate as a separate legal entity and enjoy the benefits of corporate status *as long as certain corporate formalities are observed*. The importance of following these basic corporate formalities can not be over-emphasized. All of the advantages of operating under the corporate form of business are directly dependent upon careful observance of a few basic paperwork and management requirements.

Each major action which a corporation undertakes must be carefully documented. Even if there are only a few, or even a single shareholder, complete records of corporate activities must be recorded. There must be minutes, records of shareholders meetings which outline the election of directors of the corporation. Directors meetings must also be documented and the actions of directors recorded in the form of resolutions. Stock certificates must be issued and the ownership of them must be carefully tracked. This is true regardless of the size of the corporation. In fact, as the size of the corporation decreases, the importance of careful record-keeping actually increases.

Corporate existence can be challenged in court. This will most likely happen in circumstances where a creditor of the corporation or victim of some corporate disaster is left without compensation, due to the limited liability of the corporation. Despite the fact that the corporation has been accepted by the state as a legal entity, if the formalities of corporate existence have not been carefully followed, the owners of a corporation are at risk. The court may decide that a single shareholder corporation merely used the corporation as a shell to avoid liability. The court is then empowered to *pierce the corporate veil* or declare that the corporation was actually merely the *alter ego* of the owner. In either outcome, the court can disregard the existence of the corporation and the creditors or victims can reach the personal assets of the owner. This most often will occur when a corporation is formed without sufficient capitalization to reasonably cover normal business affairs; when the corporation has not maintained sufficient insurance to cover standard contingencies; when the owner has mingled corporate funds with his/her own; and when there are no records to indicate that the corporation was actually operated as a separate entity. The results of such a lawsuit can be devastating. The loss of personal assets and the loss of corporate legal status for tax purposes can often lead to impoverishment and bankruptcy.

This difficulty is not a rarity. Each year, many corporations are found to be shams which were not operated as separate business entities. In a lawsuit against a small corporation, an attack on the use of corporate formalities is often the single most powerful weapon of the opposition. The best defense against an attack on the use of a corporate business form is to always have treated the corporation as a separate entity. This requires documenting each and every major business activity in minutes, records, and resolutions. When it is desired that the corporation undertake a particular activity, the directors should meet and adopt a resolution which clearly identifies the action and the reasons for the action. If major actions are undertaken, the shareholders may also need to meet and document their assent. This is true even if there is only one shareholder who is also the single director. With such records, it is an easy task to establish that the actions taken were done for the benefit of the corporation and not for the personal betterment of the individual owner or owners. As long as it can be clearly shown that the owners respected the corporate separateness, the corporate existence can not be disregarded by the courts, even if there is only one shareholder who is also the sole director and only officer of the corporation. It is not the size of the corporation, but rather the existence of complete corporate records which provides the protection from liability for the owners of the corporation. It is crucial to recognize this vital element in operating a corporation. Careful, detailed record-keeping is the key to enjoying the tax benefits and limited liability of the corporate business structure.

How Use To This Book

In each chapter of this book, you will find an introductory section that will give you an overview of the types of situations in which the forms or form clauses in that chapter will generally be used. Following that overview, there will be a brief explanation of the specific uses for each form. This explanation will, generally, include a listing of the information that must be compiled to complete the form.

The forms are not designed to be torn out of this book. It is expected that the forms may be used on more than one occasion. The preferable manner for using these forms is to make a photo-copy of the form, fill in the information that is necessary, and then re-type the form in its entirety on clean white letter sized paper. The trend in the legal profession is to move entirely to letter sized (8 1/2" X 11") paper. In fact, many court systems (including the entire Federal court system) now refuse to accept documents on legal sized paper.

In most cases, masculine and feminine terms have been eliminated and the generic *it* or *them* used instead. In the few situations in which this leads to awkward sentence construction, *her/his* or *she/he* may be used instead.

It is recommended that you review the table of contents of this book in order to gain a broad overview of the range and type of legal documents that are available. Then, before you prepare any of the forms for use, you should carefully read the introductory information and instructions in the chapter in which the particular form is contained. Try to be as detailed and specific as possible as you fill in these forms. The more precise the description, the less likelihood that later disputes may develop over what was actually intended by the language chosen. The forms may be carefully adopted to a particular situation which may confront your corporation. However, be very careful in altering the Articles of Incorporation and corporate By-Laws. Certain clauses are mandatory in these documents and must be included.

The careful preparation and use of the legal forms in this book should provide the typical business corporation with most of the legal documents necessary for day-to-day operations. If in doubt as to whether a particular form will work in a specific application, please consult a competent lawyer. It may also be wise to consult with an experienced accountant as you begin to organize the corporation. The tax laws regarding corporations are very complex and must be carefully complied with in order to obtain the maximum tax benefits. Understanding the use of the corporate business entity and the use of corporate forms will enable you to intelligently discuss your corporation with the professionals which you choose to assist you in your business.

Corporate Paperwork Checklist

The following checklist outlines the various corporate documents which should be prepared and maintained during the life of a corporation:

- ❏ Pre-Incorporation Checklist (see Chapter 4)
- ❏ Reservation of corporate name (filed with state)
- ❏ Articles of Incorporation (filed with state)
- ❏ Amendments to Articles of Incorporation (filed with state)
- ❏ Certificate of Good Standing (requested from state)
- ❏ By-Laws of the corporation (in corporate record book)
- ❏ Amendments to the By-Laws of the corporation (in corporate record book)
- ❏ Minutes of first meeting of the board of directors (in corporate record book)
- ❏ Minutes of the first meeting of the shareholders (in corporate record book)
- ❏ Minutes of annual board of directors meetings (in corporate record book)
- ❏ Minutes of the annual meetings of the shareholders (in corporate record book)
- ❏ Minutes of any special board of directors meetings (in corporate record book)
- ❏ Minutes of any special shareholders meetings (in corporate record book)
- ❏ Shareholder proxies (in corporate record book)
- ❏ Shareholder voting agreements (in corporate record book)
- ❏ Resolutions of the board of directors (in corporate record book)
- ❏ Resolutions of the shareholders (in corporate record book)
- ❏ Corporate loans to officers or directors (in corporate record book)
- ❏ Corporate pension or profit-sharing plans (in corporate record book)
- ❏ Corporate insurance or health benefit plans (in corporate record book)
- ❏ Form and content of stock certificates (in corporate record book)
- ❏ Stock transfer book (in corporate record book)
- ❏ Corporate accounting books
- ❏ Annual financial reports (in corporate record book)
- ❏ Annual reports (filed with the state)
- ❏ Articles of Merger (filed with the state)
- ❏ Articles of Dissolution (filed with the state)
- ❏ Corporate tax records (filed with state and federal tax authorities)
- ❏ Applications to qualify as foreign corporation (filed with other states in which the corporation desires to conduct active business operations)

Chapter 3

The Mechanics of Operating a Corporation

The corporate business structure has three levels: shareholders, directors, and officers. In order to understand the requirements for corporate record-keeping, it is necessary to understand how a corporation actually functions. Each level has different rights and different responsibilities. Each level also generates different types of paperwork. Although all three levels of corporate management may often work together and may even be the same individual, they must be treated as separate parts of the corporate structure.

Shareholders

The shareholders are the persons or other business entities who actually own the corporation. The corporation ownership is divided into shares of stock in the corporation. Each share may be then sold to shareholders who are then issued a stock certificate which represents their ownership of a percentage of the corporation, represented by numbers of shares of stock. Although many different levels and classes of stock ownership may be designated, the forms and discussions in this book will deal with only one class of stock: common stock. Each share of stock is, generally, afforded one vote in shareholder decisions. Although it is perfectly acceptable to provide for non-voting classes of stock, the forms and discussion in this book will only relate to voting shares of stock.

The ownership of stock certificates of the corporation is recorded in the corporate *stock transfer book*. This "book" can simply consist of a few pages in the corporate record book with places to note the issuance and transfer of certificates. Stock and stock transfer records are detailed in Chapter 10. The corporate record book which will contain all of the corporate records (except the accounting records) can consist of a simple 3-ring binder in which the records are organized. It is possible to purchase fancy corporate record books, but they are not a legal requirement.

Ownership of shares of stock in a corporation brings with it both benefits and responsibilities. The benefits stem from the right to a share of ownership in the assets of the corporation. In a manner, the business profits of the corporation may also be shared with the shareholders in the form of dividends. The decision of the corporation to issue dividends on stock, however, is within the realm of the board of directors. The main responsibility of the shareholders is to elect the directors of the corporation. The shareholders also have authority to vote on extraordinary business actions of the corporation. These actions are generally limited to decisive activities of the corporation, such as the sale of all of the assets of the corporation, the merger of the corporation, or the dissolution of the corporation. Shareholders, finally, also generally have the right to approve any amendments to the Articles of Incorporation. Shareholders authority to direct the business only comes from the right to undertake these few actions. Their power must also always be exercised as a group. An individual shareholder has no power to direct the management of the corporation in any way, other than to buy or sell shares of stock.

The election of the directors of the corporation takes place at the annual meeting of the shareholders, although directors can be elected for terms which last for more than one year. At the annual meeting, the president and treasurer of the corporation (both officers of the corporation) will present their annual reports on the activities and financial state of the corporation. The shareholders will then elect (generally by secret ballot majority vote) the directors for the following year. If there are any major business decisions, these may also be addressed. The minutes of this meeting and any shareholders resolutions are typically the only shareholder records to be maintained, other than the stock transfer book. Shareholders meetings and paperwork are generally contained in Chapter 8. Specific shareholder resolutions regarding "S" corporation statues and amendments to Articles of Incorporation and By-Laws are contained in Chapters 12 and 13, respectively. Shareholders may also choose to enter into various shareholders agreements regarding stock rights or voting. Shareholders agreements are explained in Chapter 11.

Directors

As explained, the directors are elected by the shareholders at their annual meetings. Please note, however, that in the forms contained in this book, the initial board of directors is specified in the Articles of Incorporation which are prepared and filed with the state. This is to comply with many state's statutes which require this. The directors which are selected in the Articles may then be approved by the shareholders at their first meeting or may be rejected and new directors elected.

The directors of the corporation must act as members of the board of directors. Individual directors, acting alone, have no authority to bind the corporation or, for example, to enter into contracts or leases for the corporation. The directors must act as a board of directors. Most states, however, allow corporations to have only a single director. This sole director must, however, continue to act as a board of directors. Please check the Appendix for the specific requirements in your state. The board of directors of a corporation has two main responsibilities. The first is to appoint and oversee the officers who will handle the day-to-day actions of actually running the business. The second responsibility is for setting out the corporate policies and making most major decisions on corporate financial and business matters. The policies of the corporation are first contained in the corporate By-Laws which will be prepared by the board of directors. Subsequent corporate policies can be outlined in board of director's resolutions, unless they conflict with the By-Laws. In such a case, the By-Laws must be formally amended by the board of directors, with the consent and approval of the shareholders. Thus, it is the directors who have the actual central authority and responsibility in a corporation.

This differentiation of responsibilities in corporate management is crucial and often difficult to grasp. The shareholders only have the right elect the directors and to vote on major extraordinary business of the corporation (merger, complete sale of the corporation, dissolution, or amendments of the Articles of Incorporation). The director's role is much wider. They have the power to authorize the corporation to enter into contracts, to purchase property, to open bank accounts, to borrow or loan money, and other such significant actions. The board can also delegate this authority to its officers, but—and this is crucial—it must do so in writing with a specific board of directors resolution. In many corporations, in fact, much of the actual operations are handled by the officers. However, all of the officer's authority to operate on behalf of the corporation stems directly from the board of directors.

The bulk of the records of the corporation will consist of matters within the province of the board of directors. The directors will hold annual meetings for the purpose of appointing corporate officers and conducting any other business. They may also hold, with proper notice, special meetings to transact other corporate business which may develop from time to time. The minutes of all directors meetings are very important in establishing that a separate corporate entity has been respected by the persons involved with the corporate management. These minutes must be detailed, complete and must be kept up to date. The various actions of the directors must be documented in formal resolutions. These resolutions are often required by banks and other businesses with which the corporation does business in order to verify that the corporation has authorized the particular transaction. The details of directors meetings and resolutions are outlined in Chapters 7 and 9. Directors resolutions regarding amendments to the Articles of Incorporation and By-Laws are included in Chapter 13. It should be noted that a few states have chosen to allow the shareholders of a corporation to actively participate in the management of the corporation. Although this may allow for ease of management in certain instances, it will not lessen the requirement for corporate record-keeping. The forms in this book are all designed for use in traditional three-tiered corporate management: shareholders, directors, and officers.

Officers

To the officers of a corporation falls the responsibilities of running the business. Their powers, however, are dictated solely by the board of directors. They can be given very broad powers to transact virtually all business for the corporation, or they can be tightly limited in their authority. A single shareholder can act as both the sole director and the sole officer of a corporation in most states. The officers, however, even in this circumstance, still derive their authority from resolutions of the board of directors. Prudent businesses often require copies of the authorizing resolutions in the course of large transactions.

There may be many levels of corporate officers. Traditionally, there are four main officers: president, vice-president, treasurer, and secretary. Their specific powers should be outlined by the directors in the corporate By-Laws and their authority to transact individual business deals should be detailed in board of director's resolutions. In general, the president acts as the corporation's general manager, handling the day-to-day operations. The vice-president normally acts only in the absence of the president, although this officer can be given specific responsibilities. The treasurer handles the corporate funds and is responsible for the accounting books. The secretary handles the corporate records (minutes, resolutions, etc.) and is also generally responsible for the corporate stock and stock transfer book.

The officers are appointed by the board of directors at annual meetings, although special meetings can be called for this purpose. The officers may be required to report individually to the board. Often the president will be called upon to present an annual report regarding the overall condition of the corporation. The treasurer will present an annual financial report at the directors meeting. The secretary will handle all of the records, including copies of these annual reports. In many corporations, the president keeps in contact with the board of directors on a much more continual basis. However, any major decisions which affect the corporation should be carefully documented and, if necessary, a special meeting of the board of directors should be called and a formal resolution adopted.

The formalities of corporate structure may seem complex for small businesses and even foolish for corporations with a single owner/director/officer. It is important to understand that it is the recognition of this structure and the documentation of corporate actions taken within this structure which afford the corporation with its limited liability protection and taxation benefits. The specific formalities for preparing Articles of Incorporation are contained in Chapter 5; for adopting By-Laws, Chapter 6; for Directors meetings, Chapter 7; and for Shareholders meetings, Chapter 8.

Chapter 4

Pre-Incorporation Matters

The planning stage of incorporation is vital to the success of any corporation. The structure of a new corporation, including the number of directors, number of shares of stock, and other matters, must be carefully tailored to the specific needs of the business. Attorneys typically use a pre-incorporation worksheet to assemble all of the necessary information from which to plan the incorporation process.

By filling out a pre-incorporation worksheet, potential business owners will be able to have before them all of the basic data to use in preparing the necessary incorporation paperwork. The process of preparing this worksheet will also help uncover any potential differences of opinion among the persons who are desiring to form the corporation. Often conflicts and demands are not known until the actual process of determining the corporate structure begins. Frank discussions regarding the questions of voting rights, number of directors, and other management decisions often will enable potential associates to resolve many of the difficult problems of corporate management in advance. The use of a written worksheet will also provide all persons involved with a clear and permanent record of the information. This may provide the principals of the corporation with vital support for later decisions that may be required.

All persons involved in the planned corporation should participate in the preparation of the following worksheet. Please take the time to carefully and completely fill in all of the spaces. Following the worksheet, there is a pre-incorporation checklist which provides a clear listing of all of the required actions necessary to incorporate a business. Follow this checklist carefully as the incorporation process proceeds. After this pre-incorporation checklist, there is a document filing checklist which provides a listing of the corporate documents which are normally required to be filed with the state corporation office. Finally, there is a discussion and form for reserving the corporate name with the state corporation department. If required, this will be the first form filed with the state corporation department.

Unfamiliar terms relating to corporations are explained in the glossary of this book. As the pre-incorporation worksheet is filled in, please refer to the following explanations:

Address of state corporation department: The Appendix of this book provides this address. You should write to this department immediately, requesting all available information on incorporation of a for-profit business corporation in your state. Although the forms in this book are designed for use in all states and the Appendix provides up-to-date information on state requirements, state laws and fees charged for incorporation are subject to change. Having the latest available information will save you time and trouble.

Parties involved: This listing should provide the names, addresses, and phone numbers of all of the people who are involved in the planning stages of the corporation.

Corporate name: The selection of a corporate name is often crucial to the success of a corporation. The name must not conflict with any existing company names, nor must it be deceptively similar to other names. It is often wise to clearly explain the business of the corporation through the choice of name. All states allow for a reservation of the corporate name in advance of actual incorporation. Check the Appendix listing for your state.

Principal place of business: This must be the address of the actual physical location of the main business. It may not be a post office box. If the corporation is home-based, this address should be the home address.

Purpose of corporation: Many states allow the use of an "all-purpose" business purpose clause in describing the main activity of the business; for example—to conduct any lawful business. The Articles of Incorporation which are used in this book provide this type of form. However, a few states require a specific business purpose to be identified in the Articles of Incorporation. Please check in the Appendix to see if this is a requirement in your state. If you must specify a purpose, be concise and specific but broad enough to allow for flexibility in operating your business.

State/local licenses required: Here you should note any specific requirements for licenses to operate your type of business. Most states require obtaining a tax ID number and a retail, wholesale, or sales tax license. A federal tax ID number must be obtained by all corporations. Additionally, certain types of businesses will require health department approvals, state board licensing, or other forms of licenses. If necessary, check with a competent local attorney for details regarding the types of licenses required for your locality and business type.

Patents/copyrights/trademarks: If patents, copyrights or trademarks will need to be transferred into the corporation, they should be noted here.

State of incorporation: In general, the corporation should be incorporated in the state in which it will conduct business. In the past, the state of Delaware was regarded as the best state in which to incorporate. This was due to the fact that Delaware was the first state to modernize its corporation laws to reflect the realities of present-day corporate business. This is no longer the case. Virtually all states have now enacted corporate laws very similar to those in Delaware. In the vast majority of situations, it is preferable to be incorporated in your home state.

Corporate existence: The choices here are perpetual (forever) or limited to a certain length. In virtually all cases, you should choose perpetual.

Incorporators: This should be the person (or persons) who will prepare and file the Articles of Incorporation. Most states allow for one incorporator. However, a few require more than one. Please check the Appendix for the requirements in your particular state.

Date of first directors meeting: This will be the date proposed for holding the first meeting of the board of directors, at which the corporate By-Laws will be officially adopted.

Proposed date to begin corporate business: This should be the date on which you expect the corporation to begin its legal existence. Until this date (actually, until the state formally accepts the Articles of Incorporation), the incorporators of your corporation will continue to be legally liable for any business conducted on behalf of the proposed corporation.

Proposed bank for corporate bank account: In advance of incorporation, you should determine the bank which will handle the corporate accounts. Obtain from the bank the necessary bank resolution, which will be signed by the board of directors at the first directors meeting.

Cost of incorporation: The state fees for incorporation are listed in the Appendix. This cost should also reflect the cost of obtaining professional assistance (legal or accounting); the cost of procuring the necessary supplies; and any other direct costs of the incorporation process.

Number of directors: Most states allow a corporation to have a single director. A number of states require three directors unless there are fewer than three shareholders, in which case they allow for the number of directors to equal the number of shareholders. Please check the Appendix for the requirements in your particular state.

Proposed directors: Here you should list the names and addresses of the proposed members of the first board of directors. Although not a requirement in every state, the Articles of Incorporation used in this book provides that these persons be listed. It is not possible to keep the names of the directors of a corporation secret.

Proposed officers: This information is not provided in the Articles of Incorporation and need not be made public. You should list here the persons who are proposed as the first officers of the business.

Corporation's registered agent and address: Here you should list the name and actual street address of the person who will act as the registered agent of the corporation. All states (except New York) require that a specific person be available as the agent of the corporation for the service of process (that is: to accept subpoenas or summons on behalf of the corporation). The person need not be a shareholder, director, or officer of the corporation. The registered agent need not be a lawyer. Normally, the main owner, chairperson of the board of directors, or president of the corporation is selected as the registered agent.

Out-of-state qualification: If the corporation desires to actively conduct business in a state other that the main state of incorporation, it is necessary to "qualify" the corporation in that state. This generally requires obtaining a Certificate of Authority to Transact Business from the other state. In this context, a corporation from another state is referred to as a "foreign" corporation. If you desire that your corporation qualify for activities in another state, you are advised to consult a competent business attorney.

Annual shareholders meeting: The date, time, and place of the annual shareholders meeting should be specified.

Required quorum: This is the percentage of ownership of shares of issued stock in the corporation which must be represented at a shareholders meeting in order to officially transact any shareholder business. This is normally set at a "majority" (over 50%), although this figure can be set higher.

Required vote for shareholder action: Once it is determined that a quorum of shareholders is present at a meeting, this is the percentage of ownership of shares of issued stock in the corporation which must vote in the affirmative in order to officially pass any shareholder business. This is normally set at a "majority" (over 50%), although this figure can be set higher and can be made to be unanimous.

Fiscal year and accounting type: For accounting purposes, the fiscal year and accounting type (cash or accrual) of the corporation should be chosen in advance. Please consult with a competent accounting professional.

Amendments to Articles of Incorporation: Here should be the determination of which bodies of the corporation will have the authority to amend the Articles of Incorporation. The forms in this book are designed to allow the Articles of the corporation to be amended by the board of directors only upon approval by the shareholders.

Amendments to By-Laws: Here should be the determination of which bodies of the corporation will have the authority to amend the By-Laws. The forms in this book are designed to allow the By-Laws of the corporation to be amended by the board of directors only upon approval by the shareholders.

Annual directors meeting: The date, time, and place of the annual board of directors meeting should be specified.

Required quorum: This is the percentage of directors which must be present at a board of directors meeting in order to officially transact any directors business. This is normally set at a "majority" (over 50%), although this figure can be set higher.

Required vote for director action: Once it is determined that a quorum of directors is present at a meeting, this is the percentage of directors which must vote in the affirmative in order to officially pass any board of director's business. This is normally set at a "majority" (over 50%), although this figure can be set higher and can be made to be unanimous.

Initial investment: This figure is the total amount of money or property which will be transferred to the corporation upon its beginning business. This transfer will be in exchange for the issuance of shares of stock in the corporation. This is also referred to as "paid-in capital".

Initial indebtedness: If there is to be any initial indebtedness for the corporation, please list here.

Initial authorized number of shares: This figure is required to be listed in the Articles of Incorporation. The number of shares of stock to be authorized should be listed. For small corporations, this number may be influenced by the incorporation fee structure of the state of incorporation. For example, some states allow for a minimum incorporation fee when only a certain minimum number of stock shares are authorized. Please see the Appendix for the requirements in your state and check with your state corporation department.

Par value or no par value? This refers to an arbitrary indication as to the value of the stock. The designation of stock as having a certain "par" value is *not* an indication of the actual value of the shares of stock. Shares must be sold for a price at or below par value. If no par value is assigned, the shares are issued for the actual price paid per share. The choice of par or no par value stock may affect the issuance of dividends and should be referred to the corporate accountant.

Proposed sales of shares of stock: Here should be listed the names, cash or property, and value of potential sales of shares of stock which may be approved by the board of directors once the corporation is officially authorized to issue stock.

Pre-Incorporation Worksheet

Name and address of state corporation department

_____
_____
_____

Parties Involved

Name	Address	Phone
_____	_____	_____
_____	_____	_____
_____	_____	_____
_____	_____	_____
_____	_____	_____

Proposed Name of the Corporation:

First choice _____

Alternate choices: _____
_____

Location of Business:

Address of principal place of business: _____
_____

Description of principal place of business: _____
_____
_____

Ownership of principal place of business: (Own/lease ?) _____

Other places of business: _____
_____
_____
_____

Type of Business

Purpose of corporation: _____
_____

State/local licenses required: _____
_____

Patents/copyrights/trademark: _____

Incorporation Matters

State of incorporation: _____

Corporate existence (limited or perpetual?): _____

Names and addresses of those who will act as incorporators:
      Name   Address

_____   _____
_____   _____
_____   _____

Proposed date of first directors meeting: _____

Proposed date to begin corporate business: _____

Proposed bank for corporate bank account: _____

Cost of incorporation: _____

Corporate Management

Proposed number of directors: _____

Proposed first board of directors:
      Name   Address

_____   _____
_____   _____
_____   _____

Proposed first officers:
      Name   Address

President: _____ _____

Vice President: _____ _____

Secretary: _____ _____

Treasurer: _____ _____

Corporation's registered agent and office address? _____
_____

Is qualification in other states necessary?: _____

Corporate By-Laws

Annual Shareholders Meeting
      Place   Date   Time

_____ _____ _____

Required quorum for shareholders meetings: _____

Required vote for shareholders actions: (majority/%/unanimous?): _____

Fiscal year: _____

Accounting type: (cash or accrual?): _____

Amendments to Articles: _____ directors; _____ shareholders; ____ either

Amendments to By-Laws: _____ directors; _____ shareholders; ____ either

Annual Directors Meeting
      Place   Date   Time

_____ _____ _____

Required quorum for directors meetings: _____

Required vote for directors actions: (majority/%/unanimous?): _____

Corporate Stock:

Initial investment total: $_____

Initial indebtedness: $_____

Initial authorized number of shares: _____

Par value or no par value? _____

Proposed sales of shares of stock:

Name	Cash/Property	Amount
_____	_____	_____
_____	_____	_____
_____	_____	_____
_____	_____	_____
_____	_____	_____
_____	_____	_____
_____	_____	_____

Pre-Incorporation Checklist

❑ Write state corporation office for information (see Appendix).
❑ Complete pre-incorporation checklist.
❑ Check annual fees and filing requirements.
❑ Prepare Articles of Incorporation.
❑ If desired, have attorney review Articles prior to filing.
❑ Review tax impact of incorporation with accountant.
❑ Check state tax, employment, licensing, unemployment, and worker's compensation requirements.
❑ Check insurance requirements.
❑ Procure corporate seal.
❑ Prepare stock certificates.
❑ Prepare corporate accounting ledgers.
❑ Prepare corporate record book (looseleaf binder).

Document Filing Checklist

❑ Application for Reservation of Corporate Name (if desired)
❑ Articles of Incorporation (mandatory)
❑ Amendments to Articles of Incorporation (mandatory, if applicable)
❑ Annual Corporate Reports (mandatory)
❑ Change of Address or Registered Agent (mandatory)
❑ Articles of Merger (mandatory, if applicable)
❑ Articles of Dissolution (mandatory, if applicable)
❑ Any other required state forms (see Appendix)

Once all of the persons involved have completed the Pre-Incorporation Worksheet, agreed on all of the details, and reviewed the Pre-incorporation and document filing checklists, the actual process of incorporation may begin. If the choice for a corporate name may be similar to another business or if the incorporators wish to insure that the name will be available, an Application for Reservation of Corporate Name may be filed. This is a simple form which requests that the state corporation department hold a chosen corporate name until the actual Articles of Incorporation are filed, at which time the name will become the official registered name of the corporation. The next page contains a sample of this form. There will be a fee required for the filing of this form and some states prefer that pre-printed state forms be used. Please check in the Appendix and with the specific state corporation department for information. In any event, the information required will be the same as is necessary for this sample form.

Application for Reservation of Corporate Name

Application for Reservation of Corporate Name

TO:

I , _____ , with office located at

_____ ,

acting as an incorporator, apply for reservation of the following corporate name:

_____

This corporate name is intended to be used to incorporate a for-profit corporation in the State of _____ , County of _____ .

I request that this corporate name be reserved for a period of _____ days. Please issue a certificate of reservation of this corporate name.

Dated _____ , 19 ___

_____
Signature of Incorporator

Chapter 5

Articles of Incorporation

The central legal document for any corporation is the Articles of Incorporation. In some states, this document may be called a Certificate of Incorporation, Articles of Association, or Articles of Organization. Please check the Appendix for the requirements in your particular state. This form outlines the basic structure of the corporation and details those matters which are relevant to the public registration of the corporation. The name, purpose, owners, registered agent, address, and other vital facts relating to the existence of the corporation are filed with the state by using this form. Upon filing of the Articles of Incorporation, payment of the proper fee, and acceptance by the state corporation department, the corporation officially begins its legal existence. Until the state has accepted the Articles, the incorporators are not shielded from liability by the corporate form. Some states have chosen to confuse matters slightly by referring to another form which may be issued by the state as a Certificate of Incorporation. Please check the Appendix for the state requirements for the state of your potential incorporation. For clarity, however, this book will refer to the incorporator-prepared document as the Articles of Incorporation.

There are a number of items which are required to be noted in all Articles of Incorporation. The Articles may also include many other details of the corporation's existence. Please check the Appendix and with your state incorporation department for specific details. Following is a Checklist of items which are mandatory or optional for Articles of Incorporation.

Articles of Incorporation Checklist

The mandatory details for Articles of Incorporation under most state laws are:

❏ The name of the corporation
❏ The purpose of the corporation
❏ The duration of the corporation
❏ The name and address of each incorporator
❏ The name of the registered agent of the corporation
❏ The office of the registered agent of the corporation
❏ The number of shares of stock that the corporation is authorized to issue to shareholders
❏ Amount of initial capital of corporation (optional some states)
❏ The number, names, and addresses of the first board of directors
❏ Par value or no par value for shares of stock
❏ The signature of the incorporators
❏ The signature of the registered agent

In addition, the following items may also be included at your option:

❏ The terms and qualifications for board members
❏ Provisions relating to the powers of the directors, officers, or shareholders
❏ Designation of different classes of stock
❏ Voting and other rights or restrictions on stock
❏ Preemptive or cumulative voting rights
❏ Election to be a close corporation under state law
❏ Provisions indemnifying corporate officers and directors

The Articles of Incorporation for your corporation should include all of the required information. Since Articles are a public record, all of the information in them will be available for inspection. However, since the names of the directors will usually be required to be revealed in the annual reports that are filed with the state, there is no purpose in attempting to conceal identities of actual management of the corporation. Much of the information which is not required in the Articles may instead be put into the By-Laws of the corporation. In this manner, the actual management structure and details will remain unavailable for public inspection. Some states provide pre-printed Articles of Incorporation which are requested to be used for filing. The information required, however, will be the same as is noted in the sample Articles of Incorporation in this chapter. Even if state-supplied forms are used, it will be helpful to read through this chapter and fill in the information as noted on the sample forms. Transferring it to the state form will then be a simple task.

Articles of Incorporation may be amended at any time. However, this generally requires a formal filing with the state and the issuance of a Certificate of Amendment of Articles of Incorporation. It also normally requires the payment of a fee. For these reasons, it is often a good idea to only put those items in the original Articles which are unlikely to require changes in the near future. All of the necessary information and forms for amending the Articles of Incorporation are provided in Chapter 13.

This chapter contains sample clauses for preparing Articles of Incorporation. The sample clauses in this chapter are labeled as either mandatory or optional. An explanation is also provided for each clause. You should check the Appendix and any information which you have received from the state corporation department to be certain that you have included all of the necessary information for your state. A few states may require additional Articles. Most of the information required for preparing the clauses for this form will be on your Pre-Incorporation Worksheet, which you prepared in Chapter 4. Once you have chosen which of the clauses you will use, re-type the Articles of Incorporation. (Type in the correct title for this document if your state has a different name for it—check the Appendix). They should be typed in black ink on one side of 8.5" X 11" white paper, double-spaced. If state-supplied documents are used, fill them in with the information you have prepared in this book. Optional clauses may be added to state-supplied forms where necessary.

The Articles must then be properly signed. Although not required by all states, the form in this book is designed to be notarized. A few states require that the Articles be published as legal notices in newspapers. Please check the Appendix for the requirements in your particular state. The signed Articles of Incorporation and the proper fee should be sent to the proper state office. Upon receipt, the state corporation department will check for duplication or confusing conflicts with the names of any other registered corporation. They will also check to be certain that all of the statutory requirements have been fulfilled and that the proper fee has been paid. If there is a problem, the Articles will be returned with an explanation of the difficulty. Correct the problem and re-file the Articles. If everything is in order, the business will officially be incorporated and able to begin to conduct business as a corporate entity. Some states have different procedures for indicating the beginning existence of a corporation. For example, you may need to request an official Certificate of Filing, Certificate of Good Standing, or other type of Certificate and pay a fee for this record. Check with your state corporation department. A completed sample Articles of Incorporation is included at the end of this chapter.

Title and Introduction (MANDATORY)

Check in the Appendix and with your state corporation department for any changes to this clause. If your state has a different title for this document, please insert the proper title (for example: Certificate of Incorporation of _____). The name of the corporation should include the corporate designation (see below under Name of Corporation).

Articles of Incorporation of _____

The undersigned person(s), acting as incorporator(s) for the purpose of forming a stock business corporation under the laws of the State of _____ , adopts the following Articles of Incorporation:

Name of Corporation (MANDATORY)

The name of the corporation should be unique. It should not be confusingly similar to any other business name in use within your state. In addition, it should not contain any terms which might lead people to believe that it is a government or financial institution. Finally, it must generally contain an indication that the business is a corporation, such as Inc., Incorporated, Corporation, or Limited. Some states allow the use of the word Company in the name of corporations. Others do not. If you wish to use a term of corporate designation other than Corporation or Incorporated (or abbreviations of these), please check the Appendix and with your state corporation department.

Article 1. The name of the corporation is _____.

Purpose and Powers of the Corporation (MANDATORY)

Many states allows a general statement of purpose: "to transact any and all lawful business for which corporations may be incorporated under the Business Corporation Act of the State of _____". Others may require that you specifically state the purpose of your corporation, such as: "to operate a retail dry-cleaning business". Please check the Appendix for the requirements in your particular state. If you are required to state a specific purpose, try to be broad enough to allow your business flexibility without the necessity of later amending the Articles of Incorporation to reflect a change in direction of your business. Chose the clause appropriate for your state and circumstances. (Please note that Kentucky and Massachusetts are referred to as "Commonwealths", rather than "States".)

Article 2. The purpose for which this corporation is organized is to transact any and all lawful business for which corporations may be organized under the laws of the State of _____ , and to have all powers which are afforded corporations under the laws of the State of _____ .

Or:

Article 2. The purpose for which this corporation is organized is:_____
_____.
This corporation shall have all powers under the laws of the State of
_____ .

Duration of Corporation (MANDATORY)

All states allow for a perpetual duration for corporations, meaning that the corporation can continue in existence forever. Unless there is a specific business reason to indicate otherwise, this is generally the safest choice. A limited duration statement is not an acceptable method to dissolve a corporation. Please see Chapter 15 regarding corporate dissolutions.

Article 3. The duration of this corporation shall be perpetual.

Minimum Capitalization (MANDATORY; may be optional)

This clause refers to the amount of capital which will form the initial basis for operating the corporation. Several states have specific dollar amounts of minimum capital which is required for a corporation to be incorporated, ranging from $500 to $1,000. All other states have no minimum and you may delete this clause. Please check the Appendix and check with your state corporation department.

Article 4. The total amount of initial capitalization of this corporation is $ _____ .

Authorization to Issue Stock (MANDATORY)

The number of shares of stock which will be issued is a business determination. There is no specific reason that the number of shares should be large. In fact, in some states the amount of fees charged for incorporation is based upon the number of shares which are authorized to be issued. Please check the Appendix for the requirements in your particular state.

Article 5. The total number of shares of common capital stock that this corporation is authorized to issue is _____ .

Par or No Par Value (MANDATORY; may be optional)

This refers to the arbitrary value which has been assigned to your shares of stock. It does not refer to the actual purchase price required for the shares of stock. Please consult with the corporation's accountant if you have questions regarding this item. Choose the clause for Article 6 which is appropriate for your state and circumstances.

Article 6. This stock shall have a par value of _____ .

Or:

Article 6. This stock shall have no par value.

Name of Registered Agent (MANDATORY)

The registered agent for a corporation is the person upon whom service of process (summons, subpoena, etc.) can be served. This person must be an adult who is a resident of the state of incorporation. The usual choice is the main owner of the corporation, unless an attorney is preferred. Residents of New York State are required to have the Secretary of State be the authorized agent for service of process. Please see the Appendix and check with your state corporation department. There is a place at the end of the Articles of Incorporation for the registered agent to sign.

> **Article 7**. The initial registered agent of this corporation is _____.
> By his/her signature at the end of this document, this person acknowledges acceptance of the responsibilities as registered agent of this corporation.

Address of Registered Agent (MANDATORY)

This address must be an actual place, generally the offices of the corporation. It may not be a post office box or other unmanned location.

> **Article 8**. The initial address of the office of the registered agent of this
> corporation is _____,
> in the County of _____ , State of _____ .

Name and Address and Age of Incorporator(s) (MANDATORY)

This is the name and address of the person or persons who are filing for incorporation. The minimum age requirement for incorporating a business is generally 18. A few states allow corporations or partnerships to act as incorporators. Please check the Appendix or with your state corporation department.

Article 9. The name(s), addresses and ages of the incorporator(s) of this corporation is/are:

Name	Address	Age
_____	_____	____
_____	_____	____
_____	_____	____

Number of Directors (MANDATORY; Optional in some states)

The minimum number of directors allowed is generally one. However, a few states require three directors if there are over two shareholders. Thus, in those states, if there is only one shareholder, then there may be one director. If there are two shareholders, there must be two directors. But if there are three shareholders or more, there must be three directors. Please check the Appendix.

Article 10. The number of directors of this corporation is _____.

Names and Addresses of Initial Directors (MANDATORY)

This clause provides for the initial directors of the corporation until the first meeting of the shareholders of the corporation either elect or approve these directors.

Article 11. The names and addresses of the initial directors of this corporation are as follows:

Name	Address
_____	_____
_____	_____
_____	_____

Preemptive Rights (Optional)

Using this clause, you may include any preemptive stock rights in the Articles, if desired. Preemptive rights are like a right of first refusal. If a corporation proposes to authorize new shares of stock, preemptive rights allow current shareholders the right to acquire a pro-rata percentage of the new shares based on their current percentage of ownership. This prevents their ownership percentage from being watered down by the authorization and issuance of new shares of stock. Under the laws of some states, preemptive rights exist unless the Articles of Incorporation specifically state that they do not. In other states, preemptive rights *do not* exist unless the Articles of Incorporation specifically state that they do. The best method of dealing with this issue is to include one of the following clauses which fits your circumstances.

Article 12. This corporation shall have preemptive rights for all shareholders.

Or:

Article 12. This corporation shall have no preemptive rights for any shareholders.

Preferences and Limitations on Stock (Optional)

In this clause, any voting preferences or limitations on transfers or other rights or restrictions on stock can be listed. This information may instead be listed in the By-Laws of the corporation, if preferred.

Article 13. The following are preferences and limitations on the common stock of this corporation:

_____
_____
_____.

Additional Articles (Optional)

This clause may be used to adopt any additional articles which may be desired.

Article 14. This corporation adopts the following additional articles:

_____

_____

_____

_____ .

Closing and Signatures (MANDATORY)

This clause provides a statement certifying that the facts as stated are true and correct. It also provides for the registered agent to sign acknowledging his acceptance of the responsibilities of this job. This should be signed in front of a Notary Public.

I certify that all of the facts stated in these Articles of Incorporation are true and correct and are made for the purpose of forming a business corporation under the laws of the State of _____ .

Dated _____

_____
Signature of Incorporator

_____
Signature of Incorporator

_____
Signature of Incorporator

I acknowledge my appointment as registered agent of this corporation and accept the appointment.

Dated _____

_____

Signature of Registered Agent

State of _____)
)   S.S.
County of _____)

Before me, on _____ , 19 ___, personally appeared
_____
_____
_____
and_____,
who are known to me to be the persons who subscribed their names to this document, and acknowledged that they did so for the purposes stated.

_____

Notary Public, in and for the County of _____ , State of
_____ . My commission expires _____ , 19 ___.

Sample Completed Articles of Incorporation

Articles of Incorporation of ABCXYZ Corporation

The undersigned person, acting as incorporator for the purpose of forming a stock business corporation under the laws of the State of Superior, adopts the following Articles of Incorporation:

Article 1. The name of the corporation is ABCXYZ Corporation.

Article 2. The purpose for which this corporation is organized is to transact any and all lawful business for which corporations may be organized under the laws of the State of Superior, and to have all powers which are afforded to corporations under the laws of the state of Superior.

Article 3. The duration of this corporation shall be perpetual.

Article 4. The total amount of initial capitalization of this corporation is $ 1,000.

Article 5. The total number of shares of common capital stock that this corporation is authorized to issue is 100.

Article 6. This stock shall have no par value.

Article 7. The initial registered agent of this corporation is Mary Celeste.

Article 8. The initial address of the office of the registered agent of this corporation is 1234 Main Street, in the County of Inferior, State of Superior.

Article 9. The name, address, and age of the incorporator of this corporation is Mary Celeste, 1234 Main Street, County of Inferior, State of Superior, age 25 years.

Article 10. The number of directors of this corporation is 2 (two).

Article 11. The names and addresses of the initial directors of this corporation are as follows:

Name	Address
Mary Celeste	1234 Main Street, Capitol City, Superior
John Celeste	1234 Main Street, Capitol City, Superior

Article 12. This corporation shall have preemptive rights for all shareholders.

Article 13. The following are preferences and limitations on the common stock of this corporation: none.

Article 14. This corporation adopts the following additional articles: none.

I certify that all of the facts stated in these Articles of Incorporation are true and correct and are made for the purpose of forming a business corporation under the laws of the State of Superior.

Dated June 4, 1994

Mary Celeste
Signature of Incorporator

I acknowledge my appointment as registered agent of this corporation and accept the appointment.

Dated June 4, 1994

Mary Celeste
Signature of Registered Agent

State of Superior   )
)   S.S.
County of Inferior   )

Before me, on June 4, 1994, personally appeared Mary Celeste, who is known to me to be the person who subscribed his/her name to this document, and acknowledged that he/she did so for the purposes stated.

Andrea Doria
Notary Public, in and for the County of Inferior, State of Superior. My commission expires June 5, 1994.

Chapter 6

Corporate By-Laws

The By-Laws of a corporation are the third part of the triangle that provides the framework for the management of the corporate business. Along with state law and the Articles of Incorporation, the By-Laws provide a clear outline of the rights and responsibilities of all parties to a corporation. In particular, the By-Laws provide the actual details of the operational framework for the business. The By-Laws are the internal document that will contain the basic rules on how the corporation is to be run. Every corporation must have a set of By-Laws. Many of the provisions cover relatively standard procedural questions, relating to quorums, voting and stock. Other provisions may need to be specifically tailored to the type of business for which the By-Laws are intended. They are generally able to be amended by vote of the board of directors, unless the Articles of Incorporation or the By-Laws themselves have transferred that authority to the shareholders. The By-Laws provided in this book specify that the power to amend the By-Laws is vested in the board of directors, but that the shareholders have the power to approve or reject any amendment. For more information regarding the amendment of By-Laws, refer to Chapter 13.

The By-Laws can contain very specific or very general provisions for the internal management of the company. Typically, the By-Laws cover 5 general areas:

- ❏ The rights and responsibilities of the shareholders
- ❏ The rights and responsibilities of the directors
- ❏ The rights and responsibilities of the officers
- ❏ Financial matters
- ❏ Methods for amending the By-Laws

This chapter contains sample clauses for preparing your corporate By-Laws. Once you have chosen which of the clauses you will use and have filled in any required information, re-type the By-Laws in black ink on one side of 8.5" X 11" white paper, double-spaced. A completed sample set of By-Laws is included at the end of this chapter. Your completed By-Laws should be both formally adopted at the first board of directors meeting and approved at the first shareholders meeting. The following is a Checklist for use in preparing your By-Laws:

By-Laws Checklist

❑ Power to designate the location of principal office of corporation
❑ Power to designate the registered office and agent of corporation
❑ Date, time, and place of annual shareholders meeting
❑ Procedures for special shareholders meetings
❑ Notice and waivers for shareholders meetings
❑ Voting eligibility requirements for shareholders
❑ Quorum and votes required for actions for shareholders
❑ Shareholders proxy requirements
❑ Shareholder consent resolutions
❑ Cumulative voting requirements
❑ Powers of the directors
❑ How many directors?
❑ Term of office for directors
❑ Directors election procedures
❑ Date, time and, place of annual directors meeting
❑ Procedures for special directors meetings
❑ Notice and waivers for directors meetings
❑ Quorum and votes required for actions for directors
❑ Directors consent resolutions
❑ Removing and filling vacancies of directors
❑ Salaries of directors
❑ Fiduciary duties of directors
❑ How many officers and how long the term of office?
❑ Removing and filling vacancies of officers
❑ Salaries of officers
❑ Duties of the officers
❑ How are stock certificates handled?
❑ Are there any restrictions on the rights to transfer shares of stock?
❑ How are corporate financial matters to be handled?
❑ Can officers or directors borrow money from the corporation?
❑ By-Law amendment procedures

Title

> **By-Laws of** _____ **, a corporation**
> **incorporated under the laws of the State of** _____ **.**

Corporate Office and Registered Agent

> **1. Corporate Office and Registered Agent**. The board of directors has the
> power to determine the location of the corporation's principal place of
> business and registered office, which need not be the same location. The board
> of directors also has the power to designate the corporation's registered agent,
> who may be an officer or director.

Date and Time of Shareholders Annual Meeting

> **2. Date and Time of Shareholders Annual Meeting**. The annual shareholders
> meeting will be held on the _____ of every year at _____
> ___ m. This meeting is for the purpose of electing directors and for transacting
> any other necessary business. If this day is a legal holiday, the meeting will be
> held on the next day.

Shareholders Special Meetings

> **3. Shareholders Special Meetings**. Special meetings of the shareholders may
> be called at any time and for any purpose. These meetings may be called by
> either the president or the board of directors or upon request of _____
> percent of the shareholders of the corporation. The request for a special
> meeting must be made in writing which states the time, place, and purpose of
> the meeting. The request should be given to the secretary of the corporation
> who will prepare and send written notice to all shareholders of record who
> are entitled to vote at the meeting.

Place of Shareholders Meetings

4. Place of Shareholders Meetings. The board of directors has the power to designate the place for shareholders meetings, unless a waiver of notice of the meeting signed by all shareholders designates the place for the meeting. If no place is designated, either by the board of directors or all of the shareholders, then the place for the meeting will be the principal office of the corporation.

Notice of Shareholders Meetings

5. Notice of Shareholders Meetings. Written notice of shareholders meetings must be sent to each shareholder of record entitled to vote at the meeting. The notice must be sent no less than _____ days nor more than _____ days before the date of the meeting. The notice should be sent to the shareholder's address as shown in the corporate Stock Transfer Book. The notice will include the place, date, and time of the meeting. Notices for special meetings must also include the purpose of the meeting. When notices are sent, the secretary of the corporation must prepare an Affidavit of Mailing of Notices. Shareholders may waive notice of meetings if done in writing, except that attendance at a meeting is considered a waiver of notice of the meeting.

Shareholders Entitled to Notice, to Vote, or to Dividends

6. Shareholders Entitled to Notice, to Vote, or to Dividends. For the purpose of determining which shareholders are entitled to notice, to vote at meetings, or to receive dividends, the board of directors may order that the corporate Stock Transfer Books be closed for _____ days prior to a meeting or the issuance of a dividend. The shareholders entitled to receive notice, vote at meetings, or receive dividends are those who are recorded in the Stock Transfer Book upon the closing of the Book. Instead of closing the Books, the board of directors may also set a Record Date. The shareholders recorded in the Stock Transfer Book at the close of business on the Record Date will be entitled to receive notice, vote at meetings, or receive dividends. A list of shareholders entitled to receive notice, vote at meetings, or receive dividends will be prepared by the secretary when necessary and provided to the officers of the corporation. Every shareholder who is entitled to receive notice, vote, or receive dividends is also entitled to examine this list and the corporate stock transfer book.

Shareholders Quorum

7. Shareholders Quorum. A quorum for shareholders meeting will be a majority of the outstanding shares which are entitled to vote at the meeting, whether in person or represented by proxy. Once a quorum is present, business may be conducted at the meeting, even if shareholders leave prior to adjournment.

Shareholders Proxies

8. Shareholders Proxies. At all meetings of shareholders, a shareholder may vote by signed proxy or by power of attorney. To be valid, a proxy must be filed with the secretary of the corporation prior to the stated time of the meeting. No proxy may be valid for over 11 months, unless the proxy specifically states otherwise. Proxies may always be revokable prior to the meeting for which it is intended. Attendance at the meeting for which a proxy has been authorized always revokes the proxy.

Shareholders Voting

9. Voting. Each outstanding share of the corporation which is entitled to vote as shown on the Stock Transfer Book will have one vote. The vote of the holders of a majority of the shares entitled to vote will be sufficient to decide any matter, unless a greater number is required by the Articles of Incorporation or by state law. Adjournment shall be by majority vote of those shares entitled to vote.

Shareholders Consent Resolutions

10. Shareholder Consent Resolutions. Any action which may be taken at a shareholders meeting may be taken instead without a meeting if a resolution is consented to, in writing, by all shareholders who would be entitled to vote.

Shareholders Cumulative Voting Rights

11. Shareholders Cumulative Voting rights. For the election of directors, each shareholder may vote in a cumulative manner, if desired, which will mean that if each shareholder has one vote per director to be elected, the shareholder may vote all votes for a single director or spread the votes among the directors.

Powers of the Board of Directors

12. Powers of the Board of Directors. The affairs of the corporation will be managed by the board of directors. The board of directors will have all powers available under state law, including the power to appoint and remove officers, agents, and employees; the power to change the offices, registered agent, and registered office of the corporation; the power to issue shares of stock; the power to borrow money on behalf of the corporation, including the power to execute any evidence of indebtedness on behalf of the corporation; and the power to enter into contracts on behalf of the corporation.

Number of Directors and Term of Office

13. Number of Directors and Term of Office. The number of directors will be as shown in the Articles of Incorporation and may be amended. The number is currently _____ . Each director will hold office for _____ year(s) and will be elected at the annual meeting of the shareholders.

Date and Time of Annual Meeting of the Board of Directors

14. Date and Time of Annual Meeting of the Board of Directors. The annual board of directors meeting will be held on the _____ of every year at _____ ____ m. This meeting is for the purpose of appointing officers and for transacting any other necessary business. If this day is a legal holiday, the meeting will be held on the next day.

Special Meetings of the Board of Directors

15. Special Meetings of the Board of Directors. Special meetings of the board of directors may be called at any time and for any purpose. These meetings may be called by either the president or the board of directors. The request for a special meeting must be made in writing which states the time, place, and purpose of the meeting. The request should be given to the secretary of the corporation who will prepare and send written notice to all directors.

Place of Board of Directors Meetings

16. Place of Board of Directors Meetings. The board of directors has the power to designate the place for directors meetings. If no place is designated, then the place for the meeting will be the principal office of the corporation.

Notice of Board of Directors Meetings

17. Notice of Board of Directors Meetings. Written notice of board of directors meetings must be sent to each director. The notice must be sent no less than _____ days nor more than _____ days before the date of the meeting. The notice should be sent to the director's address as shown in the corporate records. The notice will include the place, date, and time of the meeting, and for special meetings the purpose of the meeting. When notices are sent, the secretary of the corporation must prepare an Affidavit of Mailing of Notices. directors may waive notice of meetings if done in writing, except that attendance at a meeting is considered a waiver of notice of the meeting.

Board of Directors Quorum

18. Board of Directors Quorum. A quorum for directors meetings will be a majority of the directors. Once a quorum is present, business may be conducted at the meeting, even if directors leave prior to adjournment.

Board of Directors Voting

19. Board of Directors Voting. Each director will have one vote. The vote of a majority of the directors will be sufficient to decide any matter, unless a greater number is required by the Articles of Incorporation or state law. Adjournment shall be by majority vote.

Board of Directors Consent Resolutions

20. Board of Directors Consent Resolutions. Any action which may be taken at a directors meeting may be taken instead without a meeting if a resolution is consented to, in writing, by all directors.

Removal of Directors

21. Removal of Directors. A director may be removed from office, with or without cause, at a special meeting of the shareholders called for that purpose.

Filling Directors Vacancies

> **22. Filling Directors Vacancies**. A vacancy on the board of directors may be filled by majority vote of the remaining directors, even if technically less than a quorum. A director elected to fill a remaining term will hold office until the next annual shareholders meeting.

Salaries of Directors

> **23. Salaries of Directors**. The salaries of the directors will be fixed by the board of directors and may be altered at any time by the board. A director may receive a salary even if she/he receives a salary as an officer.

Fiduciary Duty of Directors

> **24. Fiduciary Duty of Directors**. Each director owes a a fiduciary duty of good faith and reasonable care with regard to all actions taken on behalf of the corporation. Each director must perform her/his duties in good faith in a manner which she/he reasonably believes to be in the best interests of the corporation, using ordinary care and prudence.

Number of Officers

> **25. Number of Officers**. The officers of the corporation will include a president, vice-president, treasurer, and secretary. Any two or more offices may be held by the same person.

Appointment and Terms of Officers

26. Appointment and Terms of Officers. The officers of the corporation will be appointed by the directors at the first meeting of the board of directors. Each officer will hold office until death, resignation, or removal by the board of directors.

Removal of Officers

27. Removal of Officers. Any officer may be removed by the board of directors, with or without cause. Appointment of an officer does not create any contract rights for the officer.

Filling Officers Vacancies

28. Filling Officers Vacancies. A vacancy in any office for any reason may be filled by the board of directors for the unexpired term.

Duties of the President

29. Duties of the President. The president is the principal executive officer of the corporation and is subject to control by the board of directors. The president will supervise and control all of the business and activities of the corporation. The president will preside at all shareholders and directors meetings, and perform any other duties as prescribed by the board of directors.

Duties of the Vice-President

30. Duties of the Vice-President. If the president is absent, dies, or is incapacitated, the vice-president will perform the duties of the president. When acting for the president, the vice-president will have all of the powers and authority of the president. The vice-president will also perform any other duties as prescribed by the board of directors.

Duties of the Secretary

31. Duties of the Secretary. The secretary will keep the minutes of all shareholders and directors meetings. The secretary will provide notices of all meetings as required by the By-Laws. The secretary will be the custodian of the corporate records, corporate stock transfer book, and corporate seal. The secretary will keep a list of all shareholders, directors, and officers addresses. The secretary will sign, along with other officers, the corporation's stock certificates. The secretary will also perform any other duties as prescribed by the board of directors.

Duties of the Treasurer

32. Duties of the Treasurer. The treasurer will be custodian of all corporate funds and securities. The treasurer will receive and pay out funds which are receivable or payable to the corporation from any source. The treasurer will deposit all corporate funds received into the corporate bank accounts as designated by the board of directors. The treasurer will also perform any other duties as prescribed by the board of directors.

Salaries of Officers

33. Salaries of Officers. The salaries of the officers will be fixed by the board of directors and may be altered at any time by the board. An officer may receive a salary even if she/he receives a salary as a director.

Stock Certificates

34. Stock Certificates. Certificates which represent shares of ownership in the corporation will be in the form designated by the board of directors. Certificates will be signed by all officers of the corporation. Certificates will be consecutively numbered. The name and address of the person receiving the issued shares, the certificate number, the number of shares and the date of issue will be recorded by the secretary of the corporation in the corporate stock transfer book. Shares of the corporation's stock may only be transferred on the stock transfer book of the corporation by the holder of the shares in whose name they were issued as shown on the stock transfer book, or by his or her legal representative.

Financial Matters

35. Financial Matters. The board of directors will determine the accounting methods and fiscal year of the corporation. All checks, drafts, or other methods for payment shall be signed by an officer determined by resolution of the board of directors. All notes, mortgages, or other evidence of indebtedness shall be signed by an officer determined by resolution of the board of directors. No money will be borrowed or loaned by the corporation unless authorized by a resolution of the board of directors. No contracts will be entered into on behalf of the corporation unless authorized by a resolution of the board of directors. No documents may be executed on behalf of the corporation unless authorized by a resolution of the board of directors. A board of Director's resolution may be for specific instances or a general authorization.

Loans to Officers or Directors

36. Loans to Officers or Directors. The corporation may not lend any money to an officer or director of the corporation unless the loan has been approved by a majority of the shares of all stock of the corporation, including those shares that do not have voting rights.

Amendments to the By-Laws

37. Amendments to the By-Laws. These By-Laws may be amended in any manner by majority vote of the board of directors at any annual or special meeting. Any amendments by the board of directors are subject to approval by majority vote of the shareholders at any annual or special meeting.

Signatures Clause

Dated _____

_____
Secretary of the Corporation

Adopted by the board of directors on _____ , 19 __

_____ _____
Chairperson of the board

Approved by the Shareholders on _____ , 19 __

_____
Secretary of the Corporation

Sample Corporate By-Laws

By-Laws of ABCXYZ Corporation, a corporation incorporated under the laws of the State of Superior.

1. Corporate Office and Registered Agent. The board of directors has the power to determine the location of the corporation's principal place of business and registered office, which need not be the same location. The board of directors also has the power to designate the corporation's registered agent, who may be an officer or director.

2. Date and Time of Shareholders Annual Meeting. The annual shareholders meeting will be held on the First Tuesday in October of every year at 10:00 a.m. This meeting is for the purpose of electing directors and for transacting any other necessary business. If this day is a legal holiday, the meeting will be held on the next day.

3. Shareholders Special Meetings. Special meetings of the shareholders may be called at any time and for any purpose. These meetings may be called by either the president or the board of directors or upon request of 25% percent of the shareholders of the corporation. The request for a special meeting must be made in writing which states the time, place and purpose of the meeting. The request should be given to the secretary of the corporation who will prepare and send written notice to all shareholders of record who are entitled to vote at the meeting.

4. Place of Shareholders Meetings. The board of directors has the power to designate the place for shareholders meetings, unless a waiver of notice of the meeting signed by all shareholders designates the place for the meeting. If no place is designated, either by the board of directors or all of the shareholders, then the place for the meeting will be the principal office of the corporation.

5. Notice of Shareholders Meetings. Written notice of shareholders meetings must be sent to each shareholder of record entitled to vote at the meeting. The notice must be sent no less than 7 days nor more than 21 days before the date of the meeting. The notice should be sent to the shareholder's address as shown in the corporate Stock Transfer Book. The notice will include the place, date, and time of the meeting. Notices for special meetings must also include the purpose of the meeting. When notices are sent, the secretary of the corporation must prepare an Affidavit of Mailing of Notices. Shareholders

71

may waive notice of meetings if done in writing, except that attendance at a meeting is considered a waiver of notice of the meeting.

6. Shareholders Entitled to Notice, to Vote, or to Dividends. For the purpose of determining which shareholders are entitled to notice, to vote at meetings, or to receive dividends, the board of directors may order that the corporate Stock Transfer Books be closed for 30 days prior to a meeting or the issuance of a dividend. The shareholders entitled to receive notice, vote at meetings, or receive dividends are those who are recorded in the Stock Transfer Book upon the closing of the Book. Instead of closing the Books, the board of directors may also set a Record Date. The shareholders recorded in the Stock Transfer Book at the close of business on the Record Date will be entitled to receive notice, vote at meetings, or receive dividends. A list of shareholders entitled to receive notice, vote at meetings, or receive dividends will be prepared by the secretary when necessary and provided to the officers of the corporation. Every shareholder who is entitled to receive notice, vote, or receive dividends is also entitled to examine this list and the corporate stock transfer book.

7. Shareholders Quorum. A quorum for shareholders meeting will be a majority of the outstanding shares which are entitled to vote at the meeting, whether in person or represented by proxy. Once a quorum is present, business may be conducted at the meeting, even if shareholders leave prior to adjournment.

8. Shareholders Proxies. At all meetings of shareholders, a shareholder may vote by signed proxy or by power of attorney. To be valid, a proxy must be filed with the secretary of the corporation prior to the stated time of the meeting. No proxy may be valid for over 11 months, unless the proxy specifically states otherwise. Proxies may always be revokable prior to the meeting for which it is intended. Attendance at the meeting for which a proxy has been authorized always revokes the proxy.

9. Shareholders Voting. Each outstanding share of the corporation which is entitled to vote as shown on the Stock Transfer Book will have one vote. The vote of the holders of a majority of the shares entitled to vote will be sufficient to decide any matter, unless a greater number is required by the Articles of Incorporation or by state law. Adjournment shall be by majority vote of those shares entitled to vote.

10. Shareholder Consent Resolutions. Any action which may be taken at a shareholders meeting may be taken instead without a meeting if a resolution is consented to, in writing, by all shareholders who would be entitled to vote on the matter.

11. Shareholders Cumulative Voting. For the election of directors, each shareholder may vote in a Cumulative manner, if desired. Cumulative voting will mean that if each shareholder has one vote per director to be elected, the shareholder may vote all votes for a single director or spread the votes among directors in any manner.

12. Powers of the Board of Directors. The affairs of the corporation will be managed by the board of directors. The board of directors will have all powers available under state law, including the power to appoint and remove officers, agents, and employees; the power to change the offices, registered agent, and registered office of the corporation; the power to issue shares of stock; the power to borrow money on behalf of the corporation, including the power to execute any evidence of indebtedness on behalf of the corporation; and the power to enter into contracts on behalf of the corporation.

13. Number of Directors and Term of Office. The number of directors will be as shown in the Articles of Incorporation and may be amended. The number is currently three (3). Each director will hold office for one (1) year and will be elected at the annual meeting of the shareholders.

14. Date and Time of Annual Meeting of the Board of Directors. The annual board of directors meeting will be held on the First Tuesday of October of every year at 11:00 p.m. This meeting is for the purpose of appointing officers and for transacting any other necessary business. If this day is a legal holiday, the meeting will be held on the next day.

15. Special Meetings of the Board of Directors. Special meetings of the board of directors may be called at any time and for any purpose. These meetings may be called by either the president or the board of directors. The request for a special meeting must be made in writing which states the time, place and purpose of the meeting. The request should be given to the secretary of the corporation who will prepare and send written notice to all directors.

16. Place of Board of Directors Meetings. The board of directors has the power to designate the place for directors meetings. If no place is designated, then the place for the meeting will be the principal office of the corporation.

17. Notice of Board of Directors Meetings. Written notice of board of directors meetings must be sent to each director. The notice must be sent no less than 7 days nor more than 21 days before the date of the meeting. The notice should be sent to the director's address as shown in the corporate records. The notice will include the place, date, and time of the meeting, and for special meetings the purpose of the meeting. When notices are sent, the secretary of the corporation must prepare an Affidavit of Mailing of Notices. directors may waive notice of meetings if done in writing, except that attendance at a meeting is considered a waiver of notice of the meeting.

18. Board of Directors Quorum. A quorum for directors meetings will be a majority of the directors. Once a quorum is present, business may be conducted at the meeting, even if directors leave prior to adjournment.

19. Board of Directors Voting. Each director will have one vote. The vote of a majority of the directors will be sufficient to decide any matter, unless a greater number is required by the Articles of Incorporation or state law. Adjournment shall be by majority vote.

20. Board of Directors Consent Resolutions. Any action which may be taken at a directors meeting may be taken instead without a meeting if a resolution is consented to, in writing, by all directors.

21. Removal of Directors. A director may be removed from office, with or without cause, at a special meeting of the shareholders called for that purpose.

22. Filling Directors Vacancies. A vacancy on the board of directors may be filled by majority vote of the remaining directors, even if technically less than a quorum. A director elected to fill a remaining term will hold office until the next annual shareholders meeting.

23. Salaries of Directors. The salaries of the directors will be fixed by the board of directors and may be altered at any time by the board. A director may receive a salary even if she/he receives a salary as an officer.

24. Fiduciary Duty of Directors. Each director owes a a fiduciary duty of good faith and reasonable care with regard to all actions taken on behalf of the corporation. Each director must perform her/his duties in good faith in a manner which she/he reasonably believes to be in the best interests of the corporation, using ordinary care and prudence.

25. Number of Officers. The officers of the corporation will include a president, vice-president, treasurer, and secretary. Any two or more offices may be held by the same person.

26. Appointment and Terms of Officers. The officers of the corporation will be appointed by the directors at the first meeting of the board of directors. Each officer will hold office until death, resignation or removal by the board of directors.

27. Removal of Officers. Any officer may be removed by the board of directors, with or without cause. Appointment of an officer does not create any contract rights for the officer.

28. Filling Officers Vacancies. A vacancy in any office for any reason may be filled by the board of directors for the unexpired term.

29. Duties of the President. The president is the principal executive officer of the corporation and is subject to control by the board of directors. The president will supervise and control all of the business and activities of the corporation. The president will preside at all shareholders and directors meetings, and perform any other duties as prescribed by the board of directors.

30. Duties of the Vice-President. If the president is absent, dies, or is incapacitated, the vice-president will perform the duties of the president. When acting for the president, the vice-president will have all of the powers and authority of the president. The vice-president will also perform any other duties as prescribed by the board of directors.

31. Duties of the Secretary. The secretary will keep the minutes of all shareholders and directors meetings. The secretary will provide notices of all meetings as required by the By-Laws. The secretary will be the custodian of the corporate records, corporate stock transfer book, and corporate seal. The secretary will keep a list of all shareholders, directors, and officers addresses. The secretary will sign, along with other officers, the corporation's stock certificates. The secretary will also perform any other duties as prescribed by the board of directors.

32. Duties of the Treasurer. The treasurer will be custodian of all corporate funds and securities. The treasurer will receive and pay out funds which are receivable or payable to the corporation from any source. The treasurer will deposit all corporate funds received into the corporate bank accounts as designated by the board of directors. The treasurer will also perform any other duties as prescribed by the board of directors.

33. Salaries of Officers. The salaries of the officers will be fixed by the board of directors and may be altered at any time by the board. An officer may receive a salary even if she/he receives a salary as a director.

34. Stock Certificates. Certificates which represent shares of ownership in the corporation will be in the form designated by the board of directors. Certificates will be signed by all officers of the corporation. Certificates will be consecutively numbered. The name and address of the person receiving the issued shares, the certificate number, the number of shares and the date of issue will be recorded by the secretary of the corporation in the corporate stock transfer book. Shares of the corporation's stock may only be transferred on the stock transfer book of the corporation by the holder of the shares in whose name they were issued as shown on the stock transfer book, or by his or her legal representative.

35. Financial Matters. The board of directors will determine the accounting methods and fiscal year of the corporation. All checks, drafts, or other methods for payment shall be signed by an officer determined by resolution of the board of directors. All notes, mortgages, or other evidence of indebtedness shall be signed by an officer determined by resolution of the board of directors. No money will be borrowed or loaned by the corporation unless authorized by a resolution of the board of directors. No contracts will be entered into on behalf of the corporation unless authorized by a resolution of the board of directors. No documents may be executed on behalf of the corporation unless authorized by a resolution of the board of directors. A board of Director's resolution may be for specific instances or a general authorization.

36. Loans to Officers or Directors. The corporation may not lend any money to an officer or director of the corporation unless the loan has been approved by a majority of the shares of all stock of the corporation, including those shares that do not have voting rights.

37. Amendments to the By-Laws. These By-Laws may be amended in any manner by majority vote of the board of directors at any annual or special meeting. Any amendments by the board of directors are subject to approval by majority vote of the shareholders at any annual or special meeting.

Dated June 10, 1994

Mary Celeste
Secretary of the Corporation

Approved by the board of directors on June 14, 1994

John Celeste
Chairperson of the board

Approved by the Shareholders on June 14, 1994

Mary Celeste
Secretary of the Corporation

Chapter 7

Corporate Directors Meetings

The board of directors of a corporation transacts business as a group. Each individual director has no authority to bind the corporation (unless the board of directors as a group has previously authorized him or her to exercise that power). Even in a corporation with a single director, there must be formal records of meetings and of the resolutions adopted by the board.

Corporate boards of directors must, at a minimum, hold an annual meeting to appoint the officers of the corporation for the coming year, decide if dividends will be declared for the year, and make any other annual decisions regarding the financial matters of the business. Typically, boards will hold special meetings for specific topics much more frequently. Whenever official corporate matters are discussed as a group, the board of directors should hold a meeting, keep minutes, and record the decisions made as corporate resolutions. This is not a difficult task and it will provide a clear record of the agreements made by the board for future reference.

Prior to any annual or special meetings of the board, notice must be given to each board member according to the time limits set in the By-Laws. A formal affidavit of mailing of notice should also be prepared. If all board members are in agreement, an easier method to fulfill the notice requirement is to have the board sign waivers of notice. This document and all of the other documents necessary to conduct and record board meetings are contained in this chapter. Before each type of board meeting is a Checklist of the information necessary to fill in the minutes and other forms. Follow the appropriate Checklist for each meeting.

First Directors Meeting Checklist

The following information should be covered and documented in the minutes of the first board of directors meeting:

❏ Name of corporation
❏ Date of meeting
❏ Location of meeting
❏ Officers present at meeting
❏ Others present at meeting
❏ Name of temporary Chairperson presiding over meeting
❏ Name of temporary Secretary acting at meeting
❏ Meeting called to order and quorum present
❏ Proper notification of meeting
      ❏ Notices sent and affidavit filed / or waivers filed
❏ Articles of Incorporation filed with state
      ❏ Date of filing
      ❏ Effective date of incorporation
❏ Approve and ratify any acts of incorporators taken on behalf of the corporation prior to effective date of incorporation.
❏ Elect officers of corporation.
❏ Fix annual salaries of officers.
❏ Direct that any organizational expenses be reimbursed to incorporators.
❏ Authorize opening of corporate bank account.
❏ Approve corporate seal, stock certificate, and stock transfer book.
❏ Approve corporate By-Laws.
❏ Approve issuance of stock in exchange for transfers of property or money.
❏ Designate fiscal year dates.
❏ Designate accounting basis (cash or accrual basis).
❏ Document any other necessary business.
❏ Adjournment of meeting
❏ Date and Secretary signature on minutes

Notice of First Board of Directors Meeting

Notice of First Board of Directors Meeting of

_____

TO:

In accordance with the By-Laws of this corporation, the first organizational meeting of the board of directors will be held at _____
___ m., on _____ , 19 ___ , at the offices of the corporation located at _____
_____ .

Dated _____

_____
Signature
Incorporator: _____

_____
Signature
Incorporator: _____

_____
Signature
Incorporator: _____

Affidavit of Mailing of Notice of First Directors Meeting

Affidavit of Mailing of Notice of First Directors Meeting of

_____

State of _____)

)

County of _____)

Being duly sworn, _____ states:
I am the Secretary of _____ , a
corporation organized under the laws of the State of _____ .
On _____ , 19 ___ , I personally deposited stamped and
sealed copies of Notice of the First Directors Meeting of this corporation in a
post-office box in the City of _____ , in the State of
_____ . The copies were correctly addressed to the following
persons:

Name   Address

_____   _____

_____   _____

_____   _____

_____
Secretary of the corporation

Subscribed and Sworn to before me on _____ , 19 ___ .

_____
Notary Public in and for the County of _____ and the State of
_____ . My commission expires _____ .

Waiver of Notice of First Directors Meeting

Waiver of Notice of First Directors Meeting of

_____

We, the undersigned Incorporators of this corporation, waive any required notice and consent to the holding of the first meeting of the board of directors of this corporation on _____ , 19 ___ , at _____ ___ m., at the offices of the corporation, located at

_____

_____ .

Dated _____

Name   Signature

_____   _____

_____   _____

_____   _____

_____   _____

Minutes of First Board of Directors Meeting

Minutes of the First Board of Directors Meeting of

_____

The first meeting of the board of directors of this corporation was held on
_____ , 19 ___ , at _____ _____
m., at _____ . Present at the meeting
were the following people: _____
_____ ,
all of whom are designated as directors of this corporation in the Articles of
Incorporation. The following other persons were also present _____
_____ .

1.   _____ was elected as the
     temporary Chairperson of the board and _____
     was elected as the temporary Secretary of the board.

2.   The Chairperson announced that the meeting had been duly called by
     the Incorporators of the corporation, called the meeting to order, and
     determined that a quorum was present.

3.   The Secretary then presented an Affidavit of Mailing of Notice or a
     Waiver of Notice of the meeting which was signed by all directors.
     Upon motion made and carried, the Secretary was ordered to attach the
     Affidavit of Notice or the Waiver of Notice to the minutes of this
     meeting.

4.   The Chairperson reported that the Articles of Incorporation had been
     duly filed with the State of _____ on _____ ,
     19 ___ , and that the incorporation was effective as of _____ ,
     19 ___ . Upon motion made and carried, a copy of the Articles of
     Incorporation were ordered to be attached to the minutes of this
     meeting.

5.   Upon motion made and carried, the board of directors
     RESOLVED that:
     The joint and individual acts of _____
     and _____ , the incorporators of
     this corporation, which were taken on behalf of the corporation are
     approved, ratified, and adopted as acts of the corporation.

6.   The following persons were elected as officers of the corporation to
     serve until the first annual board of directors meeting:

     _____ , President;

     _____ , Vice-President;

     _____ , Treasurer;

     _____ , Secretary.

7.   Upon motion made and carried, the annual salaries of the officers were
     fixed at the following rates until the next annual meeting of the board of
     directors:

     President $_____ ;

     Vice-President $_____ ;

     Secretary $_____ ;

     Treasurer $_____ .

8.   Upon motion made and carried, the board of directors
     RESOLVED that:
     The officers of this corporation are authorized and directed to pay all
     fees and expenses necessary for the organization of this corporation. The
     officers are also directed to procure and prepare the necessary books for
     corporate accounting.

9.   Upon motion made and carried, the board of directors
     RESOLVED that:
     The officers of this corporation be authorized and directed to open a
     bank account with _____ located
     at _____ and to deposit all funds

of the corporation into this account, with checks payable upon the corporate signature of _____
only.
Further RESOLVED that the officers of this corporation are authorized to execute any formal Bank Resolutions and documents which may be necessary to open such an account. A copy of the formal Bank Resolution for opening this account is hereby adopted and ordered to be attached to the minutes of this meeting.

10. A proposed corporate Seal, corporate Stock Certificate, and Corporate Stock Transfer Book were presented.
Upon motion made and carried, the board of directors
RESOLVED that:
The Seal, Stock Certificates, and Stock Transfer Book presented at this meeting are adopted and approved as the Seal, Stock Certificates, and Stock Transfer Book of this corporation. A specimen copy of the Stock Certificate is ordered to be attached to the minutes of this meeting.

11. A copy of the proposed By-Laws of the corporation was presented at the meeting and read by each director.
Upon motion made and carried, the board of directors
RESOLVED that:
The proposed By-Laws of this corporation are approved and adopted. A copy of these By-Laws are ordered to be attached to the minutes of this meeting.

12. The following persons have offered to transfer the property or money listed below to the corporation in exchange for the following number of shares of common capital stock in the corporation:

Name	Property or Money	# Shares
_____	_____	_____
_____	_____	_____
_____	_____	_____
_____	_____	_____
_____	_____	_____

Upon motion made and carried, the board of directors
RESOLVED that:
The assets proposed for transfer are good and sufficient consideration
and the officers are directed to accept the assets on behalf of the
corporation and to issue and deliver the appropriate number of shares
of stock in this corporation to the respective persons. The shares of stock
issued shall be fully-paid and non-assessable common capital stock of
this corporation.

13. Upon motion made and carried, the board of directors
RESOLVED that:
The fiscal year of this corporation shall begin on _____
and end on _____ . This corporation shall report its
income and expenses on a(n)_____ basis.

14. The following other business was conducted:

There being no further business, upon motion made and carried, the
meeting was adjourned.

Dated _____

Seal

_____
Secretary of the corporation

Annual Directors Meeting Checklist

The following information should be covered and documented in the minutes of the annual board of directors meeting:

❏ Name of corporation
❏ State of incorporation
❏ Date of meeting
❏ Location of meeting
❏ Notification of meeting
      ❏ Notices sent and affidavit filed / or waivers filed
❏ Officers present at meeting
❏ Others present at meeting
❏ Officers presiding over meeting
❏ Meeting called to order and quorum present
Annual matters:
❏ Date last state corporate tax return filed
❏ Date last federal corporate tax return filed
❏ Date last state annual report filed
❏ Date last federal pension/profit-sharing returns filed
❏ Date any other required reports/returns filed
❏ Date of last financial statement
❏ Review current employment agreements
❏ Review current insurance coverage
❏ Review stock transfer ledger
❏ Review current Financial Statement
      ❏ Review current year-to-date income and expenses
      ❏ Review current salaries
      ❏ Review current pension/profit-sharing plans
      ❏ Review other employee fringe benefit plans
      ❏ Review accounts receivable
            ❏ Determine if collection procedures are warranted
      ❏ Review status of any outstanding loans
      ❏ Ascertain net profit
      ❏ Determine if a stock dividend should be declared
      ❏ Discuss any major items requiring board action:
            ❏ Major purchases
            ❏ Lawsuits
            ❏ Loans
            ❏ Real estate sales or leases
❏ Adjournment of meeting
❏ Date and Secretary signature on minutes

Notice of Annual Board of Directors Meeting

Notice of Annual Board of Directors Meeting of

_____

TO:

In accordance with the By-Laws of this corporation, an official regular meeting of the board of directors will be held at _____ ___ m., on _____ , 19 ___ , at the offices of the corporation located at _____ _____.

Dated _____

Seal

_____
Secretary of the corporation

Affidavit of Mailing of Notice of Annual Directors Meeting

Affidavit of Mailing of Notice of Annual Directors Meeting of

_____

State of _____)

)

County of _____)

Being duly sworn, _____ states:
I am the Secretary of _____ , a
corporation organized under the laws of the State of _____ .
On _____ , 19 ___ , I personally deposited stamped and
sealed copies of Notice of the Annual Directors Meeting of this corporation in
a post-office box in the City of _____ , in the State of
_____ . The copies were correctly addressed to the following
persons:

Name   Address

_____   _____

_____   _____

_____   _____

_____

Secretary of the corporation

Subscribed and Sworn to before me on _____ , 19 ___ .

_____

Notary Public in and for the County of _____ and the State of
_____ . My commission expires _____ .

Waiver of Notice of Annual Directors Meeting

Waiver of Notice of Annual Directors Meeting of

_____

We, the undersigned directors of this corporation, waive any required notice and consent to the holding of the annual meeting of the board of directors of this corporation on _____ , 19 ___ , at _____ ___ m., at the offices of the corporation, located at _____ _____.

Dated _____

Name   Signature

_____   _____

_____   _____

_____   _____

_____   _____

Minutes of Annual Board of Directors Meeting

Minutes of the Annual Board of Directors Meeting of

_____

The annual meeting of the board of directors of this corporation was held on
_____ , 19 ___ , at _____
_____ m., at _____ . Present at the
meeting were the following people: _____
_____ ,
all of whom are directors of this corporation. Present also were the following
people: _____
_____ .
_____ , the President of the corporation
presided over the meeting. _____ ,
the Secretary of the corporation served as secretary for the meeting.

1.   The President called the meeting to order. The President determined
      that a quorum was present and that the meeting could conduct
      business.

2.   The Secretary reported that notice of the meeting had been properly
      given or waived by each Director in accordance with the By-Laws. Upon
      motion made and carried, the Secretary was directed to attach the
      appropriate Notice and Affidavit or Waiver to these minutes.

3.   The Secretary distributed copies of the minutes of the previous meeting
      of the board of directors which had been held on _____ ,
      19 ___ . Upon motion made and carried, these minutes were approved.

4.   The President presented the annual President's Report. Upon motion
      made and carried, the President's Report was approved and the
      Secretary was directed to attach a copy of the President's Report to these
      minutes.

5.   _____ , the Treasurer of the
      corporation, presented the Treasurer's Report, which stated that as of

_____ , 19 ___ , the corporation had a net profit of
$_____ . Upon motion made and carried, the
Treasurer's Report was approved and the Secretary was directed to
attach a copy of the Treasurer's Report to these minutes.

6. Upon motion made and carried, the board of directors
   RESOLVED that:
   A dividend of $_____ per share of common stock is
   declared on the stock of this corporation. This dividend shall be paid to
   the shareholders of record as of _____ , 19 ___ and shall
   be paid on _____ , 19 ___ . The officers of this
   corporation are directed to take all necessary actions to carry out this
   resolution.

7. Upon motion made and carried, the following persons were elected as
   officers of this corporation for a term of one year:

   _____ , President;

   _____ , Vice President;

   _____ , Treasurer;

   _____ , Secretary.

8. Upon motion made and carried, the salaries of the officers were fixed for
   the term of one year at the following rates:

   President $_____

   Vice-President $_____

   Secretary $_____

   Treasurer $_____

9.   The following other business was transacted:

There being no further business, upon motion made and carried, the meeting was adjourned.

Dated _____

Seal

_____
Secretary of the corporation

Special Directors Meeting Checklist

The following information should be covered and documented in the minutes of any special board of directors meeting:

❑ Name of corporation
❑ State of incorporation
❑ Date of meeting
❑ Location of meeting
❑ Specific purpose of meeting
❑ Proper notification of meeting
      ❑ Notices sent and affidavit filed / or waivers filed
❑ Officers present at meeting
❑ Others present at meeting
❑ Name of President presiding over meeting
❑ Name of Secretary acting at meeting
❑ Meeting called to order and quorum present
Business Transacted:
❑ Specific business discussed at meeting
❑ Resolutions passed at meeting
❑ Adjournment of meeting
❑ Date and Secretary signature on minutes

Notice of Special Board of Directors Meeting

Notice of Special Board of Directors Meeting of

_____

TO:

In accordance with the By-Laws of this corporation, a special meeting of the board of directors will be held at _____ ___ m., on _____ , 19 ___ , at the offices of the corporation located at _____ .

The purpose of this special meeting will be to discuss and take any required action regarding the following matter: _____ _____ .

Dated _____

Seal

_____
Secretary of the corporation

Affidavit of Mailing of Notice of Special Directors Meeting

Affidavit of Mailing of Notice of Special Directors Meeting of

_____

State of _____)
)
County of _____)

Being duly sworn, _____ states:
I am the Secretary of _____ , a
corporation organized under the laws of the State of _____ .
On _____ , 19 ___ , I personally deposited stamped and
sealed copies of Notice of the Special Directors Meeting of this corporation in
a post-office box in the City of _____ , in the State of
_____ . The copies were correctly addressed to the following
persons:

Name   Address

_____   _____

_____   _____

_____   _____

_____
Secretary of the corporation

Subscribed and Sworn to before me on _____ , 19 ___ .

_____
Notary Public in and for the County of _____ and the State of
_____ . My commission expires _____ .

Waiver of Notice of Special Directors Meeting

Waiver of Notice of
Special Directors Meeting of

_____

We, the undersigned directors of this corporation waive any required notice and consent to the holding of a special meeting of the board of directors of this corporation on _____ , 19 ___ , at _____ ___ m., at the offices of the corporation, located at _____
_____.

Dated _____

Name   Signature

_____   _____

_____   _____

_____   _____

_____   _____

Minutes of Special Board of Directors Meeting

Minutes of Special Board of Directors Meeting of

_____

A special meeting of the board of directors of this corporation was held on
_____ , 19 ___ , at _____
_____ m., at _____ . The purpose of
this special meeting was to _____
_____.
Present at the meeting were the following people:_____
_____,
all of whom are directors of this corporation. Present also were the following
people: _____.
_____ , the President of the corporation
presided over the meeting. _____,
the Secretary of the corporation served as secretary for the meeting.

1.   The President called the meeting to order. The President determined
      that a quorum was present and that the meeting could conduct
      business.

2.   The Secretary reported that notice of the meeting had been properly
      given or waived by each Director in accordance with the By-Laws. Upon
      motion made and carried, the Secretary was directed to attach the
      appropriate Notice and Affidavit or Waiver to these minutes.

3.   The following business was then discussed:

4.	Upon motion made and carried, the board of directors
	RESOLVED that:

		There being no further business, upon motion made and carried, the
		meeting was adjourned.

Dated _____

								Seal

_____
Secretary of the corporation

Chapter 8

Corporate Shareholders Meetings

The main responsibility of the shareholders of a corporation is to elect the directors of the business. This election is conducted at the annual meeting of the shareholders which is held on the date, time, and place as specified in the corporate By-Laws. In addition, specific corporate business at other times of the year may occasionally need shareholder approval. For example, shareholders must vote on the dissolution of the corporation (see Chapter 15), on amendments to the By-Laws or Articles of Incorporation (see Chapter 13), and on any extraordinary business transactions, such as the sale of all of the assets of the corporation. For these purposes, a special meeting of the shareholders must be held.

The initial meeting of the shareholders also has a slightly different agenda. At this meeting, the shareholders approve and ratify the adoption of the corporate By-Laws, and ratify the election or appointment of the initial board of directors who will serve until the first annual meeting of the shareholders. The shareholders also approve the election of the first officers of the corporation by the board of directors.

On the following pages, there are Checklists and forms for the initial, annual, and special shareholders meetings. Please follow the Checklists in preparing the forms. The notice requirements for shareholders meetings are identical to those for directors meetings, however, the forms are slightly different.

First Shareholders Meeting Checklist

The following information should be covered and documented in the minutes of the first shareholders meeting:

❑ Name of corporation
❑ Date of meeting
❑ Location of meeting
❑ Officers present at meeting
❑ Others present at meeting
❑ Meeting called to order and quorum present
❑ Shareholders present at meeting
❑ Shareholders represented by proxy at meeting
❑ Name of President acting at meeting
❑ Name of Secretary acting at meeting
❑ Name of Chairperson elected to preside over meeting
❑ Proper notification of meeting
　　　❑ Notice sent and affidavit filed / or waivers filed
❑ Minutes of first directors meeting read
❑ Minutes of first directors meeting approved and ratified
❑ Election of directors and officers approved and ratified
❑ Adoption of corporate By-Laws approved and ratified
❑ Any other business
❑ Meeting adjourned
❑ Secretary dated and signed minutes

Notice of First Shareholders Meeting

Notice of First Shareholders Meeting of

_____

TO:

In accordance with the By-Laws of this corporation, a first official meeting of the shareholders will be held at _____ ___ m., on _____ , 19 ___ , at the offices of the corporation located at

_____ .

The purpose of this meeting is to approve adoption of the By-Laws of this corporation, approve election of the officers, approve continuation of the directors of this corporation, and to transact any other necessary business.

The Stock Transfer Book of this corporation will remain closed from _____ , 19 ___ until _____ , 19 ___ .

Dated _____

                                        Seal

_____
Secretary of the corporation

Affidavit of Mailing of Notice of First Shareholders Meeting

Affidavit of Mailing of Notice of First Shareholders Meeting of

_____

State of _____)

)

County of _____)

Being duly sworn, _____ states:
I am the Secretary of _____ , a
corporation organized under the laws of the State of _____ .
On _____ , 19 ___ , I personally deposited stamped and
sealed copies of Notice of the First Shareholders Meeting of this corporation in
a post-office box in the City of _____ , in the State of
_____ . The copies were correctly addressed to all
shareholders of this corporation as of _____ , 19 ___ as shown
in the Stock Transfer Book of this corporation. The list of names and addresses
of the shareholders is attached to this Affidavit.

_____
Secretary of the corporation

Subscribed and Sworn to before me on _____ , 19 ___ .

_____
Notary Public in and for the County of _____ and the State of
_____ . My commission expires _____ .

Waiver of Notice of First Shareholders Meeting

Waiver of Notice of First Shareholders Meeting of

_____

We, the undersigned shareholders of this corporation, waive any required notice and consent to the holding of the first meeting of the shareholders of this corporation on _____ , 19 ___ , at _____ ___ m., at the offices of the corporation, located at _____

_____.

Dated _____

Name   Signature

_____   _____

_____   _____

_____   _____

_____   _____

_____   _____

_____   _____

Authorization to Vote Shares (Proxy)

Authorization to Vote Shares (PROXY)

_____

I, _____ , the record owner of this
corporation's stock certificate # _____ , which represents
_____ shares in this corporation, authorize
_____ to vote all of these shares at the
meeting of the shareholders of this corporation which is scheduled to be held
on _____ , 19 ___ at _____ ___ m. at the
offices of this corporation, which are located at: _____
_____.

Through the use of this proxy and authorization, _____ ,
has the right to vote these shares at any business conducted at this meeting as
if I personally were present.

This proxy and authorization may be revoked by me at any time prior to the
meeting and will be void if I personally attend the meeting.

Dated _____

_____
Name of Shareholder

_____
Signature of Shareholder

Minutes of First Shareholders Meeting

Minutes of the First Shareholders Meeting of

_____

The first meeting of the shareholders of this corporation was held on
_____ , 19 ___ , at _____
_____ m., at _____ .

The President of this corporation, _____ ,
and the Vice-President of this corporation, _____ ,
and the Secretary of this corporation, _____ ,
and the Treasurer of this corporation, _____ ,
were present. Other than shareholders of this corporation, the following other
persons were also present _____
_____ .

1. The President of this corporation called the meeting to order and
    determined that a quorum was present, either in person or by proxy.

    The following shareholders were present in person:

    Name   Number of shares

    _____   _____

    _____   _____

    _____   _____

    _____   _____

    _____   _____

    _____   _____

    _____   _____

The following shareholders were represented by proxy:

Name   Number of shares

_____   _____

_____   _____

_____   _____

_____   _____

_____   _____

2.   The Secretary of this corporation reported that notice of the meeting had been properly given or waived by each shareholder in accordance with the By-Laws. Upon motion made and carried, the Secretary was directed to attach the appropriate Notice and Affidavit or Waiver to these minutes.

3.   _____ was then elected Chairperson of this meeting.

4.   The Secretary read the minutes of the first meeting of the board of directors of this corporation which was held on _____, 19 ___.

Upon motion made and carried, the shareholders RESOLVED that:

All acts taken and decisions made at the first meeting of the board of directors of this corporation are approved and ratified, specifically that the shareholders approve and ratify the adoption of the By-Laws of this corporation and that the shareholders approve and ratify the election of the following persons as officers for the terms as stated in the minutes of the first meeting of the board of directors:

_____ , President;

_____ , Vice-President;

_____ , Treasurer;

_____ , Secretary;

5.   Upon motion made and carried, the shareholders
RESOLVED that:
The following persons are designated as the initial directors of this
corporation in the Articles of Incorporation and the shareholders
approve and ratify this designation of the following persons as directors
of this corporation until the first annual meeting of the shareholders of
this corporation:

_____ , Director;

_____ , Director;

_____ , Director.

6.   The following other business was transacted:

There being no further business, upon motion made and carried, the
meeting was adjourned.

Dated _____

Seal

_____
Secretary of the corporation

Annual Shareholders Meeting Checklist

The following information should be covered and documented in the minutes of the annual shareholders meetings:

- ❏ Name of corporation
- ❏ Date of meeting
- ❏ Location of meeting
- ❏ Officers present at meeting
- ❏ Others present at meeting
- ❏ Meeting called to order and quorum present
- ❏ Shareholders present at meeting
- ❏ Shareholders represented by proxy at meeting
- ❏ Name of President acting at meeting
- ❏ Name of Secretary acting at meeting
- ❏ Name of Chairperson elected to preside over meeting
- ❏ Proper notification of meeting
    - ❏ Notices sent and affidavit filed / or waivers filed
- ❏ Minutes of previous shareholders meeting read
- ❏ Minutes of previous shareholders meeting approved
- ❏ Presidents report read and approved and directed to be attached to minutes
- ❏ Treasurers report read and approved and directed to be attached to minutes
- ❏ Nomination of persons to serve as directors
- ❏ Election of directors
- ❏ Any other business
- ❏ Meeting adjourned
- ❏ Secretary dated and signed minutes

Notice of Annual Shareholders Meeting

Notice of Annual Shareholders Meeting of

_____

TO:

In accordance with the By-Laws of this corporation, an official annual meeting of the shareholders will be held at _____ ___ m., on _____ , 19 ___ , at the offices of the corporation located at _____ .

The purpose of this meeting is to elect directors of this corporation and to transact any other necessary business.

The Stock Transfer Book of this corporation will remain closed from _____ , 19 ___ until _____ , 19 ___ .

Dated _____

Seal

_____
Secretary of the corporation

Affidavit of Mailing of Notice of Annual Shareholders Meeting

Affidavit of Mailing of Notice of Annual Shareholders Meeting of

_____

State of _____)
_____)
County of _____)

Being duly sworn, _____ states:
I am the Secretary of _____ , a
corporation organized under the laws of the State of _____ .
On _____ , 19 ___ , I personally deposited stamped and
sealed copies of Notice of the Annual Shareholders Meeting of this
corporation in a post-office box in the City of _____ , in the
State of _____ . The copies were correctly addressed to all
shareholders of this corporation as of _____ , 19 ___ as shown
in the Stock Transfer Book of this corporation. The list of names and addresses
of the shareholders is attached to this Affidavit.

_____
Secretary of the corporation

Subscribed and Sworn to before me on _____ , 19 ___ .

_____
Notary Public in and for the County of _____ and the State of
_____ . My commission expires _____ .

Waiver of Notice of Annual Shareholders Meeting

Waiver of Notice of Annual Shareholders Meeting of

_____

We, the undersigned shareholders of this corporation, waive any required notice and consent to the holding of the annual meeting of the shareholders of this corporation on _____ , 19 ___ , at _____ ___ m., at the offices of the corporation, located at _____
_____.

Dated _____

Name   Signature

_____   _____

_____   _____

_____   _____

_____   _____

_____   _____

_____   _____

Minutes of Shareholders Annual Meeting

Minutes of the Annual Shareholders Meeting of

_____

The annual meeting of the shareholders of this corporation was held on
_____ , 19 ___ , at _____
_____ m., at _____ .

The President of this corporation, _____ ,
and the Vice-President of this corporation, _____ ,
and the Secretary of this corporation, _____ ,
and the Treasurer of this corporation, _____ ,
were present. Other than shareholders, the following other persons were also
present _____
_____ .

1. The President of this corporation called the meeting to order and
    determined that a quorum was present, either in person or by proxy.

    The following shareholders were present in person:

    Name   Number of Shares

    _____   _____

    _____   _____

    _____   _____

    _____   _____

    _____   _____

    _____   _____

The following shareholders were represented by proxy:

Name   Number of Shares

_____   _____

_____   _____

_____   _____

_____   _____

_____   _____

2.   The Secretary of this corporation reported that notice of the meeting had been properly given or waived by each shareholder in accordance with the By-Laws. Upon motion made and carried, the Secretary was directed to attach the appropriate Notice and Affidavit or Waiver to these minutes.

3.   _____ was then elected Chairperson of this meeting.

4.   The Secretary distributed copies of the minutes of the previous meeting of the shareholders which had been held on _____, 19 ___ . Upon motion made and carried, these minutes were approved.

4.   The President presented the annual President's Report. Upon motion made and carried, the President's Report was approved and the Secretary was directed to attach a copy of the President's Report to these minutes.

5.   The Treasurer of the corporation presented the Treasurer's Report. Upon motion made and carried, the Treasurer's Report was approved and the Secretary was directed to attach a copy of the Treasurer's Report to these minutes.

6.   The following persons were nominated as directors of this corporation for a term of _____ year(s):

Name

_____

_____

_____

_____

7.   In accordance with the By-Laws of this corporation, an election of directors was held, with each shareholder stating their choices for director by secret ballot and the number of shares held personally or by proxy.

8.   The votes were tallied by the Secretary and, by a majority vote of the outstanding shares entitled to vote in this election, the following persons were elected as directors of this corporation for a term of _____ year(s):

_____ ;

_____ ;

_____ .

9.   On motion made and carried, it was directed that a report of the election be filed with the Clerk of _____ County, State of _____, if required.

10. The following other business was transacted:

There being no further business, upon motion made and carried the meeting was adjourned.

Dated _____

Seal

_____
Secretary of the corporation

Special Shareholders Meeting Checklist

The following information should be covered and documented in the minutes of any special shareholders meetings:

❑ Name of corporation
❑ Date of meeting
❑ Location of meeting
❑ Officers present at meeting
❑ Others present at meeting
❑ Meeting called to order and quorum present
❑ Shareholders present at meeting
❑ Shareholders represented by proxy at meeting
❑ Name of President acting at meeting
❑ Name of Secretary acting at meeting
❑ Name of Chairperson elected to preside over meeting
❑ Proper notification of meeting
     ❑ Notices sent and affidavit filed / or waivers filed
❑ Specific business discussed
❑ Specific shareholders resolutions adopted
❑ Meeting adjourned
❑ Secretary dated and signed minutes

Notice of Special Shareholders Meeting

Notice of Special Shareholders Meeting of

_____

TO:

In accordance with the By-Laws of this corporation, an official special meeting of the shareholders will be held at _____ ___ m., on _____ , 19 ___ , at the offices of the corporation located at _____ .

The purpose of this meeting is the following: _____
_____ .

The Stock Transfer Book of this corporation will remain closed from _____ , 19 ___ until _____ , 19 ___ .

Dated _____

                                                    Seal

_____
Secretary of the corporation

Affidavit of Mailing of Notice of Special Shareholders Meeting

Affidavit of Mailing of Notice of Special Shareholders Meeting of

_____

State of _____)

)   S.S.

County of _____)

Being duly sworn, _____ states:
I am the Secretary of _____ , a
corporation organized under the laws of the State of _____ .
On _____ , 19 ___ , I personally deposited stamped and
sealed copies of Notice of the Special Shareholders Meeting of this corporation
in a post-office box in the City of _____ , in the State of
_____ . The copies were correctly addressed to all
shareholders of this corporation as of _____ , 19 ___ as shown
in the Stock Transfer Book of this corporation. The list of names and addresses
of the shareholders is attached to this Affidavit.

_____
Secretary of the corporation

Subscribed and Sworn to before me on _____ , 19 ___ .

_____
Notary Public in and for the County of _____ and the State of
_____ . My commission expires _____ .

Waiver of Notice of Special Shareholders Meeting

Waiver of Notice of Special Shareholders Meeting of

_____

We, the undersigned shareholders of this corporation, waive any required notice and consent to the holding of the special meeting of the shareholders of this corporation on _____ , 19 ___ , at _____ ___ m., at the offices of the corporation, located at _____
_____.

Dated _____

Name   Signature

_____   _____

_____   _____

_____   _____

_____   _____

_____   _____

_____   _____

Minutes of Special Shareholders Meeting

Minutes of the Special Shareholders Meeting of

_____

A special meeting of the shareholders of this corporation was held on
_____ , 19 ___ , at _____ _____
m., at the offices of the corporation located at _____
_____ .

The President of this corporation, _____ ,
and the Vice-President of this corporation, _____ ,
and the Secretary of this corporation, _____ ,
and the Treasurer of this corporation, _____ ,
were present. Other than shareholders, the following other persons were also
present _____
_____ .

1. The President of this corporation called the meeting to order and
    determined that a quorum was present, either in person or by proxy.

    The following shareholders were present in person:

    Name   Number of Shares

    _____   _____

    _____   _____

    _____   _____

    _____   _____

    _____   _____

The following shareholders were represented by proxy:

Name   Number of Shares

_____   _____

_____   _____

_____   _____

_____   _____

_____   _____

2.   The Secretary of this corporation reported that notice of the meeting had been properly given or waived by each shareholder in accordance with the By-Laws. Upon motion made and carried, the Secretary was directed to attach the appropriate Notice and Affidavit or Waiver to these minutes.

3.   _____ was then elected Chairperson of this meeting.

4.   The following business was discussed:

5. Upon motion made and carried, the following resolution was approved by a majority of the outstanding shares entitled to vote on this measure: RESOLVED that:

6. The President declared that this shareholders resolution was duly adopted.

There being no further business, upon motion made and carried, the meeting was adjourned.

Dated _____

Seal

_____
Secretary of the corporation

Chapter 9

Corporate Resolutions

Corporate resolutions are records of official acts of either the shareholders of the corporation or the board of directors. They are a permanent record of actions taken by either of these bodies as a group. In most situations and for most corporations, a majority vote of the directors or shareholders present at an official meeting (as long as the number present constitutes a quorum) is required to adopt a corporate resolution. The resolutions adopted should be kept permanently in the corporate record book. In some cases, a copy of the resolution will be required by a third party. For example, a financial institution will usually require a copy of the corporate resolution which authorizes an officer to bind the corporation in a loan transaction.

Two Checklists follow which specify the general circumstances in which corporate resolutions are required. They are not required for all of the normal day-to-day transactions of a business. In general, directors resolutions are only necessary to document the major decisions or transactions of a corporation. Shareholders resolutions are even more rare, used only for extraordinary corporate matters.

In recent years, the use of consent resolutions has increased among businesses. These resolutions are used in lieu of formal meetings and can simplify corporate management. They require, however, the written consent of all of the directors (or shareholders) of a corporation in order to be valid. Any of the resolutions in this chapter can be used as consent resolutions by adapting them using the Consent Resolution instructions located at the end of this chapter.

Corporate Resolutions Checklists

Formal corporate resolutions are generally required in the following circumstances. Most sample directors resolutions are contained in this chapter. Additional directors and shareholders resolutions relating to amendments to the Articles of Incorporation and amendments to By-Laws are contained in Chapter 13. Resolutions relating to the dissolution of a corporation are found in Chapter 15.

Directors resolutions:

❑ Authorizing of major contracts
❑ Authorizing the sale of corporate real estate
❑ Authorizing the purchase of real estate
❑ Authorizing the corporation to borrow money
❑ Authorizing the corporation to enter into a real estate lease
❑ Authorizing a lawsuit
❑ Authorizing the appointment of a lawyer
❑ Authorizing the appointment of an accountant
❑ Authorizing stock dividends
❑ Authorizing stock dividends to be declared and paid annually
❑ Authorizing stock dividends to be declared and paid quarterly
❑ Authorizing the reimbursement of expenses to an employee
❑ Authorizing the retention of corporate earnings
❑ Authorizing employee stock option plans
❑ Authorizing pension plans
❑ Authorizing profit-sharing plans
❑ Authorizing health care plans
❑ Authorizing group insurance plans
❑ Authorizing death benefit plans
❑ Authorizing other employee benefit plans
❑ Authorizing recision of prior resolutions
❑ Authorizing loans to directors or officers
❑ Authorizing the payment of officer's salaries
❑ Authorizing a restricted stock transfer
❑ Authorizing a registered office address change
❑ Authorizing the corporate president to make purchases
❑ Authorizing the payment of a bonus to employees

Shareholders resolutions:

❑ Approving the sale of all of the corporate assets
❑ Approving the dissolution of the corporation (see Chapter 15)

General Directors Resolution

Resolution of the Board of Directors of

_____

A meeting of the board of directors of this corporation was duly called and held on _____ , 19 ___. A quorum of the board of directors was present and at the meeting it was decided, by majority vote, that

Therefore, it is
RESOLVED, that this corporation

The officers of this corporation are hereby authorized to perform all necessary acts to carry out this resolution.

The undersigned, _____ , certifies that he or she is the duly elected Secretary of this corporation and that the above is a true and correct copy of the resolution that was duly adopted at a meeting of the board of directors which was held in accordance with state law and the By-Laws of the corporation on _____ , 19 ___ .
I further certify that such resolution is now in full force and effect.

Dated _____

                                                              Seal

_____
Secretary of the corporation

Directors Resolution Authorizing Contract

Resolution of the Board of Directors of

_____

A meeting of the board of directors of this corporation was duly called and held on _____ , 19 ___ . A quorum of the board of directors was present and at the meeting it was decided, by majority vote, that it is necessary for the corporation to enter into a contract with

_____ of _____

for the purpose of _____.

Therefore, it is
RESOLVED, that this corporation enter into a contract with _____ of _____ for the stated purpose. The officers of this corporation are hereby authorized to perform all necessary acts to carry out this resolution.

The undersigned, _____ , certifies that he or she is the duly elected Secretary of this corporation and that the above is a true and correct copy of the resolution that was duly adopted at a meeting of the board of directors which was held in accordance with state law and the By-Laws of the corporation on _____ , 19 ___ .
I further certify that such resolution is now in full force and effect.

Dated _____

Seal

_____
Secretary of the corporation

Directors Resolution Authorizing Sale of Real Estate

Resolution of the Board of Directors of

_____

A meeting of the board of directors of this corporation was duly called and held on _____ , 19 ___. A quorum of the board of directors was present and at the meeting it was decided, by majority vote, that it has become necessary, for the benefit of the corporation, to sell the real estate described as _____

_____

_____.

Therefore, it is
RESOLVED, that the corporation sell the real estate described as _____

_____

_____

to _____ of _____ for the price of $_____ . The officers of this corporation are hereby authorized to perform all necessary acts to carry out such sale.

The undersigned, _____ , certifies that he or she is the duly elected Secretary of this corporation and that the above is a true and correct copy of the resolution that was duly adopted at a meeting of the board of directors which was held in accordance with state law and the By-Laws of the corporation on _____ , 19 ___.
I further certify that such resolution is now in full force and effect.

Dated _____

Seal

_____
Secretary of the corporation

Directors Resolution Authorizing Purchase of Real Estate

Resolution of the Board of Directors of

_____

A meeting of the board of directors of this corporation was duly called and held on _____ , 19 ___ . A quorum of the board of directors was present and at the meeting it was decided, by majority vote, that it has become necessary for the corporation to purchase the real estate described as

_____

_____

_____ .

Therefore, it is
RESOLVED, that the corporation purchase the real estate described as _____

_____

_____

from _____ of _____

for the price of $ _____ . The officers of this corporation are hereby authorized to perform all necessary acts to carry out such purchase.

The undersigned, _____ , certifies that he or she is the duly elected Secretary of this corporation and that the above is a true and correct copy of the resolution that was duly adopted at a meeting of the board of directors which was held in accordance with state law and the By-Laws of the corporation on _____ , 19 ___ .
I further certify that such resolution is now in full force and effect.

Dated _____

Seal

_____
Secretary of the corporation

Directors Resolution Authorizing Borrowing Money

Resolution of the Board of Directors of

_____

A meeting of the board of directors of this corporation was duly called and held on _____ , 19 ___. A quorum of the board of directors was present and at the meeting it was decided, by majority vote, that it has become necessary for the corporation to borrow money for the purpose of

_____

_____ .

Therefore, it is
RESOLVED, that this corporation borrow $_____ from
_____ of _____ on the
following terms _____
_____
_____ .
The officers of this corporation are hereby authorized to perform all necessary acts to carry out such transaction.

The undersigned, _____ , certifies that he or she is the duly elected Secretary of this corporation and that the above is a true and correct copy of the resolution that was duly adopted at a meeting of the board of directors which was held in accordance with state law and the By-Laws of the corporation on _____ , 19 ___.
I further certify that such resolution is now in full force and effect.

Dated _____

Seal

_____
Secretary of the corporation

Directors Resolution Authorizing Lease

Resolution of the Board of Directors of

_____

A meeting of the board of directors of this corporation was duly called and held on _____ , 19 ___. A quorum of the board of directors was present and at the meeting it was decided, by majority vote, that it has become necessary to enter into a lease of the real estate located at

_____
_____.

Therefore, it is
RESOLVED, that this corporation enter into a lease for the period from
_____ , 19 ___ to _____ , 19 ___ with
_____ of _____ for the real estate located at
_____
_____.
The lease payments shall be $_____ each _____.
The officers of this corporation are hereby authorized to perform all necessary acts to enter into such lease.

The undersigned, _____ , certifies that he or she is the duly elected Secretary of this corporation and that the above is a true and correct copy of the resolution that was duly adopted at a meeting of the board of directors which was held in accordance with state law and the By-Laws of the corporation on _____ , 19 ___.
I further certify that such resolution is now in full force and effect.

Dated _____

Seal

_____
Secretary of the corporation

Directors Resolution Authorizing Commencement of Lawsuit

Resolution of the
Board of Directors of

_____

A meeting of the board of directors of this corporation was duly called and held on _____ , 19 ___. A quorum of the board of directors was present and at the meeting it was decided, by majority vote, that it has become necessary to file a lawsuit against _____ for the purpose of _____
_____.

Therefore, it is
RESOLVED, that this corporation file a lawsuit in the jurisdiction of
_____ against _____
of _____ on the grounds of
_____
_____.
The officers of this corporation are hereby authorized to perform all necessary acts to carry out this resolution.

The undersigned, _____ , certifies that he or she is the duly elected Secretary of this corporation and that the above is a true and correct copy of the resolution that was duly adopted at a meeting of the board of directors which was held in accordance with state law and the By-Laws of the corporation on _____ , 19 ___.
I further certify that such resolution is now in full force and effect.

Dated _____

Seal

_____
Secretary of the corporation

Directors Resolution Authorizing Appointment of Lawyer

Resolution of the Board of Directors of

_____

A meeting of the board of directors of this corporation was duly called and held on _____ , 19 ___. A quorum of the board of directors was present and at the meeting it was decided, by majority vote, that it has become necessary to appoint a lawyer for the purpose of

_____

_____   _____.

Therefore, it is
RESOLVED, that this corporation appoint _____
of _____ to represent the corporation
in the following matter: _____
_____.
The officers of this corporation are hereby authorized to perform all necessary acts to carry out this resolution.

The undersigned, _____ , certifies that
he or she is the duly elected Secretary of this corporation and that the above is a true and correct copy of the resolution that was duly adopted at a meeting of the board of directors which was held in accordance with state law and the By-Laws of the corporation on _____ , 19 ___.
I further certify that such resolution is now in full force and effect.

Dated _____

Seal

_____
Secretary of the corporation

Directors Resolution Authorizing Appointment of Accountant

Resolution of the Board of Directors of

_____

A meeting of the board of directors of this corporation was duly called and held on _____ , 19 ___ . A quorum of the board of directors was present and at the meeting it was decided, by majority vote, that it has become necessary to appoint an accountant for the purpose of

_____

_____.

Therefore, it is
RESOLVED, that this corporation appoint _____
of _____ in the following matter:

_____

_____.

The officers of this corporation are hereby authorized to perform all necessary acts to carry out this resolution.

The undersigned, _____ , certifies that he or she is the duly elected Secretary of this corporation and that the above is a true and correct copy of the resolution that was duly adopted at a meeting of the board of directors which was held in accordance with state law and the By-Laws of the corporation on _____ , 19 ___ .
I further certify that such resolution is now in full force and effect.

Dated _____

Seal

_____
Secretary of the corporation

Directors Resolution Authorizing Stock Dividends

Resolution of the Board of Directors of

_____

A meeting of the board of directors of this corporation was duly called and held on _____ , 19 ___ . A quorum of the board of directors was present and at the meeting it was decided, by majority vote, that since the corporation has $ _____ of undistributed surplus funds, $_____ should be distributed as a stock dividend.

Therefore, it is
RESOLVED, that this corporation declares a stock dividend in the amount of $_____ per share of common stock and that this dividend be paid to the stockholders of record as of _____ , 19 ___ , and that the dividend by paid on _____ , 19 ___ . The officers of this corporation are hereby authorized to perform all necessary acts to carry out this resolution.

The undersigned, _____ , certifies that he or she is the duly elected Secretary of this corporation and that the above is a true and correct copy of the resolution that was duly adopted at a meeting of the board of directors which was held in accordance with state law and the By-Laws of the corporation on _____ , 19 ___ .
I further certify that such resolution is now in full force and effect.

Dated _____

Seal

_____
Secretary of the corporation

Directors Resolution Authorizing Automatic Annual Dividends

Resolution of the
Board of Directors of

_____

A meeting of the board of directors of this corporation was duly called and held on _____ , 19 ___. A quorum of the board of directors was present and at the meeting it was decided, by majority vote, that the corporation pay an annual dividend of $_____ per share of common stock, payable on _____ of each year.

Therefore, it is
RESOLVED, that this corporation pay an annual dividend of
$_____ per share of common stock, providing its earnings should warrant. This dividend shall be payable on _____ of each year to stockholders of record on _____ of each year. The officers of this corporation are hereby authorized to perform all necessary acts to carry out this resolution.

The undersigned, _____ , certifies that he or she is the duly elected Secretary of this corporation and that the above is a true and correct copy of the resolution that was duly adopted at a meeting of the board of directors which was held in accordance with state law and the By-Laws of the corporation on _____ , 19 ___.
I further certify that such resolution is now in full force and effect.

Dated _____

Seal

_____
Secretary of the corporation

Directors Resolution Authorizing Quarterly Dividends

Resolution of the Board of Directors of

_____

A meeting of the board of directors of this corporation was duly called and held on _____ , 19 ___. A quorum of the board of directors was present and at the meeting it was decided, by majority vote, that the corporation pay a quarterly dividend of $_____ per share of common stock.

Therefore, it is
RESOLVED, that this corporation pay a quarterly dividend of $_____
per share of common stock, providing its earnings should warrant. This dividend shall be payable on _____/ _____ ,
_____ , and _____ of each year to stockholders of record on _____/ _____ , _____ , and
_____ of each year. The officers of this corporation are hereby authorized to perform all necessary acts to carry out this resolution.

The undersigned, _____ , certifies that he or she is the duly elected Secretary of this corporation and that the above is a true and correct copy of the resolution that was duly adopted at a meeting of the board of directors which was held in accordance with state law and the By-Laws of the corporation on _____ , 19 ___.
I further certify that such resolution is now in full force and effect.

Dated _____

Seal

_____
Secretary of the corporation

Directors Resolution Authorizing Expense Reimbursement

Resolution of the Board of Directors of

_____

A meeting of the board of directors of this corporation was duly called and held on _____ , 19 ___ . A quorum of the board of directors was present and at the meeting it was decided, by majority vote, that it is necessary for the benefit of the corporation that the corporation reimburse _____ , who is the _____ of this corporation, for expenses incurred on behalf of the corporation.

Therefore, it is
RESOLVED, that this corporation reimburse _____
the amount of $_____ for expenses incurred on behalf of the corporation between the periods of _____ , 19 ___ and _____ , 19 ___ . The officers of this corporation are authorized to perform all necessary acts to carry out this resolution.

The undersigned, _____ , certifies that he or she is the duly elected Secretary of this corporation and that the above is a true and correct copy of the resolution that was duly adopted at a meeting of the board of directors which was held in accordance with state law and the By-Laws of the corporation on _____ , 19 ___ .
I further certify that such resolution is now in full force and effect.

Dated _____

Seal

_____
Secretary of the corporation

Directors Resolution Authorizing Retention of Earnings

Resolution of the Board of Directors of

_____

A meeting of the board of directors of this corporation was duly called and held on _____ , 19 ___. A quorum of the board of directors was present and at the meeting it was decided, by majority vote, that, to improve the financial condition of the corporation, it is advisable that no dividends be paid and that corporate earnings be retained by the corporation for the fiscal year 19 ___ .

Therefore, it is
RESOLVED, that this corporation retain the earnings of the corporation for the fiscal year 19 ___ ; and that such earnings be credited to the corporate Surplus Account; and that no dividends be paid for the fiscal year 19 ___ . The officers of this corporation are authorized to perform all necessary acts to carry out this resolution.

The undersigned, _____ , certifies that he or she is the duly elected Secretary of this corporation and that the above is a true and correct copy of the resolution that was duly adopted at a meeting of the board of directors which was held in accordance with state law and the By-Laws of the corporation on _____ , 19 ___.
I further certify that such resolution is now in full force and effect.

Dated _____

Seal

_____
Secretary of the corporation

Directors Resolution Authorizing Employee Stock Option Plan

Resolution of the Board of Directors of

_____

A meeting of the board of directors of this corporation was duly called and held on _____ , 19 ___. A quorum of the board of directors was present and at the meeting it was decided, by majority vote, that it is advisable to provide an employee stock option plan for employees of the corporation.

Therefore, it is
RESOLVED, that this corporation adopts and approves the Employee Stock Option Plan dated _____ , 19 ___ , a copy of which is attached to this resolution and is made a part of the permanent records of this corporation. The officers of this corporation are authorized to perform all necessary acts to carry out this resolution.

The undersigned, _____ , certifies that he or she is the duly elected Secretary of this corporation and that the above is a true and correct copy of the resolution that was duly adopted at a meeting of the board of directors which was held in accordance with state law and the By-Laws of the corporation on _____ , 19 ___.
I further certify that such resolution is now in full force and effect.

Dated _____

Seal

_____
Secretary of the corporation

Directors Resolution Authorizing Pension Plan

Resolution of the Board of Directors of

_____

A meeting of the board of directors of this corporation was duly called and held on _____ , 19 ___ . A quorum of the board of directors was present and at the meeting it was decided, by majority vote, that it is advisable that the corporation adopt a pension plan for its employees.

Therefore, it is

RESOLVED, that this corporation adopts and approves the Corporate Pension Plan dated _____ , 19 ___ , a copy of which is attached to this resolution and is made a part of the permanent records of this corporation. The officers of this corporation are authorized to perform all necessary acts to carry out this resolution.

The undersigned, _____ , certifies that he or she is the duly elected Secretary of this corporation and that the above is a true and correct copy of the resolution that was duly adopted at a meeting of the board of directors which was held in accordance with state law and the By-Laws of the corporation on _____ , 19 ___ .
I further certify that such resolution is now in full force and effect.

Dated _____

Seal

_____
Secretary of the corporation

Directors Resolution Authorizing Profit-Sharing Plan

Resolution of the Board of Directors of

_____

A meeting of the board of directors of this corporation was duly called and held on _____ , 19 ___ . A quorum of the board of directors was present and at the meeting it was decided, by majority vote, that it is advisable that the corporation provide its employees with a profit-sharing plan.

Therefore, it is
RESOLVED, that this corporation adopts and approves the Corporate Profit-Sharing Plan dated _____ , 19 ___ , a copy of which is attached to this resolution and which is made a part of the permanent records of this corporation. The officers of this corporation are authorized to perform all necessary acts to carry out this resolution.

The undersigned, _____ , certifies that he or she is the duly elected Secretary of this corporation and that the above is a true and correct copy of the resolution that was duly adopted at a meeting of the board of directors which was held in accordance with state law and the By-Laws of the corporation on _____ , 19 ___ .
I further certify that such resolution is now in full force and effect.

Dated _____

Seal

_____
Secretary of the corporation

Directors Resolution Authorizing Health Care Plan

Resolution of the
Board of Directors of

_____

A meeting of the board of directors of this corporation was duly called and held on _____ , 19 ___ . A quorum of the board of directors was present and at the meeting it was decided, by majority vote, that it is advisable that the corporation provide a health care plan for its employees.

Therefore, it is
RESOLVED, that this corporation adopts and approves the Corporate Health Care Plan dated _____ , 19 ___ , a copy of which is attached to this resolution and which is made a part of the permanent records of this corporation. The officers of this corporation are authorized to perform all necessary acts to carry out this resolution.

The undersigned, _____ , certifies that he or she is the duly elected Secretary of this corporation and that the above is a true and correct copy of the resolution that was duly adopted at a meeting of the board of directors which was held in accordance with state law and the By-Laws of the corporation on _____ , 19 ___ .
I further certify that such resolution is now in full force and effect.

Dated _____

Seal

_____
Secretary of the corporation

Directors Resolution Authorizing Group Insurance Plan

Resolution of the Board of Directors of

_____

A meeting of the board of directors of this corporation was duly called and held on _____ , 19 ___. A quorum of the board of directors was present and at the meeting it was decided, by majority vote, that it is advisable for the corporation to provide group insurance for its employees.

Therefore, it is
RESOLVED, that this corporation adopts and approves the Corporate Group Insurance Plan dated _____ , 19 ___ , a copy of which is attached to this resolution and which is made a part of the permanent records of this corporation. The officers of this corporation are authorized to perform all necessary acts to carry out this resolution.

The undersigned, _____ , certifies that he or she is the duly elected Secretary of this corporation and that the above is a true and correct copy of the resolution that was duly adopted at a meeting of the board of directors which was held in accordance with state law and the By-Laws of the corporation on _____ , 19 ___.
I further certify that such resolution is now in full force and effect.

Dated _____

Seal

_____
Secretary of the corporation

Directors Resolution Authorizing Death Benefit Plan

Resolution of the Board of Directors of

_____

A meeting of the board of directors of this corporation was duly called and held on _____ , 19 ___. A quorum of the board of directors was present and at the meeting it was decided, by majority vote, that it is advisable that the corporation provide a death benefit plan for its employees.

Therefore, it is

RESOLVED, that this corporation adopts and approves the Corporate Death Benefit Plan dated _____ , 19 ___ , a copy of which is attached to this resolution and which is made a part of the permanent records of this corporation. The officers of this corporation are authorized to perform all necessary acts to carry out this resolution.

The undersigned, _____ , certifies that he or she is the duly elected Secretary of this corporation and that the above is a true and correct copy of the resolution that was duly adopted at a meeting of the board of directors which was held in accordance with state law and the By-Laws of the corporation on _____ , 19 ___.
I further certify that such resolution is now in full force and effect.

Dated _____

Seal

_____
Secretary of the corporation

Directors Resolution Authorizing Employee Benefit Plan

Resolution of the
Board of Directors of

_____

A meeting of the board of directors of this corporation was duly called and held on _____ , 19 ___ . A quorum of the board of directors was present and at the meeting it was decided, by majority vote, that it is advisable that the corporation provide an employee benefit plan for its employees.

Therefore, it is
RESOLVED, that this corporation adopts and approves the Corporate Employee Benefit Plan dated _____ , 19 ___ , a copy of which is attached to this resolution and which is made a part of the permanent records of this corporation. The officers of this corporation are authorized to perform all necessary acts to carry out this resolution.

The undersigned, _____ , certifies that he or she is the duly elected Secretary of this corporation and that the above is a true and correct copy of the resolution that was duly adopted at a meeting of the board of directors which was held in accordance with state law and the By-Laws of the corporation on _____ , 19 ___ .
I further certify that such resolution is now in full force and effect.

Dated _____

Seal

_____
Secretary of the corporation

Directors Resolution Rescinding Prior Resolution

Resolution of the
Board of Directors of

_____

A meeting of the board of directors of this corporation was duly called and
held on _____ , 19 ___ . A quorum of the board of directors
was present and at the meeting it was decided, by majority vote, that it is in
the best interests of the corporation that the resolution of the board of
directors dated _____ , 19 ___ , relating to _____
_____
no longer be in effect.

Therefore, it is
RESOLVED, that this corporation rescinds and revokes the resolution of the
board of directors dated _____ , 19 ___ , relating to _____
_____ .
The officers of this corporation are hereby authorized to perform all necessary
acts to carry out this resolution rescinding and revoking the prior resolution.

The undersigned, _____ , certifies that
he or she is the duly elected Secretary of this corporation and that the above is
a true and correct copy of the resolution that was duly adopted at a meeting of
the board of directors which was held in accordance with state law and the
By-Laws of the corporation on _____ , 19 ___ .
I further certify that such resolution is now in full force and effect.

Dated _____

Seal

_____
Secretary of the corporation

Directors Resolution Authorizing Loan to Corporate Officer

Resolution of the
Board of Directors of

_____

A meeting of the board of directors of this corporation was duly called and held on _____ , 19 ___. A quorum of the board of directors was present and at the meeting it was decided, by majority vote, that _____ , the _____ of this corporation, shall be allowed to borrow $_____ from this corporation.

Therefore, it is
RESOLVED, that this corporation loan $_____ to _____ , an officer of this corporation on the following terms: _____

_____
_____.

The officers of this corporation are hereby authorized to perform all necessary acts to carry out this resolution.

The undersigned, _____ _____ , certifies that he or she is the duly elected Secretary of this corporation and that the above is a true and correct copy of the resolution that was duly adopted at a meeting of the board of directors which was held in accordance with state law and the By-Laws of the corporation on _____ , 19 ___.
I further certify that such resolution is now in full force and effect.

Dated _____

                                                        Seal

_____
Secretary of the corporation

Directors Resolution Fixing Salary of Corporate Officer

Resolution of the
Board of Directors of

_____

A meeting of the board of directors of this corporation was duly called and held on _____ , 19 ___ . A quorum of the board of directors was present and at the meeting it was decided, by majority vote, that it is advisable that the annual salary of the _____ of the corporation be $ _____ .

Therefore, it is
RESOLVED, that this corporation provide an annual salary of
$_____ to the _____ of this corporation. The officers of this corporation are hereby authorized to perform all necessary acts to carry out this resolution.

The undersigned, _____ , certifies that he or she is the duly elected Secretary of this corporation and that the above is a true and correct copy of the resolution that was duly adopted at a meeting of the board of directors which was held in accordance with state law and the By-Laws of the corporation on _____ , 19 ___ .
I further certify that such resolution is now in full force and effect.

Dated _____

Seal

_____
Secretary of the corporation

Directors Resolution Authorizing Stock Transfer

Resolution of the Board of Directors of

_____

A meeting of the board of directors of this corporation was duly called and held on _____ , 19 ___ . A quorum of the board of directors was present and at the meeting it was decided, by majority vote, that _____ shares of the common stock of the corporation be transferred from _____ to

_____ .

Therefore, it is
RESOLVED, that this corporation approves the transfer of _____ shares of the common stock of this corporation from _____ to _____ .
Such transfer shall be entered into the Stock Transfer Records of this corporation. The officers of this corporation are hereby authorized to perform all necessary acts to carry out this resolution.

The undersigned, _____ , certifies that he or she is the duly elected Secretary of this corporation and that the above is a true and correct copy of the resolution that was duly adopted at a meeting of the board of directors which was held in accordance with state law and the By-Laws of the corporation on _____ , 19 ___ .
I further certify that such resolution is now in full force and effect.

Dated _____

Seal

_____
Secretary of the corporation

**Directors Resolution Authorizing Change of Address
    of Registered Office of Corporation**

Resolution of the
Board of Directors of

_____

A meeting of the board of directors of this corporation was duly called and held on _____ , 19 ___ . A quorum of the board of directors was present and at the meeting it was decided, by majority vote, that it is necessary to change the location of the registered office of this corporation from _____
to _____ .

Therefore, it is
RESOLVED, that this corporation changes its registered office from the location of _____
to _____ .
This address change shall be entered into the corporate records on file with the State of _____ . The officers of this corporation are hereby authorized to perform all necessary acts to carry out this resolution.

The undersigned, _____ , certifies that he or she is the duly elected Secretary of this corporation and that the above is a true and correct copy of the resolution that was duly adopted at a meeting of the board of directors which was held in accordance with state law and the By-Laws of the corporation on _____ , 19 ___ .
I further certify that such resolution is now in full force and effect.

Dated _____

                                                      Seal

_____
Secretary of the corporation

Directors Resolution Authorizing President to Make Purchases

Resolution of the Board of Directors of

_____

A meeting of the board of directors of this corporation was duly called and held on _____ , 19 ___. A quorum of the board of directors was present and at the meeting it was decided, by majority vote, that it is advisable to authorize the President of this corporation to have the authority to make day-to-day purchases for the corporation.

Therefore, it is
RESOLVED, that this corporation authorizes the President of this corporation to make all day-to-day purchases for the benefit of the corporation that the President deems necessary. The officers of this corporation are hereby authorized to perform all necessary acts to carry out this resolution.

The undersigned, _____ , certifies that he or she is the duly elected Secretary of this corporation and that the above is a true and correct copy of the resolution that was duly adopted at a meeting of the board of directors which was held in accordance with state law and the By-Laws of the corporation on _____ , 19 ___.
I further certify that such resolution is now in full force and effect.

Dated _____

Seal

_____
Secretary of the corporation

Directors Resolution Authorizing Bonus

Resolution of the Board of Directors of

_____

A meeting of the board of directors of this corporation was duly called and held on _____ , 19 ___ . A quorum of the board of directors was present and at the meeting it was decided, by majority vote, that it is advisable to provide a bonus to the following employee of this corporation:

_____ .

Therefore, it is
RESOLVED, that this corporation pay a bonus in the amount of
$_____ to _____ ,
an employee of the corporation. The officers of this corporation are hereby authorized to perform all necessary acts to carry out this resolution.

The undersigned, _____ , certifies that he or she is the duly elected Secretary of this corporation and that the above is a true and correct copy of the resolution that was duly adopted at a meeting of the board of directors which was held in accordance with state law and the By-Laws of the corporation on _____ , 19 ___ .
I further certify that such resolution is now in full force and effect.

Dated _____

Seal

_____
Secretary of the corporation

Shareholders Resolution Approving Sale of All Corporate Assets

Resolution of the Shareholders of

_____

A meeting of the shareholders of this corporation was duly called and held on
_____ , 19 ___. A quorum of the shareholders was present, in
person or by proxy, and at the meeting it was decided, by majority vote, that it
is in the best interests of the corporation that all of the corporate assets,
consisting of those items listed on the List of Corporate Assets which is
attached to this resolution, be sold to _____
of _____ .

Therefore, it is
RESOLVED, that this corporation sell all of the corporate assets listed on the
List of Corporate Assets which is attached to this resolution, be sold to
_____ of _____
_____ .
The officers of this corporation are hereby authorized to perform all necessary
acts to carry out this resolution.

The undersigned, _____ , certifies that
he or she is the duly elected Secretary of this corporation and that the above is
a true and correct copy of the resolution that was duly adopted at a meeting of
the shareholders which was held in accordance with state law and the By-
Laws of the corporation on _____ , 19 ___. I further certify
that such resolution is now in full force and effect.

Dated _____

Seal

_____
Secretary of the corporation

Consent Resolutions

Any of the resolution forms which are contained in this chapter can easily be adapted for use as consent resolutions. First, however, it must be verified that the By-Laws of the corporation allow the use of consent resolutions for directors and shareholders. The By-Laws which are presented in this book contain the following clauses which allow consent resolutions to be used:

> For shareholders: "Any action which may be taken at a shareholders meeting may be taken instead without a meeting if a resolution is consented to, in writing, by all shareholders who would be entitled to vote on the matter."

> For directors: "Any action which may be taken at a directors meeting may be taken instead without a meeting if a resolution is consented to, in writing, by all directors."

If you are operating under different By-Laws, be certain that your By-laws contains a substantially similar authorization for consent resolutions.

The use of consent resolutions allows for a much greater flexibility in the management of corporations. Formal meetings are not necessary, although for many issues, meetings may be highly recommended as a method to record the remarks and positions of board members or shareholders who may oppose the action. Consent resolutions are most useful in those situations where the board of directors or number of shareholders is small and all of the directors or shareholders are in complete agreement regarding the action to be taken.

In order to adapt the standard resolutions in this and other chapters of this book for use as consent resolutions, simply alter the form in the following three ways (substitute *shareholders* where appropriate if you are preparing a shareholders consent resolution):

> 1. Add the word "Consent" to the title (For example: Consent Resolution of the Board of Directors of the ABCXYZ Corporation).

> 2. Substitute the following for the first paragraph of the resolution:

>> The undersigned, being all of the directors (*or shareholders*) of this corporation and acting in accordance with state law and the By-Laws of this corporation, consent to the adoption of the

following as if it was adopted at a duly called meeting of the board of directors (*or shareholders*) of this corporation. By unanimous consent of the board of directors (*or shareholders*) of this corporation, it is decided that

3. Add signature lines for all of the directors (or shareholders) of the corporation. After all of the signatures, insert the following phrase:

Being all of the directors (*or shareholders*) of the corporation.

4. Substitute the following for the last paragraph of the resolution:

The undersigned, _____, certifies that he or she is the duly elected Secretary of this corporation and that the above is a true and correct copy of the resolution that was duly adopted by consent of the board of directors (*or shareholders*) in accordance with state law and the By-Laws of the corporation on _____ , 19 ___ . I further certify that such resolution is now in full force and effect.

On the following pages, you will find a General Directors Consent Resolution which has been adapted with these instructions from the General Directors Resolution form which was shown on page 125.

General Directors Consent Resolution

Consent Resolution of the Board of Directors of

_____

The undersigned, being all of the directors of this corporation and acting in accordance with state law and the By-Laws of this corporation, consent to the adoption of the following as if it was adopted at a duly called meeting of the board of directors of this corporation. By unanimous consent of the board of directors of this corporation, it is decided that

Therefore, it is
RESOLVED, that this corporation

The officers of this corporation are hereby authorized to perform all necessary acts to carry out this resolution.

Dated _____

_____
Director of the corporation

_____
Director of the corporation

_____
Director of the corporation

Being all of the Directors of this corporation.

The undersigned, _____ , certifies that
he or she is the duly elected Secretary of this corporation and that the above is
a true and correct copy of the resolution that was duly adopted by consent of
the board of directors in accordance with state law and the By-Laws of the
corporation on _____ , 19 ___ . I further certify that such
resolution is now in full force and effect.

Dated _____

Seal

_____
Secretary of the corporation

Chapter 10

Corporate Stock

Corporate stock represents the money or property which is invested in a corporation. It is a representation of the share of ownership in a corporate business. When a corporation files its Articles of Incorporation with the state, it states how many shares of stock it will be authorized to issue (For example: 500 shares). When the authorized shares are sold or transferred to a shareholder for something of value (money, property, or labor), the shares are said to be "issued and outstanding". All of the authorized shares need not be issued. The ownership of the shares in the corporation is then evidenced by a stock certificate describing the number of shares owned. The value of the shares can be a specific "par" value (for example: $1.00 per share) or they can be "no par" value, which allows the board of directors to fix the value of the shares by resolution. If the shares are given a par value, the stock must be sold for at least the stated par value. The concept of par value is gradually being eliminated from modern business corporation acts, allowing board of director discretion to fix the value of the shares. All states allow the use of no-par stock.

An example may best illustrate the use of stock. A corporation is formed and 500 shares of no-par value common stock are authorized in the Articles of Incorporation. 3 people will form the initial shareholders of the corporation, with one desiring to own 50% of the shares and the other two desiring to own 25% each. All three comprise the board of directors. As a board, they decide to issue 300 shares of stock and they decide to fix the value per share at $10.00. Thus, the majority owner will pay the corporation $1,500.00 ($10.00 X 150 shares or 50% of the issued and outstanding shares—*not* 50% of the authorized shares). The other two shareholders will pay $750.00 each for 75 shares apiece of the issued shares. The ownership of the shares which have been issued will be represented by stock certificates which will be delivered to each of the owners. The transactions will be recorded in the corporation's stock transfer book. At the close of these transactions, the corporation will have 3 shareholders: one with 150 shares of issued and outstanding stock and two with 75 shares of issued and outstanding stock. The corporation will have $3,000.00 of paid-in capital. 200 shares will remain as authorized but not issued or outstanding. At shareholder meetings, each share of issued and outstanding stock will represent one vote. (See Chapter 8).

The above scenario presents stock ownership at its most basic. The shares described were no-par value common stock. There are many, many variable characteristics which can be given to stock. The forms in this book are based on basic single-class common stock with voting rights. Classes of stock may, however, be created with non-voting attributes, with preferences for dividends, and with many other different characteristics. Most small business corporations can operate efficiently with a single class of common stock with voting rights. There is no requirement that the stock certificate be in a particular format. The stock certificates for use in this book are a simple generic form. If you desire, you may obtain fancy blank stock certificates from most office supply stores, but these are not required. For the issuance of stock, follow the steps shown below in the Stock Checklist. Each of the steps taken at a meeting of the board of directors must be documented with a board resolution (see Chapter 9).

Stock Checklist

❑ Designate the number of authorized shares in Articles of Incorporation and whether they are par or no-par value.

❑ At a board meeting, determine the number of shares to be issued.

❑ If the shares are no-par, at a board meeting, determine the value of the shares.

❑ At a board meeting, determine who will purchase shares and how many will be sold to each person.

❑ If necessary, at a board meeting, the board of directors must fix the value of any property which will be accepted in exchange for shares of stock.

❑ At a board meeting, authorize officers to issue shares to persons designated.

❑ The Secretary will then prepare the appropriate stock certificates.

❑ If there are restrictions on the transfer of stock, note the restrictions on the back of the certificate. (See Chapter 11).

❑ All of the officers of the corporation will sign the certificates.

❑ The Secretary will receive the money or property from the purchasers and deposit any funds in the corporate bank account.

❑ The Secretary will issue the certificates and receipts for money or property and record the transaction in the corporate stock transfer book.

❑ If a certificate is lost, use the Lost Stock Affidavit at the end of the chapter.

Corporate Stock Certificate (Front)

Certificate Number: _____

Number of Shares: _____

Corporate Stock Certificate

Name of Corporation
_____

A business corporation incorporated under the laws of the State of _____

Par Value of Shares: $ _____

Number of Shares Authorized: _____

This Certifies That

_____ is the owner of _____ shares of common stock of this corporation. The shares represented are fully paid and are non-assessable. The shares represented by this Certificate are only transferable on the official books of the Corporation by the holder of this Certificate, in person or by Attorney. For transfer, this Certificate must be properly endorsed on the back and surrendered to the Corporation. This Certificate is signed by all of the Officers of this Corporation.

Dated _____

_____
President

_____
Vice-President

_____
Secretary

_____
Treasurer

Corporate Stock Certificate (Back)

For value received, I, _____ , the owner of this Certificate, transfer the number of shares represented by this Certificate to _____ , and I instruct the Secretary of this Corporation to record this transfer on the books of the Corporation. Any restrictions on the transfer of these shares are shown below.

Dated _____

Signature _____

Restrictions on Transfer:

Receipt for Stock Certificate

Receipt for Stock Certificate of

_____

On this date, _____ , a shareholder in this corporation has purchased _____ shares of common stock in this corporation, represented by Stock Certificate number _____ . This Certificate represents _____ percent of ownership in this corporation.

The shareholder has transferred to the corporation the following assets, with a fair market value of $ _____ in consideration for the receipt of the shares of stock:

Payment in full has been received for these shares and the shares have been issued by the corporation, transferred to the shareholder, and received by the shareholder. Record of this transaction has been recorded in the Stock Transfer Book of this corporation.

Date _____

_____
Secretary of the corporation

_____
Shareholder

Stock Transfer Book

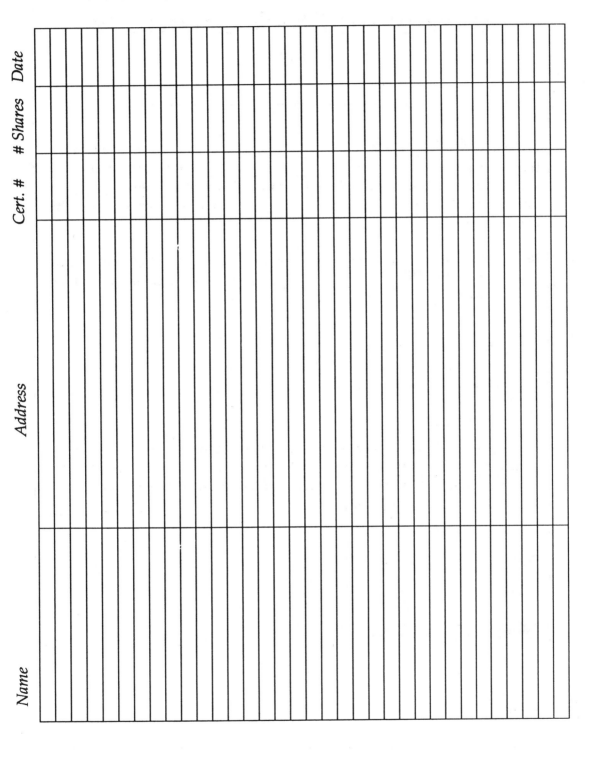

Lost Stock Affidavit

Lost Stock Affidavit

State of _____)
)   S.S.
County of _____)

Being duly sworn, the undersigned states the following on oath:

1. My name is _____ and my
    addresss is _____ , City of
    _____ , State of _____ .

2. I am the lawful owner of _____ shares of issued and
    outstanding common stock of _____ ,
    a corporation registered in the State of _____ .

3. I have not sold, exchanged, transferred or pledged any of these shares in
    any manner and the shares have been in my sole possession at my
    residence since issuance. I am now unable to locate these shares and
    believe that they have been lost, stolen, or misplaced.

4. I request the issuing corporation to issue a duplicate stock certificate for
    ownership of these shares without surrender of the original shares.

5. I agree to indemnify and hold the issuing corporation harmless from
    any liability or expenses which may result from reliance on this
    affidavit.

_____   _____
Signature   Date

Subscribed and sworn to before me on _____ , 19 ___ .

_____
Notary Public, in and for the County of _____ , State of
_____ . My commission expires _____ .

Chapter 11

Corporate Shareholder Agreement

For many smaller corporations with only a few shareholders, some form of shareholder agreement is often useful. Although shareholder agreements can take many forms, the most common specify certain restrictions on the ability to sell shares of the corporations stock to outside investors. Restrictions on the ability to transfer shares allow the corporation to have greater control regarding who is a shareholder, and, thus, ultimately who is allowed to select the board of directors of the corporation.

The agreement which is contained in this chapter addresses several of the major concerns regarding stock transfers. First, the agreement restricts the rights of shareholders to transfer their stock except by the terms of the agreement. Second, it provides a "right of first refusal" to both the corporation and to the other shareholders on any proposed sale of stock. The agreement also provides for a buy-out/sell-out restriction. This particular restriction requires that if a shareholder desires to buy all of the shares of the corporation, she/he must be willing to also sell all of her/his shares on the same terms. Thus, if a shareholder desires to total control, it becomes an all-or-nothing proposition. If the other shareholders agree, the deal will go through. But if the other shareholders desire to retain control, the one who proposed the buy-out must sell out to the remaining shareholders. Finally, the agreement provides for methods for determining the value of the shares for sales upon death or resignation.

Shareholders Stock Purchase Agreement

Shareholders Stock Purchase Agreement

This Agreement is made on _____ , 19 ___ between _____ _____ , a corporation incorporated under the laws of the State of _____ and the following shareholders of this corporation _____ _____ _____.

The shareholders listed above own all of the issued and outstanding stock of this corporation. The corporation and its shareholders desire to provide for continuity in the ownership and management of this corporation.

THEREFORE, in consideration of the mutual promises in this Agreement, and for other good and valuable consideration, the parties agree as follows:

1. *Restrictions.* No shareholder shall transfer, mortgage, encumber or dispose of any or all of their shares except as allowed in this Agreement.

2. *Transfer Outside The Corporation.* If a shareholder wishes to dispose of any shares, other than to the corporation, 30 days written notice must be given to the corporation. This notice must state the number of shares to be transferred, the name and address of the person or company to whom the transfer is proposed, the purchase price amount, and the date of the proposed transfer.

    The corporation will have 30 days after receipt of the written notice to exercise an option to buy any or all of the shares on the same terms as the proposed transfer.

If the corporation does not exercise its option, then within its 30-day option period, the corporation must provide written notice to all of the other shareholders of the corporation. Then any or all of the other shareholders of the corporation will have an additional 30 days to exercise an option to buy any or all of the shares on the same terms as the proposed transfer. Each shareholder will have an option to buy a percentage of the proposed transfer amount equal to the number of shares owned by that shareholder divided by the total number of shares issued and outstanding, not including the number of shares which are included in the proposed transfer. If a shareholder does not exercise its option to buy, then the percentage will be determined without including that shareholder's shares in the total shares outstanding.

Acting separately or together, the corporation and the shareholders must agree to purchase all of the shares offered in the proposed transfer. If neither the corporation nor the shareholders elect to buy all of the shares offered in the proposed transfer, then 60 days after the corporation's receipt of the written notice of the proposed transfer, the shareholder may sell the shares as stated in the written notice of proposed transfer.

3.   *Offer To Buy or Sell All Shares.* If a shareholder wishes to sell all of her/his shares or buy all of the shares of all the other shareholders in the corporation, the shareholder must provide written notice that she/he is willing to either sell all of his/her shares or buy all of the outstanding shares of other shareholders. The shareholder must be willing to allow either event to happen.

Within 30 days of receipt of the written notice, any or all of the other shareholders of the corporation will have an option to buy any or all of the shares on the same terms as the proposed transaction. Each shareholder will have an option to buy a percentage of the shares of the shareholder requesting the buy/sell transaction. The percentage will be the number of shares owned by that shareholder divided by the number of shares issued and outstanding, not including the number of shares which are owned by the shareholder proposing the transaction. If a shareholder does not exercise its option to buy, then the percentage will be determined without including that shareholder's shares in the total shares outstanding and the remaining shareholders will have an additional 30 days in which to exercise their own options.

Acting separately or together, the other shareholders must either agree to purchase all of the shares owned by the shareholder proposing the buy/sell transaction or allow all of their own shares to be purchased. If the shareholders do not elect to buy all of the shares offered in the proposed transfer, then 60 days after the receipt of the written notice of the proposed transaction, the shareholder proposing the transaction shall be obligated to purchase all of the shares of the other shareholders as stated in the written notice of proposed transaction and that all the other shareholders will be obligated to sell all of their shares.

4.   *Involuntary Transfer of Shares.* If a shareholder's shares are transferred by operation of law, other than by death, the corporation and other shareholders shall have 60 days to exercise an option to purchase all of such shares under the option terms of Paragraph #2 of this Agreement. If a price is paid upon the involuntary transfer, then this will be the price for the exercise of the option. If no price is paid, the price will be determined as specified under Paragraph #8 of this Agreement.

5.   *Death of a Shareholder.* On the death of a shareholder, the corporation will purchase all of the deceased shareholder's shares at the price as specified in Paragraph #8 of this Agreement. The deceased shareholder's estate must sell the shares to the corporation.

6.   *Disability of Shareholder.* If any shareholder shall suffer a permanent disability which prevents him/her from performing his/her usual duties for 1 year, the corporation may elect to purchase all of the shareholders shares. Written notice must be provided to the shareholder or his/her representatives within 30 days after the 1 year period. The purchase price will be as specified in Paragraph #8 of this Agreement. The disabled shareholder or his/her representatives must sell the shares to the corporation.

7.   *Resignation or Discharge of a Shareholder.* If any shareholder voluntarily resigns from employment with the corporation, or is discharged from employment with the corporation for reasonable cause, then the corporation will buy all of the shareholder's shares at a purchase price as specified under Paragraph #8 of this Agreement. The shareholder must sell the shares to the corporation.

8.   *Purchase Price of Shares.* For purchases under Paragraph #2, the purchase price will be as provided by Paragraph #2. For all other purchases, the purchase price will be as follows:

For shares to be sold prior to _____, 19 ___ , the purchase price will be $ _____. The shareholders agree to redetermine the purchase price prior to _____ , 19 ___ . For each succeeding year, the shareholders agree to redetermine the purchase price at a special meeting which will take place within 60 days prior to the end of the corporation's fiscal year. The valuation will be in the form of a Shareholder's Resolution and be signed by all shareholders.

If the shareholders fail to make any of the required redeterminations of purchase price, then the purchase price will be determined by the Certified Public Accountant for the corporation as of the last day of the month preceding the proposed transaction. The method for valuation will be as follows:

9.   *Closing of Transactions.* The closing of any transaction under this Agreement will take place at the offices of the corporation. The Closing Date will be determined under the appropriate paragraph or if not provided, then 90 days after the first notice of the proposed transaction. Upon closing, the buyer will deliver to the seller at least 50% of the purchase price in cash, with the other 50% in the form of a promissory note bearing 10% annual interest payable within 3 years, with payments amortized and payable on the first of each month following the closing date. The note may be prepaid without penalty and will provide that if any payment is not made by the due date, the entire note is immediately due and payable. Upon receipt of the required cash and/or promissory note, the seller shall deliver the appropriate shares to the buyer.

10.   *Certificate Endorsement.* All shares issued by the corporation will bear the following endorsement:

The ownership and transfer of the shares of stock evidenced by this Certificate are specifically restricted by the provisions of a Shareholders Stock Purchase Agreement executed by the shareholder whose name appears on the face of this Certificate and by the corporation and all remaining shareholders of the corporation. The Agreement restricts all sales or purchases of shares of stock of this corporation and provides various purchase options.

11. *Termination.* This Agreement will terminate:

a. On _____ , 19 ___; or
b. By unanimous agreement of all shareholders; or
c. On the death of all shareholders; or
d. On the corporation's filing for voluntary bankruptcy.

12. *Additional Provisions.*

13. *Miscellaneous Provisions.* This Agreement is binding on the corporation, the shareholders, their heirs, legal representatives, successors, or assigns. This Agreement will be governed by the laws of the State of _____ . This Agreement may be amended only by unanimous written consent of the corporation and all of its shareholders.

Dated _____

_____
Name of corporation

By:

Seal

_____
The President of the corporation

_____
Shareholder

_____
Shareholder

_____
Shareholder

_____
Shareholder

Being all of the shareholders of this corporation.

Chapter 12

"S" Corporation Status

An "S" corporation is a type of corporation which is recognized by the U.S. Internal Revenue Service and is treated differently than other corporations in terms of federal taxation. Some states also recognize "S" corporation status for state income taxation purposes; some states do not. The only reason for becoming an "S" corporation is to obtain a different method of taxation than other corporations.

For standard corporations, the corporation pays a federal and, perhaps, state corporate tax on the business profits. If the after-tax profit is then distributed to the shareholders as dividends, the shareholders then pay an additional personal income tax on the dividends. The amount distributed to the shareholders as dividends is not a deduction for the corporation. "S" corporations, on the other hand, are taxed similarly to partnerships. They act merely as a conduit for passing the income and deductions of the corporation directly through to the individual shareholders in much the same manner as partnerships, or even sole proprietorships. The "S" corporation does not pay a corporate tax and files a different type of tax form than does a standard corporation. (See Chapter 14). Taxation of the profits of the "S" corporation falls to the individuals who own shares in the corporation. This also allows for each individual shareholder to personally deduct their share of any corporate losses.

There are, however, certain basic requirements for qualifying a corporation for "S" corporation status. Every requirement must be met before the IRS will recognize "S" corporation status and allow for the different tax treatment.

1. The corporation must have no more than 35 shareholders. (Wives and husbands, even if they own stock separately, are considered as only one shareholder.)

2. Each of the corporation's shareholders must be a natural person or the estate of a natural person. Corporations and partnerships may not hold shares in the corporation. Each shareholder must also be a citizen or resident of the United States.

3. The corporation must only have one class of stock which is issued and outstanding. The corporation may have other classes of stock which are authorized, providing no shares are issued. Different voting rights within a class of stock (ie. voting and non-voting) do not disqualify the corporation.

4. The corporation must already be incorporated in one of the United States or its possessions. Financial institutions, foreign corporations, and certain other very specialized corporations are not eligible.

5. The corporation must not have been qualified as an "S" corporation within the previous 5 years. This restrictions prevents abrupt shifting from one type of corporation to another in order to obtain the maximum tax benefits.

6. The corporation must file *Form 2553*: **Election by a Small Business Corporation** with the IRS.

If your corporation meets all of these requirements, "S" corporation status may be elected. It may be prudent to obtain the advice of a competent accountant prior to making the election, however. The actual steps in electing "S" corporation status are detailed below in the "S" Corporation Checklist. Following the Checklist are the forms required to complete the election of "S" corporation status. Please note that *IRS Form 2553*: **Election by a Small Business Corporation** is only provided for illustration purposes and a copy of the form should be obtained from the IRS.

"S" Corporation Checklist

❑ Determine that the corporation has fewer than 35 shareholders.

❑ Determine that all shareholders are natural persons or estates.

❑ Determine that the corporation has only one class of stock issued and outstanding.

❑ Determine that the corporation is already incorporated in the U.S or one of its possessions.

❑ Determine that the corporation has not had "S" status within the past 5 years.

❑ All shareholders must consent to the election to be treated as an "S" corporation.

❑ Notice of a special shareholders meeting for the purpose of consenting to the election as an "S" corporation should be provided to all shareholders of record.

❑ A special shareholders meeting should be held at which all shareholders of the corporation consent to the election by the corporation to be treated as an "S" corporation.

❑ A shareholders resolution consenting to the election to be treated as an "S" corporation should be signed by all shareholders of record.

❑ The Secretary of the corporation should complete *IRS Form 2553*: **Election by a Small Business Corporation.**

❑ All shareholders of record must sign *IRS Form 2553*: **Election by a Small Business Corporation.**

❑ The secretary of the corporation should file *IRS Form 2553*: **Election by a Small Business Corporation.**

Notice of Special Shareholders Meeting Regarding "S" Corporation

Notice of Special Shareholders Meeting of

_____

TO:

In accordance with the By-Laws of this corporation, an official special meeting of the shareholders will be held at _____ ___ m., on _____ , 19 ___ , at the offices of the corporation located at _____ .

The purpose of this meeting is to discuss the election of "S" corporation status for the corporation, under Internal Revenue Code Section 1362.

The Stock Transfer Book of this corporation will remain closed from _____ , 19 ___ until _____ , 19 ___ .

Dated _____

Seal

_____
Secretary of the corporation

Affidavit of Mailing of Notice of Special Shareholders Meeting Regarding "S" Corporation

Affidavit of Mailing of Notice of Special Shareholders Meeting of

_____

State of _____)
)   S.S.
County of _____)

Being duly sworn, _____ states:
I am the Secretary of _____ , a
corporation organized under the laws of the State of _____ .
On _____ , 19 ___ , I personally deposited stamped and
sealed copies of Notice of the Special Shareholders Meeting of this corporation
in a post-office box in the City of _____ , in the State of
_____ . The copies were correctly addressed to all
shareholders of this corporation as of _____ , 19 ___ as shown
in the Stock Transfer Book of this corporation. The list of names and addresses
of the shareholders is attached to this Affidavit.

_____
Secretary of the corporation

Subscribed and Sworn to before me on _____ , 19 ___ .

_____
Notary Public in and for the County of _____ and the State of
_____ . My commission expires _____ .

Waiver of Notice of Special Shareholders Meeting Regarding "S" Corporation

Waiver of Notice of Special Shareholders Meeting of

_____

We, the undersigned shareholders of this corporation, waive any required notice and consent to the holding of the special meeting of the shareholders of this corporation on _____ , 19 ___ , at _____ ___ m., at the offices of the corporation, located at _____

_____.

Dated _____

Name   Signature

_____   _____

_____   _____

_____   _____

_____   _____

_____   _____

_____   _____

_____   _____

Minutes of Special Shareholders Meeting Regarding "S" Corporation

Minutes of the Special Shareholders Meeting of

_____

A special meeting of the shareholders of this corporation was held on
_____ , 19 ___ , at _____ _____
m., at the offices of the corporation located at _____
_____ .

The President of this corporation, _____ ,
and the Vice-President of this corporation, _____ ,
and the Secretary of this corporation, _____ ,
and the Treasurer of this corporation, _____ ,
were present. Other than shareholders, the following other persons were also
present _____
_____ .

1.   The President of this corporation called the meeting to order and
      determined that a quorum was present, either in person or by proxy.

      The following shareholders were present in person:

      Name   Number of Shares

      _____   _____

      _____   _____

      _____   _____

      _____   _____

      The following shareholders were represented by proxy:

Name	Number of Shares
_____	_____
_____	_____
_____	_____

2. The Secretary of this corporation reported that notice of the meeting had been properly given or waived by each shareholder in accordance with the By-Laws. Upon motion made and carried, the Secretary was directed to attach the appropriate Notice and Affidavit or Waiver to these minutes.

3. _____ was then elected Chairperson of this meeting.

4. The following business was discussed: The benefits and advantages of the shareholders electing to obtain "S" corporation status under Internal Revenue Code Section 1362.

5. Upon motion made and carried, the following resolution was approved unanimously by outstanding shares of this corporation:
   RESOLVED that:
   This corporation elects to be treated and taxed as an "S" corporation under Internal Revenue Section 1362.

6. The President declared that this shareholders resolution was duly adopted.

There being no further business, upon motion made and carried the meeting was adjourned.

Dated _____

Seal

_____
Secretary of the corporation

Shareholders Resolution Consenting to Election of "S" Corporation Status

Resolution of the Shareholders of

_____

A special meeting of the shareholders of this corporation was duly called and held on _____ , 19 ___. All of the shareholders of this corporation were present, in person or by proxy.

At the meeting it was decided, by unanimous vote, that it is in the best interests of the corporation that the corporation elect to be treated as an "S" corporation under the provisions of Internal Revenue Code Section 1362.

Therefore, it is unanimously

RESOLVED, that this corporation elects to be treated as an "S" corporation under the provisions of Internal Revenue Code Section 1362. The officers of this corporation are hereby authorized to perform all necessary acts to carry out this resolution.

The undersigned, _____ , certifies that he or she is the duly elected Secretary of this corporation and that the above is a true and correct copy of the resolution that was duly adopted at a meeting of the shareholders which was held in accordance with state law and the By-Laws of the corporation on _____ , 19 ___. I further certify that such resolution is now in full force and effect.

Dated _____

Seal

_____
Secretary of the corporation

_____
Shareholder

_____
Shareholder

_____
Shareholder

_____
Shareholder

_____
Shareholder

_____
Shareholder

Being all of the shareholders of this corporation.

Sample IRS Form 2553: Election by a Small Business Corporation

Form **2553** (Rev. December 1990) Department of the Treasury Internal Revenue Service	**Election by a Small Business Corporation** (Under section 1362 of the Internal Revenue Code) ▶ For Paperwork Reduction Act Notice, see page 1 of Instructions. ▶ See separate Instructions.	OMB No. 1545-0146 Expires 11-30-93

Notes: 1. *This election, to be treated as an "S corporation," can be accepted only if all the tests in General Instruction B are met; all signatures in Parts I and III are originals (no photocopies); and the exact name and address of the corporation and other required form information are provided.*

2. *Do not file Form 1120S until you are notified that your election is accepted. See General Instruction E.*

Part I Election Information

Please Type or Print	
Name of corporation (see instructions)	**A** Employer Identification number (see instructions)
Number, street, and room or suite no. (If a P.O. box, see instructions.)	**B** Name and telephone number (including area code) of corporate officer or legal representative who may be called for information
City or town, state, and ZIP code	**C** Election is to be effective for tax year beginning (month, day, year)

D Is the corporation the outgrowth or continuation of any form of predecessor? . . ☐ Yes ☐ No

If "Yes," state name of predecessor, type of organization, and period of its existence ▶ ....

E Date of incorporation

F Check here ▶ ☐ if the corporation has changed its name or address since applying for the employer identification number shown in item A above.

G State of incorporation

H If this election takes effect for the first tax year the corporation exists, enter month, day, and year of the **earliest** of the following: (1) date the corporation first had shareholders, (2) date the corporation first had assets, or (3) date the corporation began doing business. ▶

I Selected tax year: Annual return will be filed for tax year ending (month and day) ▶ ....

If the tax year ends on any date other than December 31, except for an automatic 52-53-week tax year ending with reference to the month of December, you **must** complete Part II on the back. If the date you enter is the ending date of an automatic 52-53-week tax year, write "52-53-week year" to the right of the date. See Temporary Regulations section 1.441-2T(e)(3).

J Name of each shareholder, person having a community property interest in the corporation's stock, and each tenant in common, joint tenant, and tenant by the entirety. (A husband and wife (and their estates) are counted as one shareholder in determining the number of shareholders without regard to the manner in which the stock is owned.)	**K** Shareholders' Consent Statement. We, the undersigned shareholders, consent to the corporation's election to be treated as an "S corporation" under section 1362(a). (Shareholders sign and date below.)*		**L** Stock owned		**M** Social security number or employer identification number (see instructions)	**N** Share-holder's tax year ends (month and day)
	Signature	Date	Number of shares	Dates acquired		

*For this election to be valid, the consent of each shareholder, person having a community property interest in the corporation's stock, and each tenant in common, joint tenant, and tenant by the entirety must either appear above or be attached to this form. (See instructions for Column K if continuation sheet or a separate consent statement is needed.)

Under penalties of perjury, I declare that I have examined this election, including accompanying schedules and statements, and to the best of my knowledge and belief, it is true, correct, and complete.

Signature of officer ▶ _____ Title ▶ _____ Date ▶ _____

See Parts II and III on back.

Form **2553** (Rev. 12-90)

Form 2553 (Rev. 12-90)   ·Page **2**

Part II Selection of Fiscal Tax Year (All corporations using this Part must complete item O and one of items P, Q, or R.)

O   Check the applicable box below to indicate whether the corporation is:

    1. ☐ A new corporation adopting the tax year entered in item I, Part I.

    2. ☐ An existing corporation retaining the tax year entered in item I, Part I.

    3. ☐ An existing corporation changing to the tax year entered in item I, Part I.

P   Complete item P if the corporation is using the expeditious approval provisions of Revenue Procedure 87-32, 1987-2 C.B. 396, to request: **(1)** a natural business year (as defined in section 4.01(1) of Rev. Proc. 87-32), or **(2)** a year that satisfies the ownership tax year test in section 4.01(2) of Rev. Proc. 87-32. Check the applicable box below to indicate the representation statement the corporation is making as required under section 4 of Rev. Proc. 87-32.

    1. Natural Business Year ► ☐ I represent that the corporation is retaining or changing to a tax year that coincides with its natural business year as defined in section 4.01(1) of Rev. Proc. 87-32 and as verified by its satisfaction of the requirements of section 4.02(1) of Rev. Proc. 87-32. In addition, if the corporation is changing to a natural business year as defined in section 4.01(1), I further represent that such tax year results in less deferral of income to the owners than the corporation's present tax year. I also represent that the corporation is not described in section 3.01(2) of Rev. Proc. 87-32. (See instructions for additional information that must be attached.)

    2. Ownership Tax Year ► ☐ I represent that shareholders holding more than half of the shares of the stock (as of the first day of the tax year to which the request relates) of the corporation have the same tax year or are concurrently changing to the tax year that the corporation adopts, retains, or changes to per item I, Part I. I also represent that the corporation is not described in section 3.01(2) of Rev. Proc. 87-32.

Note: *If you do not use item P and the corporation wants a fiscal tax year, complete either item Q or R below. Item Q is used to request a fiscal tax year based on a business purpose and to make a back-up section 444 election. Item R is used to make a regular section 444 election.*

Q   Business Purpose—To request a fiscal tax year based on a business purpose, you must check box Q1 and pay a user fee. See instructions for details. You may also check box Q2 and/or box Q3.

    1. Check here ► ☐ if the fiscal year entered in item I, Part I, is requested under the provisions of section 6.03 of Rev. Proc. 87-32. Attach to Form 2553 a statement showing the business purpose for the requested fiscal year. See instructions for additional information that must be attached.

    2. Check here ► ☐ to show that the corporation intends to make a back-up section 444 election in the event the corporation's business purpose request is not approved by the IRS. (See instructions for more information.)

    3. Check here ► ☐ to show that the corporation agrees to adopt or change to a tax year ending December 31 if necessary for the IRS to accept this election for S corporation status in the event: (1) the corporation's business purpose request is not approved and the corporation makes a back-up section 444 election, but is ultimately not qualified to make a section 444 election, or (2) the corporation's business purpose request is not approved and the corporation did not make a back-up section 444 election.

R   Section 444 Election—To make a section 444 election, you must check box R1 and you may also check box R2.

    1. Check here ► ☐ to show the corporation will make, if qualified, a section 444 election to have the fiscal tax year shown in item I, Part I. To make the election, you must complete **Form 8716**, Election To Have a Tax Year Other Than a Required Tax Year, and either attach it to Form 2553 or file it separately.

    2. Check here ► ☐ to show that the corporation agrees to adopt or change to a tax year ending December 31 if necessary for the IRS to accept this election for S corporation status in the event the corporation is ultimately not qualified to make a section 444 election.

Part III Qualified Subchapter S Trust (QSST) Election Under Section 1361(d)(2)**

Income beneficiary's name and address	Social security number
Trust's name and address	Employer identification number

Date on which stock of the corporation was transferred to the trust (month, day, year) ►

In order for the trust named above to be a QSST and thus a qualifying shareholder of the S corporation for which this Form 2553 is filed, I hereby make the election under section 1361(d)(2). Under penalties of perjury, I certify that the trust meets the definition requirements of section 1361(d)(3) and that all other information provided in Part III is true, correct, and complete.

_____   _____
Signature of income beneficiary or signature and title of legal representative or other qualified person making the election   Date

**Use of Part III to make the QSST election may be made only if stock of the corporation has been transferred to the trust on or before the date on which the corporation makes its election to be an S corporation. The QSST election must be made and filed separately if stock of the corporation is transferred to the trust after the date on which the corporation makes the S election.

Chapter 13

Amendments to Corporate Articles and By-Laws

Amendments to the Articles of Incorporation and corporate By-Laws may sometimes be required by changing business circumstances. However, in general, amendments should be infrequent and reserved only for situations which require a substantial change in the manner in which the corporation conducts its business. Generally, amendments to Articles of Incorporation require that the corporation file a Certificate of Amendment or some similar form with the state. This procedure insures that the public record of the corporation's existence reflects the actual management of the corporation. The necessity of having to file any amendments to the Articles of Incorporation with the state, however, also requires that a state fee be paid. In some states, this fee can be substantial.

Under most state corporation laws, the Articles of Incorporation are amended by a process which includes both the directors of the corporation and its shareholders. The process used in this book requires that the directors approve a resolution adopting the amendment and calling for a meeting of the shareholders. At the shareholders meeting, the shareholders then approve the amendment to the Articles. Finally, a Certificate of Amendment is prepared. The final step is the filing of the Certificate with the state. The procedure used in this book for amendments to the By-Laws provides that the board of directors may amend the By-Laws, subject to approval by the shareholders, without notification of the state. (See Chapter 6). Checklists for both procedures follow.

Amendment to Articles of Incorporation Checklist

❏ A special meeting of the board of directors is called for the purpose of proposing an amendment to the Articles of Incorporation.

❏ Proper notice (or waivers) of the meeting is provided to all directors. (See Chapter 7).

❏ At the board meeting, a resolution is adopted proposing an amendment and calling for a special shareholders meeting. (A sample resolution is included in this chapter).

❏ Proper notice (or waivers) of the meeting is provided to all shareholders. (See Chapter 8).

❏ At the shareholders meeting, a resolution is adopted approving the amendment. (A sample resolution is included in this chapter).

❏ The Secretary of the corporation prepares a Certificate of Amendment of the Articles of Incorporation. (A sample Certificate is included in this chapter).

❏ The Secretary of the corporation files the Certificate with the state corporation department and pays the proper fees.

Amendment to By-Laws Checklist

❏ A special meeting of the board of directors is called for the purpose of proposing an amendment to the By-Laws.

❏ Proper notice (or waivers) of the meeting is provided to all directors. (See Chapter 7).

❏ At the board meeting, a resolution is adopted amending the By-Laws and calling for a special shareholders meeting. (A sample resolution is included in this chapter).

❏ Proper notice (or waivers) of the meeting is provided to all shareholders. (See Chapter 8).

❏ At the shareholders meeting, a resolution is adopted approving the amendment. (A sample resolution is included in this chapter).

❏ The Secretary of the corporation attaches the amendment to the original By-Laws of the corporation.

Directors Resolution Adopting Amendment to Articles of Incorporation and Calling for Special Meeting

Resolution of the Board of Directors of

A meeting of the board of directors of this corporation was duly called and held on _____ , 19 ___. A quorum of the board of directors was present and at the meeting it was decided, by majority vote, that it is advisable to amend the Articles of Incorporation.

Therefore, it is
RESOLVED, that Articles of Incorporation of this corporation be amended in the following manner:

It is further
RESOLVED, that a special meeting of the shareholders of this corporation be held on _____ , 19 ___ at _____ ___ m. at the offices of the corporation located at _____

_____
for the purpose of obtaining shareholder approval of this amendment. The Secretary is directed to give appropriate notice to all shareholders entitled to attend this meeting. The officers of this corporation are hereby authorized to perform all necessary acts to carry out this resolution.

The undersigned, _____ , certifies that he or she is the duly elected Secretary of this corporation and that the above is a true and correct copy of the resolution that was duly adopted at a meeting of the board of directors which was held in accordance with state law and the By-Laws of the corporation on _____ , 19 ___ . I further certify that such resolution is now in full force and effect.

Dated _____

                                                        Seal

_____
Secretary of the corporation

**Shareholders Resolution and Consent Approving Amendment to
Articles of Incorporation**

Resolution and Consent of the Shareholders of

_____

A meeting of the shareholders of this corporation was duly called and held on
_____ , 19 ___. A quorum of the shareholders was present, in
person or by proxy, and at the meeting it was decided, by vote of holders of a
majority of outstanding shares, that the Articles of Incorporation of this
corporation be amended.

Therefore, it is
RESOLVED, that the Articles of Incorporation of this corporation be amended
as follows:

Shareholders holding a majority of outstanding shares of stock in this
corporation have signed this resolution and consent to this Amendment. The
Secretary of this corporation is authorized to prepare and execute an official
Certificate of Amendment to the Articles of Incorporation and file and record
this Certificate as required. The officers of this corporation are authorized to
perform all necessary acts to carry out this resolution.

Shareholder Name   Signature

_____   _____

_____   _____

_____   _____

_____   _____

_____   _____

_____   _____

_____   _____

The undersigned, _____ , certifies that he or she is the duly elected Secretary of this corporation and that the above is a true and correct copy of the resolution that was duly adopted at a meeting of the shareholders which was held in accordance with state law and the By-Laws of the corporation on _____ , 19 ___ . I further certify that such resolution is now in full force and effect.

Dated _____

Seal

_____
Secretary of the corporation

Certificate of Amendment of Articles of Incorporation

Certificate of Amendment of Articles of Incorporation

Pursuant to law and the By-Laws of this corporation, a special meeting of the shareholders of this corporation was held on _____ , 19 ___ , at _____ ___ m. at the offices of the corporation located at

_____ .

At this meeting, it was resolved by a vote of the holders of a majority of shares entitled to vote on this matter that the Articles of Incorporation of this corporation be amended to read as follows:

The undersigned, _____ , certifies that he or she is the duly elected Secretary of this corporation and that the above is a true and correct copy of the Amendment to the Articles of Incorporation that was duly adopted at a meeting of the shareholders which was held in accordance with state law and the By-Laws of the corporation on _____ , 19 ___ .

Dated _____

Seal

_____
Secretary of the corporation

Directors Resolution Amending the By-Laws of the Corporation and Calling for Shareholders Special Meeting

Resolution of the Board of Directors of

_____

A meeting of the board of directors of this corporation was duly called and held on _____ , 19 ___. A quorum of the board of directors was present and at the meeting it was decided, by majority vote, that it is advisable to amend the By-Laws of the corporation:

Therefore, it is
RESOLVED, that the By-Laws of this corporation be amended in the following manner:

It is further
RESOLVED, that a special meeting of the shareholders of this corporation be held on _____ , 19 ___ at _____ ___ m. at the offices of the corporation located at _____

_____
for the purpose of obtaining shareholder approval of this action. The Secretary is directed to give appropriate notice to all shareholders entitled to attend this meeting. The officers of this corporation are hereby authorized to perform all necessary acts to carry out this resolution.

The undersigned, _____ , certifies that he or she is the duly elected Secretary of this corporation and that the above is a true and correct copy of the resolution that was duly adopted at a meeting of the board of directors which was held in accordance with state law and the By-Laws of the corporation on _____ , 19 ___ .
I further certify that such resolution is now in full force and effect.

Dated _____

Seal

_____
Secretary of the corporation

**Shareholders Resolution and Consent Approving Amendment to
By-Laws of the Corporation**

Resolution and Consent of the Shareholders of

_____

A meeting of the shareholders of this corporation was duly called and held on
_____ , 19 ___ . A quorum of the shareholders was present, in
person or by proxy, and at the meeting it was decided, by vote of holders of a
majority of outstanding shares, that the Amendment to the By-Laws of the
corporation which was adopted at a meeting of the board of directors held on
_____ , 19 ___ , be approved.

Therefore, it is
RESOLVED, that the shareholders approve the amendment to the By-Laws of
the corporation adopted by the board of directors of this corporation as
follows:

Shareholders holding a majority of outstanding shares of stock in this corporation have signed this resolution and consent to this Amendment. The officers of this corporation are authorized to perform all necessary acts to carry out this resolution.

Shareholder Name   Signature

_____   _____

_____   _____

_____   _____

_____   _____

_____   _____

_____   _____

_____   _____

The undersigned, _____ , certifies that he or she is the duly elected Secretary of this corporation and that the above is a true and correct copy of the resolution that was duly adopted at a meeting of the Shareholders which was held in accordance with state law and the By-Laws of the corporation on _____ , 19 ___ .
I further certify that such resolution is now in full force and effect.

Dated _____

                                                              Seal

_____
Secretary of the corporation

Chapter 14

Taxation of Corporations

Corporations are a separate entity under the law and as such are subject to taxation at both the state and federal levels. In general, standard non-"S" corporations are subject to federal income tax on the annual profits in many ways similar to the tax on individual income. However, there are significant differences. The most important aspect is the "double" taxation on corporate income if it is distributed to the shareholders in the form of dividends. At the corporate level, corporate net income is subject to tax at the corporate level. Corporate funds which are distributed to officers or directors in the forms of salaries, expense reimbursements, or employee benefits may be used by a corporation as a legitimate business deduction against the income of the corporation. Corporate surplus funds, however, that are paid out to shareholders in the form of dividends on their ownership of stock in the corporation are not allowed to be used as a corporate deduction. Thus, any funds used in this manner have been subject to corporate income tax prior to distribution to the shareholders. The dividends are then also subject to taxation as income to the shareholder and so are subject to a "double" taxation. "S" corporations are taxed similarly to partnerships, with the corporation acting only as a conduit and all of the deductions and income passing to the individual shareholders where they are subject to income tax.

Corporations, however, may be used by businesses in many ways to actually lessen the federal and state income tax burdens. A competent tax professional should be consulted. The federal tax forms which are contained in this chapter are for illustrative purposes only. A brief study of them will provide you with an overview of the method by which corporations are taxed.

Form **1120**		**U.S. Corporation Income Tax Return**			OMB No. 1545-0123
Department of the Treasury Internal Revenue Service		For calendar year 1992 or tax year beginning .... , 1992, ending .... , 19 ... ▶ **Instructions are separate. See page 1 for Paperwork Reduction Act Notice.**			**1992**

A Check if a:	**Use IRS label. Other-wise, please print or type.**	Name		**B** Employer identification number
(1) Consolidated return (attach Form 851) ☐				
(2) Personal holding co. (attach Sch. PH) ☐		Number, street, and room or suite no. (If a P.O. box, see page 6 of instructions.)		**C** Date incorporated
(3) Personal service corp. (as defined in Temporary Regs. sec. 1.441-4T— see instructions) ☐		City or town, state, and ZIP code		**D** Total assets (see Specific Instructions) $

E Check applicable boxes: (1) ☐ Initial return (2) ☐ Final return (3) ☐ Change in address

Income	1a	Gross receipts or sales	⎿_____ **b** Less returns and allowances ⎿_____ **c** Bal ▶	**1c**	
	2	Cost of goods sold (Schedule A, line 8)		**2**	
	3	Gross profit. Subtract line 2 from line 1c		**3**	
	4	Dividends (Schedule C, line 19)		**4**	
	5	Interest		**5**	
	6	Gross rents		**6**	
	7	Gross royalties		**7**	
	8	Capital gain net income (attach Schedule D (Form 1120))		**8**	
	9	Net gain or (loss) from Form 4797, Part II, line 20 (attach Form 4797)		**9**	
	10	Other income (see instructions—attach schedule)		**10**	
	11	**Total income.** Add lines 3 through 10 ▶		**11**	
Deductions (See instructions for limitations on deductions.)	12	Compensation of officers (Schedule E, line 4)		**12**	
	13a	Salaries and wages ⎿_____ **b** Less jobs credit ⎿_____ **c** Balance ▶		**13c**	
	14	Repairs		**14**	
	15	Bad debts		**15**	
	16	Rents		**16**	
	17	Taxes		**17**	
	18	Interest		**18**	
	19	Charitable contributions (**see instructions for 10% limitation**)		**19**	
	20	Depreciation (attach Form 4562)	**20**		
	21	Less depreciation claimed on Schedule A and elsewhere on return	**21a**	**21b**	
	22	Depletion		**22**	
	23	Advertising		**23**	
	24	Pension, profit-sharing, etc., plans		**24**	
	25	Employee benefit programs		**25**	
	26	Other deductions (attach schedule)		**26**	
	27	**Total deductions.** Add lines 12 through 26 ▶		**27**	
	28	Taxable income before net operating loss deduction and special deductions. Subtract line 27 from line 11		**28**	
	29	**Less: a** Net operating loss deduction (see instructions)	**29a**		
		b Special deductions (Schedule C, line 20)	**29b**	**29c**	
Tax and Payments	30	**Taxable income.** Subtract line 29c from line 28		**30**	
	31	Total tax (Schedule J, line 10)		**31**	
	32	Payments: **a** 1991 overpayment credited to 1992	**32a**		
	b	1992 estimated tax payments	**32b**		
	c	Less 1992 refund applied for on Form 4466	**32c** ( ) **d** Bal ▶ **32d**		
	e	Tax deposited with Form 7004	**32e**		
	f	Credit from regulated investment companies (attach Form 2439)	**32f**		
	g	Credit for Federal tax on fuels (attach Form 4136). See instructions	**32g**	**32h**	
	33	Estimated tax penalty (see instructions). Check if Form 2220 is attached ▶ ☐		**33**	
	34	Tax due. If line 32h is smaller than the total of lines 31 and 33, enter amount owed		**34**	
	35	Overpayment. If line 32h is larger than the total of lines 31 and 33, enter amount overpaid		**35**	
	36	Enter amount of line 35 you want: **Credited to 1993 estimated tax** ▶ Refunded ▶		**36**	

Please Sign Here	Under penalties of perjury, I declare that I have examined this return, including accompanying schedules and statements, and to the best of my knowledge and belief, it is true, correct, and complete. Declaration of preparer (other than taxpayer) is based on all information of which preparer has any knowledge.		
	▶ Signature of officer	Date	▶ Title

Paid Preparer's Use Only	Preparer's signature ▶	Date	Check if self-employed ☐	Preparer's social security number
	Firm's name (or yours if self-employed) and address ▶		E.I. No. ▶	
			ZIP code ▶	

Cat. No. 11450Q

Form 1120 (1992)   Page **2**

Schedule A   Cost of Goods Sold (See instructions.)

1	Inventory at beginning of year	**1**
2	Purchases	**2**
3	Cost of labor	**3**
4	Additional section 263A costs (attach schedule)	**4**
5	Other costs (attach schedule)	**5**
6	**Total.** Add lines 1 through 5	**6**
7	Inventory at end of year	**7**
8	**Cost of goods sold.** Subtract line 7 from line 6. Enter here and on page 1, line 2	**8**

9a   Check all methods used for valuing closing inventory:

     (i) ☐ Cost   (ii) ☐ Lower of cost or market as described in Regulations section 1.471-4

     (iii) ☐ Writedown of "subnormal" goods as described in Regulations section 1.471-2(c)

     (iv) ☐ Other (Specify method used and attach explanation.) ▶ ....

   b   Check if the LIFO inventory method was adopted this tax year for any goods (if checked, attach Form 970) . . . . . ▶ ☐

   c   If the LIFO inventory method was used for this tax year, enter percentage (or amounts) of closing inventory computed under LIFO **9c**

   d   Do the rules of section 263A (for property produced or acquired for resale) apply to the corporation? . . . . . ☐ Yes   ☐ No

   e   Was there any change in determining quantities, cost, or valuations between opening and closing inventory? If "Yes," attach explanation . . . . ☐ Yes   ☐ No

Schedule C   Dividends and Special Deductions (See instructions.)

		(a) Dividends received	(b) %	(c) Special deductions: (a) × (b)
1	Dividends from less-than-20%-owned domestic corporations that are subject to the 70% deduction (other than debt-financed stock)		70	
2	Dividends from 20%-or-more-owned domestic corporations that are subject to the 80% deduction (other than debt-financed stock)		80 see instructions	
3	Dividends on debt-financed stock of domestic and foreign corporations (section 246A)			
4	Dividends on certain preferred stock of less-than-20%-owned public utilities . . .		41.176	
5	Dividends on certain preferred stock of 20%-or-more-owned public utilities . . .		47.059	
6	Dividends from less-than-20%-owned foreign corporations and certain FSCs that are subject to the 70% deduction		70	
7	Dividends from 20%-or-more-owned foreign corporations and certain FSCs that are subject to the 80% deduction		80	
8	Dividends from wholly owned foreign subsidiaries subject to the 100% deduction (section 245(b))		100	
9	**Total.** Add lines 1 through 8. See instructions for limitation	/////	/////	
10	Dividends from domestic corporations received by a small business investment company operating under the Small Business Investment Act of 1958		100	
11	Dividends from certain FSCs that are subject to the 100% deduction (section 245(c)(1))		100	
12	Dividends from affiliated group members subject to the 100% deduction (section 243(a)(3))		100	.
13	Other dividends from foreign corporations not included on lines 3, 6, 7, 8, or 11 . .		/////	/////
14	Income from controlled foreign corporations under subpart F (attach Form(s) 5471) .		/////	/////
15	Foreign dividend gross-up (section 78)		/////	/////
16	IC-DISC and former DISC dividends not included on lines 1, 2, or 3 (section 246(d)) .		/////	/////
17	Other dividends		/////	/////
18	Deduction for dividends paid on certain preferred stock of public utilities (see instructions)	/////	/////	
19	**Total dividends.** Add lines 1 through 17. Enter here and on line 4, page 1 . . ▶		/////	
20	**Total deductions.** Add lines 9, 10, 11, 12, and 18. Enter here and on line 29b, page 1 . . . . ▶			

Schedule E   Compensation of Officers (See instructions for line 12, page 1.)

Complete Schedule E only if total receipts (line 1a plus lines 4 through 10 on page 1, Form 1120) are $500,000 or more.

(a) Name of officer	(b) Social security number	(c) Percent of time devoted to business	Percent of corporation stock owned		(f) Amount of compensation
			(d) Common	(e) Preferred	
1		%	%	%	
		%	%	%	
		%	%	%	
		%	%	%	
		%	%	%	

2	Total compensation of officers	
3	Compensation of officers claimed on Schedule A and elsewhere on return	
4	Subtract line 3 from line 2. Enter the result here and on line 12, page 1	

Form 1120 (1992)   Page **3**

Schedule J — Tax Computation (See instructions.)

1   Check if the corporation is a member of a controlled group (see sections 1561 and 1563) . . . . . ▶ ☐
2   If the box on line 1 is checked:
a   Enter the corporation's share of the $50,000 and $25,000 taxable income bracket amounts (in that order):
    (i) $ _____ | | (ii) $ _____ | |
b   Enter the corporation's share of the additional 5% tax (not to exceed $11,750) ▶ $ _____ |
3   Income tax. Check this box if the corporation is a qualified personal service corporation as defined in section
    448(d)(2) (see instructions on page 14) . . . . ▶ ☐ | **3**
4a Foreign tax credit (attach Form 1118) . . . . | **4a**
b   Possessions tax credit (attach Form 5735) . . . . | **4b**
c   Orphan drug credit (attach Form 6765) . . . . | **4c**
d   Credit for fuel produced from a nonconventional source . . . . | **4d**
e   General business credit. Enter here and check which forms are attached:
    ☐ Form 3800 ☐ Form 3468 ☐ Form 5884 ☐ Form 6478
    ☐ Form 6765 ☐ Form 8586 ☐ Form 8830 ☐ Form 8826 . . . . | **4e**
f   Credit for prior year minimum tax (attach Form 8827) . . . . | **4f**
5   **Total credits.** Add lines 4a through 4f . . . . | **5**
6   Subtract line 5 from line 3 . . . . | **6**
7   Personal holding company tax (attach Schedule PH (Form 1120)) . . . . . . | **7**
8   Recapture taxes. Check if from: ☐ Form 4255 ☐ Form 8611 . . . . . . | **8**
9a Alternative minimum tax (attach Form 4626) . . . . | **9a**
b   Environmental tax (attach Form 4626) . . . . | **9b**
10 **Total tax.** Add lines 6 through 9b. Enter here and on line 31, page 1 . . . . . . | **10**

Schedule K — Other Information (See instructions.)

	Yes	No

1   Check method of accounting:
a   ☐ Cash   b   ☐ Accrual
c   ☐ Other (specify) ▶ ....
2   Refer to the list in the instructions and state the principal:
a   Business activity code no. ▶ ....
b   Business activity ▶ ....
c   Product or service ▶ ....
3   Did the corporation at the end of the tax year own, directly or indirectly, 50% or more of the voting stock of a domestic corporation? (For rules of attribution, see section 267(c).) . . . .
    If "Yes," attach a schedule showing: (a) name and identifying number; (b) percentage owned; and (c) taxable income or (loss) before NOL and special deductions of such corporation for the tax year ending with or within your tax year.
4   Did any individual, partnership, corporation, estate, or trust at the end of the tax year own, directly or indirectly, 50% or more of the corporation's voting stock? (For rules of attribution, see section 267(c).) If "Yes," complete a, b, and c below. . . . .
a   Is the corporation a subsidiary in an affiliated group or a parent-subsidiary controlled group? . . . . . .
b   Enter the name and identifying number of the parent corporation or other entity with 50% or more ownership ▶ ....
    ....
c   Enter percentage owned ▶...............................
5   During this tax year, did the corporation pay dividends (other than stock dividends and distributions in exchange for stock) in excess of the corporation's current and accumulated earnings and profits? (See secs. 301 and 316.) . . . .
    If "Yes," file Form 5452. If this is a consolidated return, answer here for the parent corporation and on **Form 851,** Affiliations Schedule, for each subsidiary.

6   Was the corporation a U.S. shareholder of any controlled foreign corporation? (See sections 951 and 957.) . . .
    If "Yes," attach Form 5471 for each such corporation. Enter number of Forms 5471 attached ▶.................
7   At any time during the 1992 calendar year, did the corporation have an interest in or a signature or other authority over a financial account in a foreign country (such as a bank account, securities account, or other financial account)? . . . .
    If "Yes," the corporation may have to file Form TD F 90-22.1.
    If "Yes," enter name of foreign country ▶ ....
8   Was the corporation the grantor of, or transferor to, a foreign trust that existed during the current tax year, whether or not the corporation has any beneficial interest in it? . . .
    If "Yes," the corporation may have to file Forms 926, 3520, or 3520-A.
9   Did one foreign person at any time during the tax year own, directly or indirectly, at least 25% of: (a) the total voting power of all classes of stock of the corporation entitled to vote, or (b) the total value of all classes of stock of the corporation? . . . .
    If "Yes," see page 17 of instructions and
a   Enter percentage owned ▶..............................
b   Enter owner's country ▶...................................
c   The corporation may have to file Form 5472. (See page 18 for penalties that may apply.) Enter number of Forms 5472 attached ▶ ....
10 Check this box if the corporation issued publicly offered debt instruments with original issue discount . ▶ ☐
    If so, the corporation may have to file Form 8281.
11 Enter the amount of tax-exempt interest received or accrued during the tax year ▶ $ _____ |
12 If there were 35 or fewer shareholders at the end of the tax year, enter the number ▶ ....
13 If the corporation has an NOL for the tax year and is electing under sec. 172(b)(3) to forego the carryback period, check here . . . . ▶ ☐

Form 1120 (1992) Page **4**

Schedule L	Balance Sheets	Beginning of tax year		End of tax year	
		(a)	(b)	(c)	(d)
	Assets				
1	Cash				
2a	Trade notes and accounts receivable				
b	Less allowance for bad debts	( )		( )	
3	Inventories				
4	U.S. government obligations				
5	Tax-exempt securities (see instructions)				
6	Other current assets (attach schedule)				
7	Loans to stockholders				
8	Mortgage and real estate loans				
9	Other investments (attach schedule)				
10a	Buildings and other depreciable assets				
b	Less accumulated depreciation	( )		( )	
11a	Depletable assets				
b	Less accumulated depletion	( )		( )	
12	Land (net of any amortization)				
13a	Intangible assets (amortizable only)				
b	Less accumulated amortization	( )		( )	
14	Other assets (attach schedule)				
15	Total assets				
	Liabilities and Stockholders' Equity				
16	Accounts payable				
17	Mortgages, notes, bonds payable in less than 1 year				
18	Other current liabilities (attach schedule)				
19	Loans from stockholders				
20	Mortgages, notes, bonds payable in 1 year or more				
21	Other liabilities (attach schedule)				
22	Capital stock: a Preferred stock				
	b Common stock				
23	Paid-in or capital surplus				
24	Retained earnings—Appropriated (attach schedule)				
25	Retained earnings—Unappropriated				
26	Less cost of treasury stock		( )		( )
27	Total liabilities and stockholders' equity				

Note: *You are not required to complete Schedules M-1 and M-2 below if the total assets on line 15, column (d) of Schedule L are less than $25,000.*

Schedule M-1	Reconciliation of Income (Loss) per Books With Income per Return (See instructions.)

1	Net income (loss) per books		7	Income recorded on books this year not included on this return (itemize):	
2	Federal income tax			Tax-exempt interest $	
3	Excess of capital losses over capital gains			....	
4	Income subject to tax not recorded on books this year (itemize):			....	
	....		8	Deductions on this return not charged against book income this year (itemize):	
5	Expenses recorded on books this year not deducted on this return (itemize):		a	Depreciation . . . . $	
a	Depreciation . . . . $		b	Contributions carryover $	
b	Contributions carryover $			....	
c	Travel and entertainment $			....	
	....		9	Add lines 7 and 8	
6	Add lines 1 through 5		10	Income (line 28, page 1)—line 6 less line 9	

Schedule M-2	Analysis of Unappropriated Retained Earnings per Books (Line 25, Schedule L)

1	Balance at beginning of year		5	Distributions: a Cash	
2	Net income (loss) per books			b Stock	
3	Other increases (itemize):			c Property	
	....		6	Other decreases (itemize):	
	....			....	
	....		7	Add lines 5 and 6	
4	Add lines 1, 2, and 3		8	Balance at end of year (line 4 less line 7)	

Form **1120-A**	**U.S. Corporation Short-Form Income Tax Return**	OMB No. 1545-0890
Department of the Treasury Internal Revenue Service	See separate instructions to make sure the corporation qualifies to file Form 1120-A. For calendar year 1992 or tax year beginning ...., 1992, ending.............., 19.....	**1992**

A Check this box if corp. is a personal service corp. (as defined in Temporary Regs. section 1.441-4T—see instructions) ▶ ☐

Use IRS label. Other-wise, please print or type.	Name	**B** Employer identification number
	Number, street, and room or suite no. (If a P.O. box, see page 6 of instructions.)	**C** Date incorporated
	City or town, state, and ZIP code	**D** Total assets (see Specific Instructions) $

E Check applicable boxes: **(1)** ☐ Initial return **(2)** ☐ Change in address
F Check method of accounting: **(1)** ☐ Cash **(2)** ☐ Accrual **(3)** ☐ Other (specify) . . ▶

Income

1a Gross receipts or sales	**b** Less returns and allowances	**c** Balance ▶ 1c
2 Cost of goods sold (see instructions)		2
3 Gross profit. Subtract line 2 from line 1c		3
4 Domestic corporation dividends subject to the 70% deduction		4
5 Interest		5
6 Gross rents		6
7 Gross royalties		7
8 Capital gain net income (attach Schedule D (Form 1120))		8
9 Net gain or (loss) from Form 4797, Part II, line 20 (attach Form 4797)		9
10 Other income (see instructions)		10
11 Total income. Add lines 3 through 10 ▶		11

Deductions (See instructions for limitations on deductions.)

12 Compensation of officers (see instructions)		12
13a Salaries and wages	**b** Less jobs credit	**c** Balance ▶ 13c
14 Repairs		14
15 Bad debts		15
16 Rents		16
17 Taxes		17
18 Interest		18
19 Charitable contributions (see instructions for 10% limitation)		19
20 Depreciation (attach Form 4562)	20	
21 Less depreciation claimed elsewhere on return	21a	21b
22 Other deductions (attach schedule)		22
23 Total deductions. Add lines 12 through 22 ▶		23
24 Taxable income before net operating loss deduction and special deductions. Subtract line 23 from line 11		24
25 Less: a Net operating loss deduction (see instructions)	25a	
b Special deductions (see instructions)	25b	25c

Tax and Payments

26 Taxable income. Subtract line 25c from line 24		26
27 Total tax (from page 2, Part I, line 7)		27
28 Payments:		
a 1991 overpayment credited to 1992	28a	
b 1992 estimated tax payments	28b	
c Less 1992 refund applied for on Form 4466	28c ( ) Bal ▶ 28d	
e Tax deposited with Form 7004	28e	
f Credit from regulated investment companies (attach Form 2439)	28f	
g Credit for Federal tax on fuels (attach Form 4136). See instructions	28g	
h Total payments. Add lines 28d through 28g		28h
29 Estimated tax penalty (see instructions). Check if Form 2220 is attached ▶ ☐		29
30 Tax due. If line 28h is smaller than the total of lines 27 and 29, enter amount owed		30
31 Overpayment. If line 28h is larger than the total of lines 27 and 29, enter amount overpaid		31
32 Enter amount of line 31 you want: Credited to 1993 estimated tax ▶ Refunded ▶		32

Please Sign Here

Under penalties of perjury, I declare that I have examined this return, including accompanying schedules and statements, and to the best of my knowledge and belief, it is true, correct, and complete. Declaration of preparer (other than taxpayer) is based on all information of which preparer has any knowledge.

▶ Signature of officer / Date / Title

Paid Preparer's Use Only

Preparer's signature ▶	Date	Check if self-employed ▶ ☐	Preparer's social security number
Firm's name (or yours if self-employed) and address ▶		E.I. No. ▶	ZIP code ▶

For Paperwork Reduction Act Notice, see page 1 of the instructions.   Cat. No. 11456E   Form **1120-A** (1992)

Form 1120-A (1992)   Page **2**

Part I — Tax Computation (See instructions.)

1	Income tax. Check this box if the corporation is a qualified personal service corporation as defined in section 448(d)(2) (see instructions on page 14) . . . . ▶ ☐	1
2a	General business credit. Check if from: ☐ Form 3800 ☐ Form 3468 ☐ Form 5884 ☐ Form 6478 ☐ Form 6765 ☐ Form 8586 ☐ Form 8830 ☐ Form 8826 **2a**	
b	Credit for prior year minimum tax (attach Form 8827) **2b**	
3	Total credits. Add lines 2a and 2b	3
4	Subtract line 3 from line 1	4
5	Recapture taxes. Check if from: ☐ Form 4255 ☐ Form 8611	5
6	Alternative minimum tax (attach Form 4626)	6
7	Total tax. Add lines 4 through 6. Enter here and on line 27, page 1	7

Part II — Other Information (See instructions.)

1 Refer to the list in the instructions and state the principal:

     a   Business activity code no. ▶ ....

     b   Business activity ▶ ....

     c   Product or service ▶ ....

2 Did any individual, partnership, estate, or trust at the end of the tax year own, directly or indirectly, 50% or more of the corporation's voting stock? (For rules of attribution, see section 267(c).) . . . . ☐ Yes ☐ No

If "Yes," attach a schedule showing name and identifying number.

3 Enter the amount of tax-exempt interest received or accrued during the tax year . . . ▶ |$

4 Enter amount of cash distributions and the book value of property (other than cash) distributions made in this tax year . . . . ▶ |$

5a If an amount is entered on line 2, page 1, see the worksheet on page 12 for amounts to enter below:

     (1) Purchases . . . . . .

     (2) Additional sec. 263A costs (see instructions—attach schedule) .

     (3) Other costs (attach schedule) .

b Do the rules of section 263A (for property produced or acquired for resale) apply to the corporation? . . . . . . ☐ Yes ☐ No

6 At any time during the 1992 calendar year, did the corporation have an interest in or a signature or other authority over a financial account in a foreign country (such as a bank account, securities account, or other financial account)? If "Yes," the corporation may have to file Form TD F 90-22.1 . . . . ☐ Yes ☐ No

If "Yes," enter the name of the foreign country ▶ ....

Part III — Balance Sheets

		(a) Beginning of tax year		(b) End of tax year	
Assets	1 Cash				
	2a Trade notes and accounts receivable				
	b Less allowance for bad debts	(	)	(	)
	3 Inventories				
	4 U.S. government obligations				
	5 Tax-exempt securities (see instructions)				
	6 Other current assets (attach schedule)				
	7 Loans to stockholders				
	8 Mortgage and real estate loans				
	9a Depreciable, depletable, and intangible assets . . .				
	b Less accumulated depreciation, depletion, and amortization	(	)	(	)
	10 Land (net of any amortization)				
	11 Other assets (attach schedule)				
	12 Total assets				
Liabilities and Stockholders' Equity	13 Accounts payable				
	14 Other current liabilities (attach schedule)				
	15 Loans from stockholders				
	16 Mortgages, notes, bonds payable				
	17 Other liabilities (attach schedule)				
	18 Capital stock (preferred and common stock) . . .				
	19 Paid-in or capital surplus				
	20 Retained earnings				
	21 Less cost of treasury stock	(	)	(	)
	22 Total liabilities and stockholders' equity				

Part IV — Reconciliation of Income (Loss) per Books With Income per Return *(You are not required to complete Part IV if the total assets on line 12, column (b) of Part III are less than $25,000.)*

1	Net income (loss) per books		6	Income recorded on books this year not included on this return (itemize)	
2	Federal income tax				
3	Excess of capital losses over capital gains . .		7	Deductions on this return not charged against book income this year (itemize)	
4	Income subject to tax not recorded on books this year (itemize)				
5	Expenses recorded on books this year not deducted on this return (itemize)		8	Income (line 24, page 1). Enter the sum of lines 1 through 5 less the sum of lines 6 and 7 . .	

Form **1120S**	**U.S. Income Tax Return for an S Corporation**	OMB No. 1545-0130

Department of the Treasury
Internal Revenue Service

For calendar year 1992, or tax year beginning ...., 1992, and ending ...., 19 .....
▶ See separate instructions.

1992

A Date of election as an S corporation

Use IRS label. Otherwise, please print or type.

Name

C Employer identification number

B Business code no. (see Specific Instructions)

Number, street, and room or suite no. (If a P.O. box, see page 8 of the instructions.)

D Date incorporated

City or town, state, and ZIP code

E Total assets (see Specific Instructions)
$

F Check applicable boxes: (1) ☐ Initial return (2) ☐ Final return (3) ☐ Change in address (4) ☐ Amended return
G Check this box if this S corporation is subject to the consolidated audit procedures of sections 6241 through 6245 (see instructions before checking this box) . ▶ ☐
H Enter number of shareholders in the corporation at end of the tax year . . . . . ▶

Caution: *Include only trade or business income and expenses on lines 1a through 21. See the instructions for more information.*

Income

1a Gross receipts or sales [____] b Less returns and allowances [____] c Bal ▶ **1c**
2 Cost of goods sold (Schedule A, line 8) . . . **2**
3 Gross profit. Subtract line 2 from line 1c . . **3**
4 Net gain (loss) from Form 4797, Part II, line 20 *(attach Form 4797)* **4**
5 Other income (loss) (see instructions) *(attach schedule)* **5**
6 Total income (loss). Combine lines 3 through 5 . . . ▶ **6**

Deductions (See instructions for limitations.)

7 Compensation of officers . . . **7**
8a Salaries and wages [____] b Less jobs credit [____] c Bal ▶ **8c**
9 Repairs . . . **9**
10 Bad debts . . . **10**
11 Rents . . . **11**
12 Taxes . . . **12**
13 Interest . . . **13**
14a Depreciation (see instructions) . . . **14a**
  b Depreciation claimed on Schedule A and elsewhere on return . . . **14b**
  c Subtract line 14b from line 14a . . . **14c**
15 Depletion (Do not deduct oil and gas depletion.) . . . **15**
16 Advertising . . . **16**
17 Pension, profit-sharing, etc., plans . . . **17**
18 Employee benefit programs . . . **18**
19 Other deductions (see instructions) *(attach schedule)* . . . **19**
20 Total deductions. Add lines 7 through 19 . . . ▶ **20**
21 Ordinary income (loss) from trade or business activities. Subtract line 20 from line 6 . . . **21**

Tax and Payments

22 Tax:
  a Excess net passive income tax *(attach schedule)* . . . **22a**
  b Tax from Schedule D (Form 1120S) . . . **22b**
  c Add lines 22a and 22b (see instructions for additional taxes) . . . **22c**
23 Payments:
  a 1992 estimated tax payments . . . **23a**
  b Tax deposited with Form 7004 . . . **23b**
  c Credit for Federal tax paid on fuels *(attach Form 4136)* . . . **23c**
  d Add lines 23a through 23c . . . **23d**
24 Estimated tax penalty (see instructions). Check if Form 2220 is attached. . . . ▶☐ **24**
25 Tax due. If the total of lines 22c and 24 is larger than line 23d, enter amount owed. See instructions for depositary method of payment . . . ▶ **25**
26 Overpayment. If line 23d is larger than the total of lines 22c and 24, enter amount overpaid ▶ **26**
27 Enter amount of line 26 you want: **Credited to 1993 estimated tax** ▶ [____] **Refunded** ▶ **27**

Please Sign Here

Under penalties of perjury, I declare that I have examined this return, including accompanying schedules and statements, and to the best of my knowledge and belief, it is true, correct, and complete. Declaration of preparer (other than taxpayer) is based on all information of which preparer has any knowledge.

▶ _____ Signature of officer Date ▶ _____ Title

Paid Preparer's Use Only

Preparer's signature ▶ | Date | Check if self-employed ▶ ☐ | Preparer's social security number
Firm's name (or yours if self-employed) and address ▶ | | E.I. No. ▶ | ZIP code ▶

For Paperwork Reduction Act Notice, see page 1 of separate instructions. Cat. No. 11510H Form **1120S** (1992)

Form 1120S (1992)   Page **2**

Schedule A   Cost of Goods Sold (See instructions.)

1	Inventory at beginning of year	1	
2	Purchases	2	
3	Cost of labor	3	
4	Additional section 263A costs (see instructions) *(attach schedule)*	4	
5	Other costs *(attach schedule)*	5	
6	**Total.** Add lines 1 through 5	6	
7	Inventory at end of year	7	
8	**Cost of goods sold.** Subtract line 7 from line 6. Enter here and on page 1, line 2	8	

9a Check all methods used for valuing closing inventory:
  (i) ☐ Cost
  (ii) ☐ Lower of cost or market as described in Regulations section 1.471-4
  (iii) ☐ Writedown of "subnormal" goods as described in Regulations section 1.471-2(c)
  (iv) ☐ Other (specify method used and attach explanation) ▶ ....
  b Check if the LIFO inventory method was adopted this tax year for any goods *(if checked, attach Form 970)*. ▶ ☐
  c If the LIFO inventory method was used for this tax year, enter percentage (or amounts) of closing inventory computed under LIFO   9c
  d Do the rules of section 263A (for property produced or acquired for resale) apply to the corporation? ☐ Yes ☐ No
  e Was there any change in determining quantities, cost, or valuations between opening and closing inventory? ☐ Yes ☐ No
  If "Yes," attach explanation.

Schedule B   Other Information

		Yes	No
1	Check method of accounting: (a) ☐ Cash (b) ☐ Accrual (c) ☐ Other (specify) ▶		
2	Refer to the list in the instructions and state the corporation's principal: (a) Business activity ▶ .... (b) Product or service ▶		
3	Did the corporation at the end of the tax year own, directly or indirectly, 50% or more of the voting stock of a domestic corporation? (For rules of attribution, see section 267(c).) If "Yes," attach a schedule showing: (a) name, address, and employer identification number and (b) percentage owned.		
4	Was the corporation a member of a controlled group subject to the provisions of section 1561?		
5	At any time during calendar year 1992, did the corporation have an interest in or a signature or other authority over a financial account in a foreign country (such as a bank account, securities account, or other financial account)? (See instructions for exceptions and filing requirements for form TD F 90-22.1.) If "Yes," enter the name of the foreign country ▶		
6	Was the corporation the grantor of, or transferor to, a foreign trust that existed during the current tax year, whether or not the corporation has any beneficial interest in it? If "Yes," the corporation may have to file Forms 3520, 3520-A, or 926.		
7	Check this box if the corporation has filed or is required to file **Form 8264,** Application for Registration of a Tax Shelter. ▶ ☐		
8	Check this box if the corporation issued publicly offered debt instruments with original issue discount ▶ ☐ If so, the corporation may have to file **Form 8281,** Information Return for Publicly Offered Original Issue Discount Instruments.		
9	If the corporation: (a) filed its election to be an S corporation after 1986, (b) was a C corporation before it elected to be an S corporation or the corporation acquired an asset with a basis determined by reference to its basis (or the basis of any other property) in the hands of a C corporation, and (c) has net unrealized built-in gain (defined in section 1374(d)(1)) in excess of the net recognized built-in gain from prior years, enter the net unrealized built-in gain reduced by net recognized built-in gain from prior years (see instructions) ▶ $		
10	Check this box if the corporation had subchapter C earnings and profits at the close of the tax year (see instructions) ▶ ☐		
11	Was this corporation in operation at the end of 1992?		
12	How many months in 1992 was this corporation in operation?		

Designation of Tax Matters Person (See instructions.)

Enter below the shareholder designated as the tax matters person (TMP) for the tax year of this return:

Name of designated TMP ▶ _____   Identifying number of TMP ▶ _____

Address of designated TMP ▶ _____

Form 1120S (1992)   Page **3**

Schedule K — Shareholders' Shares of Income, Credits, Deductions, etc.

	(a) Pro rata share items		(b) Total amount	
Income (Loss)	**1** Ordinary income (loss) from trade or business activities (page 1, line 21)	**1**		
	2 Net income (loss) from rental real estate activities *(attach Form 8825)*	**2**		
	3a Gross income from other rental activities **3a**			
	b Expenses from other rental activities *(attach schedule)*. **3b**			
	c Net income (loss) from other rental activities. Subtract line 3b from line 3a	**3c**		
	4 Portfolio income (loss):			
	a Interest income	**4a**		
	b Dividend income.	**4b**		
	c Royalty income	**4c**		
	d Net short-term capital gain (loss) *(attach Schedule D (Form 1120S))*	**4d**		
	e Net long-term capital gain (loss) *(attach Schedule D (Form 1120S))*.	**4e**		
	f Other portfolio income (loss) *(attach schedule)*	**4f**		
	5 Net gain (loss) under section 1231 (other than due to casualty or theft) *(attach Form 4797)*	**5**		
	6 Other income (loss) *(attach schedule)*	**6**		
Deductions	**7** Charitable contributions (see instructions) *(attach schedule)*	**7**		
	8 Section 179 expense deduction *(attach Form 4562)*.	**8**		
	9 Deductions related to portfolio income (loss) (see instructions) (itemize)	**9**		
	10 Other deductions *(attach schedule)*.	**10**		
Investment Interest	**11a** Interest expense on investment debts	**11a**		
	b (1) Investment income included on lines 4a through 4f above	**11b(1)**		
	(2) Investment expenses included on line 9 above	**11b(2)**		
Credits	**12a** Credit for alcohol used as a fuel *(attach Form 6478)*	**12a**		
	b Low-income housing credit (see instructions):			
	(1) From partnerships to which section 42(j)(5) applies for property placed in service before 1990	**12b(1)**		
	(2) Other than on line 12b(1) for property placed in service before 1990.	**12b(2)**		
	(3) From partnerships to which section 42(j)(5) applies for property placed in service after 1989	**12b(3)**		
	(4) Other than on line 12b(3) for property placed in service after 1989	**12b(4)**		
	c Qualified rehabilitation expenditures related to rental real estate activities *(attach Form 3468)*.	**12c**		
	d Credits (other than credits shown on lines 12b and 12c) related to rental real estate activities (see instructions).	**12d**		
	e Credits related to other rental activities (see instructions).	**12e**		
	13 Other credits (see instructions)	**13**		
Adjustments and Tax Preference Items	**14a** Depreciation adjustment on property placed in service after 1986	**14a**		
	b Adjusted gain or loss	**14b**		
	c Depletion (other than oil and gas)	**14c**		
	d (1) Gross income from oil, gas, or geothermal properties	**14d(1)**		
	(2) Deductions allocable to oil, gas, or geothermal properties	**14d(2)**		
	e Other adjustments and tax preference items *(attach schedule)*	**14e**		
Foreign Taxes	**15a** Type of income ▶			
	b Name of foreign country or U.S. possession ▶			
	c Total gross income from sources outside the United States *(attach schedule)*	**15c**		
	d Total applicable deductions and losses *(attach schedule)*.	**15d**		
	e Total foreign taxes (check one): ▶ ☐ Paid ☐ Accrued	**15e**		
	f Reduction in taxes available for credit *(attach schedule)*	**15f**		
	g Other foreign tax information *(attach schedule)*	**15g**		
Other	**16a** Total expenditures to which a section 59(e) election may apply	**16a**		
	b Type of expenditures ▶			
	17 Tax-exempt interest income	**17**		
	18 Other tax-exempt income.	**18**		
	19 Nondeductible expenses	**19**		
	20 Total property distributions (including cash) other than dividends reported on line 22 below	**20**		
	21 Other items and amounts required to be reported separately to shareholders (see instructions) *(attach schedule)*			
	22 Total dividend distributions paid from accumulated earnings and profits	**22**		
	23 Income (loss). (Required only if Schedule M-1 must be completed.) Combine lines 1 through 6 in column (b). From the result, subtract the sum of lines 7 through 11a, 15e, and 16a.	**23**		

Form 1120S (1992) Page **4**

Schedule L	Balance Sheets	Beginning of tax year		End of tax year	
	Assets	(a)	(b)	(c)	(d)
1	Cash				
2a	Trade notes and accounts receivable				
b	Less allowance for bad debts				
3	Inventories				
4	U.S. Government obligations				
5	Tax-exempt securities				
6	Other current assets (attach schedule)				
7	Loans to shareholders				
8	Mortgage and real estate loans				
9	Other investments (attach schedule)				
10a	Buildings and other depreciable assets				
b	Less accumulated depreciation				
11a	Depletable assets				
b	Less accumulated depletion				
12	Land (net of any amortization)				
13a	Intangible assets (amortizable only)				
b	Less accumulated amortization				
14	Other assets (attach schedule)				
15	Total assets				
	Liabilities and Shareholders' Equity				
16	Accounts payable				
17	Mortgages, notes, bonds payable in less than 1 year				
18	Other current liabilities (attach schedule)				
19	Loans from shareholders				
20	Mortgages, notes, bonds payable in 1 year or more				
21	Other liabilities (attach schedule)				
22	Capital stock				
23	Paid-in or capital surplus				
24	Retained earnings				
25	Less cost of treasury stock		( )		( )
26	Total liabilities and shareholders' equity				

Schedule M-1 Reconciliation of Income (Loss) per Books With Income (Loss) per Return (You are not required to complete this schedule if the total assets on line 15, column (d), of Schedule L are less than $25,000.)

1 Net income (loss) per books
2 Income included on Schedule K, lines 1 through 6, not recorded on books this year (itemize): ....
3 Expenses recorded on books this year not included on Schedule K, lines 1 through 11a, 15e, and 16a (itemize):
a Depreciation $ ....
b Travel and entertainment $ ....
4 Add lines 1 through 3

5 Income recorded on books this year not included on Schedule K, lines 1 through 6 (itemize):
a Tax-exempt interest $ ....
6 Deductions included on Schedule K, lines 1 through 11a, 15e, and 16a, not charged against book income this year (itemize):
a Depreciation $ ....
7 Add lines 5 and 6
8 Income (loss) (Schedule K, line 23). Line 4 less line 7

Schedule M-2 Analysis of Accumulated Adjustments Account, Other Adjustments Account, and Shareholders' Undistributed Taxable Income Previously Taxed (See instructions.)

		(a) Accumulated adjustments account	(b) Other adjustments account	(c) Shareholders' undistributed taxable income previously taxed
1	Balance at beginning of tax year			
2	Ordinary income from page 1, line 21			
3	Other additions			
4	Loss from page 1, line 21	( )		
5	Other reductions	( )	( )	
6	Combine lines 1 through 5			
7	Distributions other than dividend distributions			
8	Balance at end of tax year. Subtract line 7 from line 6			

Chapter 15

Dissolving a Corporation

The act of dissolving a corporation is generally based on a decision to stop the active business activities of the corporation. Dissolutions can be voluntarily adopted by the shareholders and directors of a corporation. Dissolutions can also be involuntary. Involuntary dissolution may be caused by the revocation of the corporate Articles of Incorporation by the state for failure to file the proper reports, pay the proper taxes, or maintain a registered office and agent. Bankruptcy of the corporation can also lead to involuntary dissolution of the business.

Dissolution, as a major event in the life of a corporation, requires both shareholder and director approval. The action is generally initiated by the board of directors by an authorization and recommendation for dissolution, a proposal of a plan for dissolution, and a call for a special shareholders meeting. The shareholders must then approve the dissolution plan by majority vote and order the Secretary of the corporation to prepare and file the necessary Articles of Dissolution with the state corporation department. Upon acceptance of this document by the state, the corporation is officially dissolved. However, a corporation is allowed to continue to transact business for a short period after dissolution in order to wind up its affairs, liquidate its assets, and distribute proportionate shares of the corporate funds or property to its shareholders. During the period after the filing for dissolution, however, a corporation can not transact business which is not directed towards winding up its affairs, such as entering into long-term contracts. A Dissolution Checklist follows showing the steps necessary for a voluntary dissolution of a corporation. Please contact your state corporation department or an attorney for details of state requirements in your jurisdiction.

Dissolution Checklist

❏ The board of directors call for a special meeting regarding dissolution.

❏ Proper notice of the meeting (or waiver) is provided to all of the directors. (See Chapter 7).

❏ At the meeting, the board of directors adopts a resolution approving the dissolution of the corporation and calling for a special shareholders meeting. (A sample resolution is provided in this chapter).

❏ Proper notice of the meeting (or waiver) is provided to all of the shareholders of record. (See Chapter 8).

❏ At the shareholders meeting, a majority of the shareholders entitled to vote adopt a resolution approving the directors plan for dissolution and ordering the Secretary of the corporation to prepare and file Articles of Dissolution with the appropriate state corporation department. (A sample resolution is provided in this chapter).

❏ The Secretary prepares and files the Articles of Dissolution. (A sample Articles of Dissolution is provided in this chapter).

Directors Resolution Approving Dissolution and Calling for Special Meeting

Resolution of the
Board of Directors of

_____

A meeting of the board of directors of this corporation was duly called and held on _____ , 19 ___. A quorum of the board of directors was present and at the meeting it was decided, by majority vote, that it is advisable to dissolve this corporation

Therefore, it is
RESOLVED, that this corporation be dissolved as soon as is reasonably feasible, based upon the following plan for dissolution:

It is further
RESOLVED, that a special meeting of the shareholders of this corporation be held on _____ , 19 ___ at _____ ___ m. at the offices of the corporation located at _____

_____

for the purpose of obtaining shareholder approval of this recommendation for dissolution. The Secretary is directed to give appropriate notice to all shareholders entitled to attend this meeting. The officers of this corporation are hereby authorized to perform all necessary acts to carry out this resolution.

The undersigned, _____ , certifies that he or she is the duly elected Secretary of this corporation and that the above is a true and correct copy of the resolution that was duly adopted at a meeting of the board of directors which was held in accordance with state law and the By-Laws of the corporation on _____ , 19 ___ . I further certify that such resolution is now in full force and effect.

Dated _____

Seal

_____
Secretary of the corporation

Shareholders Resolution and Consent Approving Dissolution

Resolution and Consent of the Shareholders of

_____

A meeting of the shareholders of this corporation was duly called and held on _____ , 19 ___. A quorum of the shareholders was present, in person or by proxy, and at the meeting it was decided, by vote of holders of a majority of outstanding shares, that the it is in the best interests of this corporation that the corporation be dissolved.

Therefore, it is
RESOLVED, that this corporation be dissolved under the provisions of the following plan for dissolution:

Shareholders holding a majority of outstanding shares of stock in this corporation have signed this resolution and consent to this resolution. The Secretary of this corporation is authorized to prepare and execute official Articles of Dissolution and file and record these Articles of Dissolution as required. The officers of this corporation are authorized to perform all necessary acts to carry out this resolution.

Shareholder Name   Signature

_____   _____

_____   _____

_____   _____

_____   _____

_____   _____

_____   _____

_____   _____

The undersigned, _____ , certifies that he or she is the duly elected Secretary of this corporation and that the above is a true and correct copy of the resolution that was duly adopted at a meeting of the shareholders which was held in accordance with state law and the By-Laws of the corporation on _____ , 19 ___ . I further certify that such resolution is now in full force and effect.

Dated _____

Seal

_____
Secretary of the corporation

211

Articles of Dissolution

Articles of Dissolution of

_____

The undersigned persons, being the holders of all of the issued and outstanding share of stock of this corporation, and being all of the shareholders which are entitled to vote on the dissolution of this corporation in accordance with the By-Laws of this corporation and with the laws of the State of _____ ; do adopt these Articles of Dissolution:

Article 1. The name of the corporation is _____ .

Article 2. The Articles of Incorporation for this corporation were filed with the State of _____ on _____ , 19 ___ .

Article 3. The names and addresses of the directors of this corporation are:

Name   Address

_____   _____

_____   _____

_____   _____

Article 4. The names and addresses of the officers of this corporation are:

Name   Address

_____   _____
President

_____   _____
Vice-President

_____   _____
Secretary

_____   _____
Treasurer

Article 5. The corporation has only one class of stock.

Article 6. A special meeting of the directors of this corporation was held on _____ , 19 ____. At this meeting, a majority of the directors adopted a resolution electing to dissolve this corporation.

Article 7. A special meeting of the shareholders of this corporation was held on _____ , 19 ____. At this meeting, holders of a majority of the shares entitled to vote on the issue of dissolution adopted a resolution electing to dissolve this corporation.

Article 8. This corporation elects to dissolve.

I certify that all of the facts stated in these Articles of Dissolution are true and correct and are made for the purpose of dissolving a business corporation under the laws of the State of _____ .

Dated _____

_____
Secretary of the corporation

Shareholder Name   Signature

_____   _____

_____   _____

_____   _____

_____   _____

_____   _____

_____   _____

Appendix of State Incorporation Information

On the following pages are found state listings containing relevant information regarding incorporation. You are advised to check your states listing carefully to determine the particular requirements for incorporation in your jurisdiction. Virtually every state has some differing conditions for incorporation. You are also advised to write to the state corporation department for information on incorporation. They will provide you with any necessary updates on the information contained in this Appendix. Following is an explanation of the listings:

State law reference: Should you wish to research the law in your state, this lists the name and chapter of the state statute in which the corporation laws are found in each state.

Title of corporate filing: This listing specifies the name of the document which is filed with the state for incorporation. In this book, it has always been referred to as "Articles of Incorporation". A number of states, however, use different titles. Please substitute the correct title on your form before filing it.

Filing fees: The cost of filing the Articles of Incorporation with the state. In some states, the fee is variable based on the amount of capital stock of the corporation.

Other fees: This listing details any other fees which are due at the time of filing or soon thereafter. These can be franchise taxes, organizational taxes, or various other required fees.

Name reservation: All states allow a proposed corporation to register its corporate name prior to filing in order to reserve the corporation's name. The cost and time limits, however, differ widely.

Name requirements: This listing specifies the corporate designation which is required in each state. Most states allow "corporation", "incorporated", "limited", "company" or some abbreviation of these. However, many states have variations on what designation is allowed.

Incorporator requirements: This designates how many incorporators are required. One is sufficient in most states. This listing also tells whether the incorporators must be persons, or if they can be business entities.

Corporate purpose requirements: This specifies what must be put in the Articles of Incorporation regarding the business purpose of the enterprise. If the listing states: General "all-purpose" clause; you should include the clause which is found in the sample "purpose and powers" clause in Chapter 5. If a specific business purpose is required, replace this general clause with a statement of the actual business purpose.

Director requirements: Most states allow a corporation to have only one director, who may be a non-resident. However, several states have a requirement that the corporation have three directors, unless there are fewer than three shareholders. In these states, if there are less than three shareholders, the number of directors can equal the number of shareholders (ie. a one shareholder corporation can have one director).

Paid-in-capital requirements: Most states have no requirement for paid-in-capital. A few, however, require that the corporation have $1,000 in actual paid-in-capital prior to commencing business. These states also require that you state this fact in the Articles of Incorporation.

Publication requirements: A few states require that you publish either your intention to incorporate or the actual fact of incorporation in a newspaper. Most states, however, do not have this requirement.

Other provisions: This listing details any other special incorporation requirements of each state. These range from additional items which must be added to the Articles of Incorporation to the use of different terminology. Check this listing carefully to determine the situation in your state.

Alabama

Address of State Corporation Department:
    Alabama Secretary of State
    Alabama Business Division
    Post Office Box 5616
    Montgomery AL 36103
State law reference: Alabama Business Corporation Act.
Title of corporate filing: Articles of Incorporation.
Filing fees: $40.00 to Secretary of State.
Other fees: Tax: $10 per $1000 of stock (minimum $50); Permit: minimum $10.
Name reservation: Reservable for 120 days for $10.00 fee (required).
Name requirements: Corporation, Incorporated, or abbreviation.
Incorporator requirements: One or more persons, partnerships or corporations.
Corporate purpose requirements: General "all purpose" clause (see instructions).
Director requirements: One or more (may be non-residents).
Paid-in capital requirements: None.
Publication requirements: None.
Other provisions: None.

Alaska

Address of State Corporation Department
    Alaska Department of Commerce and Economic Development
    Division of Banking, Securities, & Corporations
    Post Office Box D
    Juneau AK 99801
State law reference: Alaska Statutes, Section 10.06.
Title of corporate filing: Articles of Incorporation.
Filing fees: $150.00.
Other fees: Biennial Corporation Tax at filing: $100.00.
Name reservation: Reservable for 120 days for $ 15.00 fee.
Name requirements: Corporation, Incorporated, Company, Limited, or abbrev.
Incorporator requirements: One or more persons, 18 years or older.
Corporate purpose requirements: General "all purpose" clause (see instructions).
Director requirements: One or more (may be non-residents).
Paid-in capital requirements: None.
Publication requirements: None.
Other provisions: Articles must include a statement of codes from the Alaska Standard Industrial Classification Code List describing business type.

Arizona

Address of State Corporation Department

Arizona Corporation Commission
1200 West Washington
Post Office Box 6019
Phoenix AZ 85005

State law reference: Arizona Revised Statutes, Section 10.

Title of corporate filing: Articles of Incorporation.

Filing fees: $50.00.

Other fees: None.

Name reservation: Reservable for 120 days for $10.00 fee.

Name requirements: Corporation, Incorporated, Company, Limited or abbrev.

Incorporator requirements: Two or more persons.

Corporate purpose requirements: General "all purpose" clause (see instructions).

Director requirements: One or more.

Paid-in capital requirements: None.

Publication requirements: Articles must be published in newspaper 3 times.

Other provisions: Articles must specify ending of corporation's fiscal year.

Arkansas

Address of State Corporation Department

Arkansas Secretary of State
Corporation Department
State Capitol, Room 256
Little Rock AR 72201

State law reference: Arkansas Code, Section 4-27-400+.

Title of corporate filing: Articles of Incorporation.

Filing fees: $50.00.

Other fees: Initial Corporation Franchise Tax due upon filing: minimum $50.

Name reservation: Reservable for 120 days.

Name requirements: Corporation, Incorporated, Company, Limited, or abbrev.

Incorporator requirements: One or more persons.

Corporate purpose requirements: A specific primary purpose must be stated.

Director requirements: One or more (may be non-residents).

Paid-in capital requirements: None.

Publication requirements: None.

Other provisions: There are no preemptive rights unless granted in the Articles.

California

Address of State Corporation Department
    California Secretary of State
    Corporation Division
    1560 Broadway
    Sacramento CA 95814

State law reference: California Corporations Code, Section 200+.

Title of corporate filing: Articles of Incorporation.

Filing fees: $100.

Other fees: Franchise tax upon filing: $800.00; filing agent statement: $5.00.

Name reservation: Reservable for 60 days for $10 fee.

Name requirements: Corporation, Incorporated, Limited, or abbreviation.

Incorporator requirements: One or more persons.

Corporate purpose requirements: General "all purpose" clause (see instructions).

Director requirements: 3 (unless less than 3 shareholders, then same amount).

Paid-in capital requirements: None.

Publication requirements: None.

Other provisions: If initial directors are named in the Articles, they must sign the Articles of Incorporation. No preemptive rights unless granted in Articles.

Colorado

Address of State Corporation Department
    Colorado Secretary of State
    Corporations Section
    1560 Broadway, Suite 200
    Denver CO 80202

State law reference: Colorado Revised Statutes, Section 7-.

Title of corporate filing: Articles of Incorporation.

Filing fees: $50.00.

Other fees: None.

Name reservation: Reservable for 120 days for $10.00 fee (renewable).

Name requirements: Corporation, Incorporated, Company, Limited, or abbrev.

Incorporator requirements: One or more persons, 18 years or older.

Corporate purpose requirements: General "all purpose" clause (see instructions).

Director requirements: 3 (unless less than 3 shareholders, then same amount).

Paid-in capital requirements: None.

Publication requirements: None.

Other provisions: None.

Connecticut

Address of State Corporation Department
> Connecticut Secretary of State
> Corporation Division
> 30 Trinity Street
> Hartford CT 06115

State law reference: General Statutes of Connecticut, Section 33-.
Title of corporate filing: Certificate of Incorporation.
Filing fees: $45.00.
Other fees: Initial tax upon filing: minimum $150; Initial biennial report: $125.
Name reservation: Reservable for 120 days for a $30.00 fee.
Name requirements: Corporation, Incorporated, Company, Limited, or abbrev.
Incorporator requirements: One or more persons.
Corporate purpose requirements: General "all purpose" clause (see instructions).
Director requirements: 3 (unless less than 3 shareholders, then same amount).
Paid-in capital requirements: Articles must state minimum of $1000.00.
Publication requirements: None.
Other provisions: First corporate report due within 30 days of first organizational meeting.

Delaware

Address of State Corporation Department
> Delaware Department of State
> Corporation Division
> Post Office Box 898
> Dover DE 19903

State law reference: Delaware Code, Chapter 1, Title 8.
Title of corporate filing: Certificate of Incorporation.
Filing fees: $25.00.
Other fees: State tax: minimum $15.00.
Name reservation: Reservable for 30 days for $10.00 fee.
Name requirements: Corporation, Incorporated, Company, Limited, or abbrev.
Incorporator requirements: One or more persons, partnerships or corporations.
Corporate purpose requirements: General "all purpose" clause (see instructions).
Director requirements: One or more (may be non-residents).
Paid-in capital requirements: None.
Publication requirements: None.
Other provisions: None.

District of Columbia (Washington D.C.)

Address of State Corporation Department
> Recorder of Deeds
> Superintendent of Corporations
> 515 "D" Street
> Washington DC 20001

State law reference: District of Columbia Code, Section 29-.
Title of corporate filing: Articles of Incorporation.
Filing fees: $20.00.
Other fees: Initial License Fee: minimum $20.00; indexing: $2.00.
Name reservation: Reservable for 60 days for $7.00 fee.
Name requirements: Corporation, Incorporated, Company, Limited, or abbrev.
Incorporator requirements: Three or more persons, 18 years or older.
Corporate purpose requirements: A specific primary purpose must be stated.
Director requirements: 3 (unless less than 3 shareholders, then same amount).
Paid-in capital requirements: Articles must state minimum of $1000.00.
Publication requirements: None.
Other provisions: Corporation's name must not indicate that the corporation is organized under an Act of Congress.

Florida

Address of State Corporation Department
> Florida Department of State
> Corporation Division
> Post Office Box 6327
> Tallahassee FL 32304

State law reference: Florida Statutes, Section 607.+
Title of corporate filing: Articles of Incorporation.
Filing fees: $35.00.
Other fees: Registered Agent Designation: $35.00.
Name reservation: Reservable for 120 days for $35.00 fee.
Name requirements: Corporation, Incorporated, Company, or abbreviation.
Incorporator requirements: One or more persons.
Corporate purpose requirements: General "all purpose" clause (see instructions).
Director requirements: One or more (may be non-residents).
Paid-in capital requirements: None.
Publication requirements: None.
Other provisions: A Certificate of Designation of Registered Agent must be filed at the time of filing for incorporation.

Georgia

Address of State Corporation Department
Georgia Secretary of State
Corporation Division
2 Martin Luther King Drive SE
Atlanta GA 30334

State law reference: Official Code of Georgia Annotated, Sections 14-2-.
Title of corporate filing: Articles of Incorporation.
Filing fees: $60.
Other fees: Publication of Notice of Intent to file for incorporation: $40.00.
Name reservation: Reservable for 90 days for no fee.
Name requirements: Corporation, Incorporated, Company, Limited, or abbrev.
Incorporator requirements: One or more persons or corporations.
Corporate purpose requirements: General "all purpose" clause (see instructions).
Director requirements: One or more (may be non-residents).
Paid-in capital requirements: None.
Publication requirements: Must publish Notice of Intent to File to incorporate.
Other provisions: None.

Hawaii

Address of State Corporation Department
Hawaii Department of Commerce and Consumer Affairs
Business Registration Division
Post Office Box 40
Honolulu HI 96813

State law reference: Hawaii Revised Statutes, Section 415-.
Title of corporate filing: Articles of Incorporation.
Filing fees: $50.00.
Other fees: Expedited Service fee: $40.00 (expect long delays without this fee).
Name reservation: Reservable for 120 days.
Name requirements: Corporation, Incorporated, Limited, or abbreviation.
Incorporator requirements: One or more persons or corporations.
Corporate purpose requirements: A specific primary purpose must be stated.
Director requirements: 3 (unless less than 3 shareholders, then same amount).
Paid-in capital requirements: None.
Publication requirements: None.
Other provisions: At least one director must be state resident.

Idaho

Address of State Corporation Department
    Idaho Secretary of State
    Corporation Division
    Statehouse Room 203
    Boise ID 83720
State law reference: Idaho Code, Section 30-.
Title of corporate filing: Articles of Incorporation.
Filing fees: $60.00.
Other fees: None.
Name reservation: Reservable for 4 months for $10.00 fee.
Name requirements: Corporation, Incorporated, Company, Limited, or abbrev.
Incorporator requirements: One or more persons or corporations.
Corporate purpose requirements: A specific primary purpose must be stated.
Director requirements: One or more (may be non-residents).
Paid-in capital requirements: None.
Publication requirements: None.
Other provisions: None.

Illinois

Address of State Corporation Department
    Illinois Secretary of State
    Corporation Division
    Centennial Building, 3rd Floor
    Springfield IL 62756
State law reference: Illinois Annotated Statutes, Chapter 32.
Title of corporate filing: Articles of Incorporation.
Filing fees: $75.00.
Other fees: Initial Franchise Tax: Minimum $25.00.
Name reservation: Reservable for 90 days for $25.00 fee.
Name requirements: Corporation, Incorporated, Company, Limited, or abbrev.
Incorporator requirements: One or more persons or corporations.
Corporate purpose requirements: General "all purpose" clause (see instructions).
Director requirements: One or more (may be non-residents).
Paid-in capital requirements: None.
Publication requirements: None.
Other provisions: None.

Indiana

Address of State Corporation Department

Indiana Secretary of State

Corporation Division

201 State House

Indianapolis IN 46204

State law reference: Indiana Business Corporation Law, Section 23-1-.

Title of corporate filing: Articles of Incorporation.

Filing fees: $90.00.

Other fees: None.

Name reservation: Reservable for 120 days for $20 fee. (Renewable).

Name requirements: Corporation, Incorporated, Company, Limited, or abbrev.

Incorporator requirements: One or more persons.

Corporate purpose requirements: General "all purpose" clause (see instructions).

Director requirements: One or more (may be non-residents).

Paid-in capital requirements: None.

Publication requirements: None.

Other provisions: No preemptive rights unless granted by the Articles of Incorporation.

Iowa

Address of State Corporation Department

Iowa Secretary of State

Corporation Division

Hoover Building, 2nd Floor

Des Moines IA 50319

State law reference: Iowa Code Annotated, Section 493B.

Title of corporate filing: Articles of Incorporation.

Filing fees: $50.00.

Other fees: None.

Name reservation: Reservable for 120 days for $10.00 fee.

Name requirements: Corporation, Incorporated, Company, Limited, or abbrev.

Incorporator requirements: One or more persons or corporations.

Corporate purpose requirements: General "all purpose" clause (see instructions).

Director requirements: One or more (may be non-residents).

Paid-in capital requirements: None.

Publication requirements: None.

Other provisions: No preemptive rights unless granted in the Articles. Names of the initial Board of Directors must be given in the Articles.

Kansas

Address of State Corporation Department
 Kansas Secretary of State
 Corporation Division
 State Capitol, 2nd Floor
 Topeka KS 66612

State law reference: Kansas Statutes Annotated, Section 17-.

Title of corporate filing: Articles of Incorporation.

Filing fees: $75.00.

Other fees: None.

Name reservation: Reservable for 120 days for $20.00 fee.

Name requirements: Many business designation names allowed.

Incorporator requirements: One or more persons, partnerships or corporations.

Corporate purpose requirements: General "all purpose" clause (see instructions).

Director requirements: One or more (may be non-residents).

Paid-in capital requirements: None.

Publication requirements: None.

Other provisions: Names and addresses of initial directors must be given in Articles of Incorporation.

Kentucky

Address of State Corporation Department
 Kentucky Secretary of State
 Corporation Division
 New Capitol Building
 Frankfort KY 40601

State law reference: Kentucky Revised Statutes, Section 271B-.

Title of corporate filing: Articles of Incorporation.

Filing fees: $40.00.

Other fees: Organization Tax: minimum $10.00 (paid to State Treasurer).

Name reservation: Reservable for 120 days for $15.00 fee (renewable).

Name requirements: Corporation, Incorporated, Company, Limited, or abbrev.

Incorporator requirements: One or more persons or corporations.

Corporate purpose requirements: General "all purpose" clause (see instructions).

Director requirements: One or more (may be non-residents).

Paid-in capital requirements: None.

Publication requirements: None.

Other provisions: Number of initial directors must be stated in Articles.

Louisiana

Address of State Corporation Department
>   Louisiana Secretary of State
>   Corporation Division
>   7051 Florida Boulevard
>   Baton Rouge LA 70804

State law reference: Louisiana Revised Statutes, Section 12:.
Title of corporate filing: Articles of Incorporation.
Filing fees: $60.00.
Other fees: Notary fee in Orleans Parish: $25.00; Recording Articles: variable.
Name reservation: Reservable for 60 days for $20.00 fee.
Name requirements: Corporation, Incorporated, Company, Limited, or abbrev.
Incorporator requirements: One or more persons or corporations.
Corporate purpose requirements: General "all purpose" clause (see instructions).
Director requirements: 3 (unless less than 3 shareholders, then same amount).
Paid-in capital requirements: None.
Publication requirements: None.
Other provisions: Corporate name using "Company" can not be preceded by "and" or "&". No preemptive rights unless granted by Articles.

Maine

Address of State Corporation Department
>   Maine Secretary of State
>   Corporation Division
>   State House Station 101
>   Augusta ME 04333

State law reference: Maine Revised Statutes, Title 13-A.
Title of corporate filing: Articles of Incorporation.
Filing fees: $75.00.
Other fees: Capital Stock Fee: minimum $30.00.
Name reservation: Reservable for 120 days for $5.00 fee.
Name requirements: No requirements.
Incorporator requirements: One or more persons or corporations.
Corporate purpose requirements: General "all purpose" clause (see instructions).
Director requirements: 3 (unless less than 3 shareholders, then same amount).
Paid-in capital requirements: None.
Publication requirements: None.
Other provisions: Number of initial board of directors must be stated in Articles. Registered Agent is referred to as "Clerk" in Maine.

Maryland

Address of State Corporation Department

Maryland State Department of Assessments and Taxation
Corporation Division
301 West Preston Street, Room 809
Baltimore MD 21201

State law reference: Annotated Code of Maryland, Corp. and Assoc. Articles.
Title of corporate filing: Articles of Incorporation.
Filing fees: $40.00.
Other fees: None.
Name reservation: Reservable for 30 days for $7.00 fee.
Name requirements: Corporation, Incorporated, Company, Limited, or abbrev.
Incorporator requirements: One or more persons.
Corporate purpose requirements: General "all purpose" clause (see instructions).
Director requirements: 3 (unless less than 3 shareholders, then same amount).
Paid-in capital requirements: None.
Publication requirements: None.
Other provisions: If name includes "Company", may not be preceded by "and" or "&". Names of initial directors must be stated in Articles.

Massachusetts

Address of State Corporation Department

Massachusetts Secretary of State
Corporation Division
State House
Boston MA 02133

State law reference: Massachusetts Business Corporation Law, Chapter 156B.
Title of corporate filing: Articles of Organization.
Filing fees: Based on amount of authorized stock: minimum fee $200.00.
Other fees: None.
Name reservation: Reservable for 30 days. Renewable once.
Name requirements: Any name that indicates that business is incorporated.
Incorporator requirements: One or more persons, over 18 years old.
Corporate purpose requirements: A specific primary purpose must be stated.
Director requirements: 3 (unless less than 3 shareholders, then same amount).
Paid-in capital requirements: None.
Publication requirements: None.
Other provisions: Name of initial directors and officers must be stated in Articles of Organization. Secretary is referred to as "clerk" in Massachusetts. End date of fiscal year is required in Articles of Organization.

Michigan

Address of State Corporation Department
>   Michigan Department of Commerce
>   Corporation Bureau
>   Post Office Box 30054
>   Lansing MI 48926

State law reference: Michigan Compiled Laws, Section 450.
Title of corporate filing: Articles of Incorporation.
Filing fees: $10.00.
Other fees: Organization fee: minimum $50.00.
Name reservation: Reservable for 4 months for $10.00 fee. Renewable.
Name requirements: Corporation, Incorporated, Company, Limited, or abbrev.
Incorporator requirements: One or more persons, partnerships or corporations.
Corporate purpose requirements: General "all purpose" clause (see instructions).
Director requirements: One or more (may be non-residents).
Paid-in capital requirements: None.
Publication requirements: None.
Other provisions: Mandatory filing with Michigan Treasury for various tax licenses is required (sales, use, income withholding, and single business tax).

Minnesota

Address of State Corporation Department
>   Minnesota Secretary of State
>   Corporation Division
>   State Office Building #180
>   St Paul MN 55155

State law reference: Minnesota Statutes, Section 302A.
Title of corporate filing: Articles of Incorporation.
Filing fees: $135.00.
Other fees: None.
Name reservation: Reservable for 12 months for $35.00 fee. Renewable.
Name requirements: Corporation, Incorporated, Company, Limited, or abbrev.
Incorporator requirements: One or more persons.
Corporate purpose requirements: General "all purpose" clause (see instructions).
Director requirements: One or more.
Paid-in capital requirements: None.
Publication requirements: None.
Other provisions: If name includes "Company", can not be preceded with "and or "&". Cumulative voting allowed unless stated in Articles.

Mississippi

Address of State Corporation Department
Mississippi Secretary of State
Corporation Division
Post Office Box 136
Jackson MS 39205

State law reference: Mississippi Code Annotated, Section 79-4-.

Title of corporate filing: Articles of Incorporation.

Filing fees: $50.00.

Other fees: None.

Name reservation: Reservable for 180 days for $25.00 fee.

Name requirements: Corporation, Incorporated, Company, Limited, or abbrev.

Incorporator requirements: One or more persons.

Corporate purpose requirements: General "all purpose" clause (see instructions).

Director requirements: One or more (may be non-residents).

Paid-in capital requirements: None.

Publication requirements: None.

Other provisions: Initial directors must be named in Articles. Within 60 days of incorporation, must file for Franchise Tax Registration with State Tax Comm.

Missouri

Address of State Corporation Department
Secretary of State
Corporation Division
Post Office Box 778
Jefferson City MO 65102

State law reference: Revised Statutes of Missouri, Section 351.

Title of corporate filing: Articles of Incorporation.

Filing fees: Organization tax: minimum $53.00 based on amount of stock.

Other fees: None.

Name reservation: Reservable for 60 days for $20.00 fee.

Name requirements: Corporation, Incorporated, Company, Limited, or abbrev.

Incorporator requirements: One or more persons, 18 years or older.

Corporate purpose requirements: A specific primary purpose must be stated.

Director requirements: 3 (unless less than 3 shareholders, then same amount).

Paid-in capital requirements: None.

Publication requirements: None.

Other provisions: Number of initial directors must be stated in the Articles of Incorporation.

Montana

Address of State Corporation Department
>Montana Secretary of State
>Corporation Division
>State Capitol
>Helena MT 59601

State law reference: Montana Code Annotated, Title 35.
Title of corporate filing: Articles of Incorporation.
Filing fees: $20.00
Other fees: License Fee: minimum $50.00.
Name reservation: Reservable for 120 days for $10.00 fee.
Name requirements: Corporation, Incorporated, Company, Limited, or abbrev.
Incorporator requirements: One or more persons or corporations.
Corporate purpose requirements: General "all purpose" clause (see instructions).
Director requirements: One or more (may be non-residents).
Paid-in capital requirements: None.
Publication requirements: None.
Other provisions: Number of directors must be specified in the Articles of Incorporation.

Nebraska

Address of State Corporation Department
>Nebraska Secretary of State
>Corporation Division
>State Capitol Building, Room 2300
>Lincoln NE 68509

State law reference: Revised Statutes of Nebraska, Section 21-.
Title of corporate filing: Articles of Incorporation.
Filing fees: $40.00 minimum: variable fee based on amount of stock.
Other fees: Advertising notice approximately $30.00.
Name reservation: Reservable for 120 days.
Name requirements: Corporation, Incorporated, Company, Limited, or abbrev.
Incorporator requirements: One or more persons.
Corporate purpose requirements: General "all purpose" clause (see instructions).
Director requirements: One or more (may be non-residents).
Paid-in capital requirements: None.
Publication requirements: Notice of incorporation must be published for three consecutive weeks.
Other provisions: None.

Nevada

Address of State Corporation Department
  Nevada Secretary of State
  Corporation Division
  Capitol Complex
  Carson City NV 89701

State law reference: Nevada Revised Statutes, Section 78.

Title of corporate filing: Articles of Incorporation.

Filing fees: $125.00 minimum; variable fee based on amount of stock.

Other fees: Filing of list of officers and directors: $85.00.

Name reservation: Reservable for 90 days for $20.00 fee. Non-renewable.

Name requirements: Corporation, Incorporated, Company, Limited, or abbrev.

Incorporator requirements: One or more persons.

Corporate purpose requirements: General "all purpose" clause (see instructions).

Director requirements: One or more (may be non-residents).

Paid-in capital requirements: None.

Publication requirements: None.

Other provisions: No given names may be used in corporate name. A list of officers and directors must be filed with the state.

New Hampshire

Address of State Corporation Department
  Department of State
  Corporation Division
  107 North Main Street
  Concord NH 00301

State law reference: New Hampshire Revised Statutes Annotated, Section 293A.

Title of corporate filing: Articles of Incorporation.

Filing fees: $35.00.

Other fees: Filing of Addendum: $50.00; License fee: minimum $75.00, variable.

Name reservation: Reservable for 120 days for $15.00 fee.

Name requirements: Corporation, Incorporated, Limited, or abbreviation.

Incorporator requirements: One or more persons or corporations.

Corporate purpose requirements: A specific primary purpose must be stated.

Director requirements: One or more (may be non-residents).

Paid-in capital requirements: None.

Publication requirements: None.

Other provisions: An Addendum to the Articles must be filed stating that the stock of the corporation is either exempt or has been registered with state.

New Jersey

Address of State Corporation Department

> New Jersey Department of State
> Corporation Division
> C N 308
> Trenton NJ 08625

State law reference: New Jersey Statutes, Section 14A.

Title of corporate filing: Certificate of Incorporation.

Filing fees: $100.00.

Other fees: None.

Name reservation: Reservable for 120 days for $50.00 fee.

Name requirements: Corporation, Incorporated, or abbreviation.

Incorporator requirements: One or more persons or corporations.

Corporate purpose requirements: General "all purpose" clause (see instructions).

Director requirements: One or more (may be non-residents).

Paid-in capital requirements: None.

Publication requirements: None.

Other provisions: Number of directors on initial board must be stated in Certificate of Incorporation.

New Mexico

Address of State Corporation Department

> New Mexico Secretary of State
> Corporation Division
> Post Office Box 1269
> Santa Fe NM 87504

State law reference: New Mexico Statutes Annotated, Section 53.

Title of corporate filing: Articles of Incorporation.

Filing fees: $50.00; variable fee based on amount of stock.

Other fees: Initial Corporate Report filing fee: $20.00 (filed within 20 days).

Name reservation: Reservable for 120 days for a $10.00 fee.

Name requirements: Corporation, Incorporated, Company, Limited, or abbrev.

Incorporator requirements: One or more persons or corporations.

Corporate purpose requirements: A specific primary purpose must be stated.

Director requirements: One or more (may be non-residents).

Paid-in capital requirements: None.

Publication requirements: None.

Other provisions: None.

New York

Address of State Corporation Department
New York Department of State
Corporation Bureau
162 Washington Street
Albany NY 12231

State law reference: New York Business Corporation Law.
Title of corporate filing: Certificate of Incorporation.
Filing fees: $125.00.
Other fees: Organization tax: minimum $10.00; variable based on stock.
Name reservation: Reservable for 60 days for $20.00 fee. Renewable twice.
Name requirements: Corporation, Incorporated, Limited, or abbreviation.
Incorporator requirements: One or more persons.
Corporate purpose requirements: General "all purpose" clause (but see below).
Director requirements: 3 (unless less than 3 shareholders, then same amount).
Paid-in capital requirements: None.
Publication requirements: None.
Other provisions: Purpose must state corporation needs no approval of any state body. Articles must appoint NY Secretary of State as registered agent.

North Carolina

Address of State Corporation Department
North Carolina Secretary of State
Corporation Division
Capitol Building
Raleigh NC 27603

State law reference: General Statutes of North Carolina, Section 55.
Title of corporate filing: Articles of Incorporation.
Filing fees: $100.00.
Other fees: None.
Name reservation: Reservable for 120 days for $10 fee.
Name requirements: Corporation, Incorporated, Company, Limited, or abbrev.
Incorporator requirements: One or more persons.
Corporate purpose requirements: General "all purpose" clause (see instructions).
Director requirements: One or more (may be non-residents).
Paid-in capital requirements: None.
Publication requirements: None.
Other provisions: None.

North Dakota

Address of State Corporation Department
> North Dakota Secretary of State
> Corporation Division
> Capitol Building
> Bismarck ND 58505

State law reference: North Dakota Century Code, Section 10-19.

Title of corporate filing: Articles of Incorporation.

Filing fees: $30.00.

Other fees: Initial Franchise Fee: minimum $50.00; variable (see below also).

Name reservation: Reservable for 12 months for $10.00 fee.

Name requirements: Corporation, Incorporated, Company, Limited, or abbrev.

Incorporator requirements: One or more persons.

Corporate purpose requirements: General "all purpose" clause (see instructions).

Director requirements: One or more.

Paid-in capital requirements: None.

Publication requirements: None.

Other provisions: If "Company" is in corporate name, may not be preceded by "and" or "&". Consent to be Registered Agent must be filed with a $10.00 fee.

Ohio

Address of State Corporation Department
> Ohio Secretary of State
> Corporation Division
> 30 East Broad Street
> Columbus OH 43266

State law reference: Ohio Revised Code, Section 1701.

Title of corporate filing: Articles of Incorporation.

Filing fees: $75.00 minimum; variable fee based on amount of stock.

Other fees: None.

Name reservation: Reservable for 60 days for $5.00 fee.

Name requirements: Corporation, Incorporated, Company, or abbreviation.

Incorporator requirements: One or more persons.

Corporate purpose requirements: General "all purpose" clause (see instructions).

Director requirements: 3 (unless less than 3 shareholders, then same amount).

Paid-in capital requirements: None.

Publication requirements: None.

Other provisions: Corporate By-Laws are referred to as the corporate "Code of Regulations" in Ohio. Must also file Appointment of Statutory Agent form.

Oklahoma

Address of State Corporation Department
> Oklahoma Secretary of State
> Corporation Division
> 101 State Capitol Building
> Oklahoma City OK 73105

State law reference: Oklahoma Statutes, Title 18.
Title of corporate filing: Certificate of Incorporation.
Filing fees: $50.00 minimum; variable fee based on amount of stock.
Other fees: None.
Name reservation: Reservable for 60 days for $5.00 fee.
Name requirements: May contain various business designations.
Incorporator requirements: One or more persons, partnerships or corporations.
Corporate purpose requirements: General "all purpose" clause (see instructions).
Director requirements: One or more (may be non-residents).
Paid-in capital requirements: None.
Publication requirements: None.
Other provisions: None.

Oregon

Address of State Corporation Department
> Oregon Secretary of State
> Corporation Division
> 158 NE 12th
> Salem OR 97310

State law reference: Oregon Business Corporation Act.
Title of corporate filing: Articles of Incorporation.
Filing fees: $50.00.
Other fees: None.
Name reservation: Reservable for 120 days for $10.00 fee.
Name requirements: Corporation, Incorporated, Company, Limited, or abbrev.
Incorporator requirements: One or more persons, partnerships or corporations.
Corporate purpose requirements: General "all purpose" clause (see instructions).
Director requirements: One or more.
Paid-in capital requirements: None.
Publication requirements: None.
Other provisions: None.

Pennsylvania

Address of State Corporation Department
      Pennsylvania Department of State
      Corporation Bureau
      308 North Office Building
      Harrisburg PA 17120

State law reference: Pennsylvania Consolidated Statutes, Section 1300-.
Title of corporate filing: Articles of Incorporation.
Filing fees: $100.00.
Other fees: None.
Name reservation: Reservable for 120 days for $52.00 fee.
Name requirements: May use various business designations.
Incorporator requirements: One or more persons or corporations.
Corporate purpose requirements: General "all purpose" clause (see instructions).
Director requirements: One or more (may be non-residents).
Paid-in capital requirements: None.
Publication requirements: Must publish intent to file or filing of Articles twice.
Other provisions: Must file Docketing Statement at time of filing Articles.

Rhode Island

Address of State Corporation Department
      Rhode Island Secretary of State
      Corporation Division
      100 North Main Street
      Providence RI 20903

State law reference: General Laws of Rhode Island, Section 7-1.
Title of corporate filing: Articles of Incorporation.
Filing fees: $70.00.
Other fees: License Fee: minimum $80.00; variable based on stock amount.
Name reservation: Reservable for 120 days for $50.00 fee.
Name requirements: Corporation, Incorporated, Company, Limited, or abbrev.
Incorporator requirements: One or more persons.
Corporate purpose requirements: A specific primary purpose must be stated.
Director requirements: One or more (may be non-residents).
Paid-in capital requirements: None.
Publication requirements: None.
Other provisions: Registered Agent must sign Articles of Incorporation.

South Carolina

Address of State Corporation Department
>   South Carolina Secretary of State
>   Corporation Division
>   Post Office Box 11350
>   Columbia SC 29211

State law reference: Code of Laws of South Carolina, Section 33.

Title of corporate filing: Articles of Incorporation.

Filing fees: $10.00.

Other fees: Incorporation Tax: $100.00; License Fee and Report Fee: $25.00.

Name reservation: Reservable for 120 days for $10.00 fee.

Name requirements: Corporation, Incorporated, Company, Limited, or abbrev.

Incorporator requirements: One or more persons, partnerships or corporations.

Corporate purpose requirements: General "all purpose" clause (see instructions).

Director requirements: One or more (may be non-residents).

Paid-in capital requirements: None.

Publication requirements: None.

Other provisions: Certificate of Attorney must be signed by a South Carolina lawyer. Initial Corporate Report must state specific business purpose.

South Dakota

Address of State Corporation Department
>   South Dakota Secretary of State
>   Corporation Division
>   Capitol Building
>   Pierre SD 57501

State law reference: South Dakota Compiled Laws, Section 47.

Title of corporate filing: Articles of Incorporation.

Filing fees: $40.00 minimum; variable fee based on amount of stock.

Other fees: None.

Name reservation: Reservable for 120 days for $10.00 fee.

Name requirements: Corporation, Incorporated, Company, Limited, or abbrev.

Incorporator requirements: One or more persons, 18 years or older.

Corporate purpose requirements: General "all purpose" clause (see instructions).

Director requirements: One or more.

Paid-in capital requirements: Must have paid-in capital of at least $1,000.

Publication requirements: None.

Other provisions: Articles of Incorporation must state number, names and addresses of initial directors.

Tennessee

Address of State Corporation Department
> Tennessee Secretary of State
> Corporation Division
> State Capitol Building
> Nashville TN 37219

State law reference: Tennessee Code Annotated, Section 48.

Title of corporate filing: Certificate of Incorporation.

Filing fees: $50.00.

Other fees: Register of Deeds filing fee: $5.00/page if office is in Tennessee.

Name reservation: Reservable for four months for $10.00 fee.

Name requirements: Corporation, Incorporated, or abbreviation.

Incorporator requirements: One or more persons, partnerships or corporations.

Corporate purpose requirements: General "all purpose" clause (see instructions).

Director requirements: One or more (may be non-residents).

Paid-in capital requirements: None.

Publication requirements: None.

Other provisions: Certificate of Incorporation also referred to as the Corporate Charter in Tennessee.

Texas

Address of State Corporation Department
> Texas Secretary of State
> Corporation Section
> Post Office Box 13697
> Austin TX 78711

State law reference: Texas Business Corporation Act.

Title of corporate filing: Articles of Incorporation.

Filing fees: $300.00.

Other fees: Initial Franchise Tax: $100.00.

Name reservation: Reservable for 120 days for $40.00 fee.

Name requirements: Corporation, Incorporated, or abbreviation.

Incorporator requirements: One or more persons, partnerships or corporations.

Corporate purpose requirements: General "all purpose" clause (see instructions).

Director requirements: One or more (may be non-residents).

Paid-in capital requirements: Paid-in capital must be at least $1,000.

Publication requirements: Notice must be published if an operating company intends to incorporate without changing the firm's name.

Other provisions: Number, names and addresses of initial directors in Articles.

Utah

Address of State Corporation Department
>Utah Secretary of State
>Division of Corporations and Commercial Code
>Post Office Box 45801
>Salt Lake City UT 84103

State law reference: Utah Code Annotated, Section 16-10.
Title of corporate filing: Articles of Incorporation.
Filing fees: $50.00.
Other fees: None.
Name reservation: Reservable for 120 days for $20.00 fee.
Name requirements: Corporation, Incorporated, Company, or abbreviation.
Incorporator requirements: Three or more persons, 18 years or older.
Corporate purpose requirements: A specific primary purpose must be stated.
Director requirements: 3 (unless less than 3 shareholders, then same amount).
Paid-in capital requirements: Must have at least $1,000 of paid-in capital.
Publication requirements: None.
Other provisions: Names and addresses of the initial directors must be stated in the Articles of Incorporation. Registered Agent must sign Articles.

Vermont

Address of State Corporation Department
>Vermont Secretary of State
>Corporation Division
>109 State Street
>Montpelier VT 05602

State law reference: Vermont Statutes Annotated, Title 11.
Title of corporate filing: Articles of Association.
Filing fees: $35.00 minimum; variable fee based on amount of stock.
Other fees: None.
Name reservation: Reservable for 120 days for $10.00 fee.
Name requirements: Corporation, Incorporated, Company, Limited, or abbrev.
Incorporator requirements: One or more persons, 18 years or older.
Corporate purpose requirements: A specific primary purpose must be stated.
Director requirements: 3 (unless less than 3 shareholders, then same amount).
Paid-in capital requirements: None.
Publication requirements: None.
Other provisions: Number, names and addresses of the initial directors must be stated in the Articles of Association.

Virginia

Address of State Corporation Department

    Virginia State Corporation Commission
    1220 Bank Street
    Post Office Box 1197
    Richmond VA 23219

State law reference: Code of Virginia, Title 13.1.

Title of corporate filing: Articles of Incorporation.

Filing fees: $25.00.

Other fees: Charter fee: $50.00 minimum; variable fee based on stock amount.

Name reservation: Reservable for 120 days for $10.00 fee.

Name requirements: Corporation, Incorporated, Company, Limited, or abbrev.

Incorporator requirements: One or more persons.

Corporate purpose requirements: General "all purpose" clause (see instructions).

Director requirements: One or more (may be non-residents).

Paid-in capital requirements: None.

Publication requirements: None.

Other provisions: None.

Washington

Address of State Corporation Department

    Washington Secretary of State
    Corporation Division
    505 East Union Street
    Olympia WA 98504

State law reference: Revised Code of Washington, Title 23-B.

Title of corporate filing: Articles of Incorporation.

Filing fees: $175.00.

Other fees: Annual Report filing: $10.00 (file within 120 days of incorporation).

Name reservation: Reservable for 180 days for $20.00 fee.

Name requirements: Corporation, Incorporated, Company, Limited, or abbrev.

Incorporator requirements: One or more persons or corporations.

Corporate purpose requirements: General "all purpose" clause (see instructions).

Director requirements: One or more (may be non-residents).

Paid-in capital requirements: None.

Publication requirements: None.

Other provisions: Must state official Washington State Unified Business Identifier in Articles, if issued. Registered Agent must sign Articles.

West Virginia

Address of State Corporation Department
>   West Virginia Secretary of State
>   Corporation Division
>   State Capitol Building
>   Charleston WV 25305

State law reference: West Virginia Code, Chapter 31, Article 1.

Title of corporate filing: Articles of Incorporation.

Filing fees: $10.00.

Other fees: Annual license tax: $75 minimum; variable fee based on stock.

Name reservation: Reservable for 120 days for a $5.00 fee.

Name requirements: Corporation, Incorporated, Company, Limited, or abbrev.

Incorporator requirements: One or more persons or corporations.

Corporate purpose requirements: General "all purpose" clause (see instructions).

Director requirements: One or more (may be non-residents).

Paid-in capital requirements: None.

Publication requirements: None.

Other provisions: Number of initial directors must be stated in the Articles of Incorporation.

Wisconsin

Address of State Corporation Department
>   Wisconsin Secretary of State
>   Corporation Division
>   Post Office Box 7846
>   Madison WI 53701

State law reference: Wisconsin Statutes Annotated, Section 180.

Title of corporate filing: Articles of Incorporation.

Filing fees: $90.00 minimum; variable fee based on amount of stock.

Other fees: None.

Name reservation: Reservable for 120 days for $15.00 fee.

Name requirements: Corporation, Incorporated, Company, Limited, or abbrev.

Incorporator requirements: One or more persons.

Corporate purpose requirements: General "all purpose" clause (see instructions).

Director requirements: One or more (may be non-residents).

Paid-in capital requirements: None.

Publication requirements: None.

Other provisions: None.

Wyoming

Address of State Corporation Department
  Wyoming Secretary of State
  Corporation Division
  State Capitol Building
  Cheyenne WY 82002

State law reference: Wyoming Statutes, Section 17-16.

Title of corporate filing: Articles of Incorporation.

Filing fees: $90.00 ($30.00 credit if filed when reserving name).

Other fees: None.

Name reservation: Reservable for 120 days for $30.00 fee.

Name requirements: Corporation, Incorporated, or abbreviation.

Incorporator requirements: One or more persons or corporations.

Corporate purpose requirements: A specific primary purpose must be stated.

Director requirements: One or more (may be non-residents).

Paid-in capital requirements: None.

Publication requirements: None.

Other provisions: Written Consent to Appointment as Registered Agent must accompany filing of Articles of Incorporation.

Glossary of Corporate Legal Terms

Agent: A person who is authorized to act on behalf of another. A corporation acts only through its agents, whether they are directors, employees, or officers.

Articles of Incorporation: The charter of the corporation, this is the public filing with a state which requests that the corporation be allowed to exist. Along with the corporate By-Laws, it provides details of the organization and structure of the business. They must be consistent with the laws of the state of incorporation.

Assumed name: A name, other than the corporation's legal name as shown on the Articles of Incorporation, under which a corporation will conduct business. Most states require registration of the fictitious name if a company desires to conduct business under an assumed name. The corporation's legal name is not an assumed name.

Authorized stock: The number of shares of stock that a corporation is allowed to issue as stated in the Articles of Incorporation. All authorized shares need not be issued.

Board of directors: The group with control of the general supervision of the corporation. They are elected by the shareholders and they, in turn, appoint the officers of the corporation.

Business corporation laws: For each individual state, these provide the legal framework for the operation of corporations. The Articles of Incorporation and the By-Laws of a corporation must adhere to the specifics of state law.

By-Laws: The internal rules which govern the management of the corporation. They contain the procedures for holding meetings, appointments, elections and other management matters. If these conflict with the Articles of Incorporation, the provision in the Articles will be controlling.

Capital: Initially, the actual money or property that shareholders transfer to the corporation to allow it to operate. Once in operation, it also consists of accumulated profits. The net worth of the corporation.

Capital stock: See *Authorized stock*.

Certificate of Incorporation: See *Articles of Incorporation*. Note, however, some states will issue a Certificate of Incorporation after the filing of the Articles of Incorporation.

Close corporation: Corporation with less than 50 shareholders and which has elected to be treated as a close corporation. Not all states have close corporation statutes. (For information regarding close corporations, please consult a competent attorney).

Closely-held corporation: Not a specific state-sanctioned type of corporation, but rather a designation of any corporation in which the stock is held by a small group of people or entities and is not publicly traded.

Common stock: The standard stock of a corporation which includes the right to vote the shares and the right to proportionate dividends. See also *Preferred stock*.

Consent Resolution: Any resolution signed by all of the directors or shareholders of a corporation authorizing an action, without the necessity of a meeting.

Cumulative voting: A voting right of shareholders which allows votes for directors to be spread among the various nominees. This right protects the voting strength of minority shareholders. The amount of votes in cumulative voting is based on the number of shares held times the number of director positions to be voted on. The shareholder can then allocate the total cumulative votes in any manner.

Dissolution: Methods by which a corporation concludes its business and liquidates. Dissolutions may be involuntary because of bankruptcy or credit problems or voluntary on the initiation of the directors or shareholders of a corporation.

Dividend: A distribution of money or property paid by the corporation to a shareholder based on the amount of shares held. Dividends must be paid out of the corporations net earnings and profits. The board of directors has the authority to declare or withhold dividends based on sound business discretion.

Domestic corporation: A corporation is a domestic corporation in the state in which it is incorporated. See also *Foreign corporation*.

Fictitious name: See *Assumed name*.

Foreign corporation: A corporation is referred to as a foreign corporation in all states other than the one in which it is actually incorporated. In order to conduct active business affairs in a different state, foreign corporation must be registered with the other state for the authority to transact business and it must pay an annual fee for this privilege.

Incorporator: The person who signs the Articles of Incorporation. Usually a person, but some states allow a corporation or partnership to be an incorporator.

Indemnify: To reimburse or compensate. Directors and officers of corporations are often reimbursed or indemnified for all the expenses they may have incurred in incorporating.

Issued shares: The number of authorized shares of stock that are actually transferred to shareholders of the corporation. Also referred to as outstanding shares. See also *Treasury shares*.

Minutes: A written record of the activities of a meeting.

No-par value: Shares of stock which have no specific face value. The board of directors can assign a value to the shares for sale and can then allocate a portion of the sales price to the paid-in-capital account.

Not-for-profit corporation: A corporation formed under state law which exists for a socially-worthwhile purpose. Profits are not distributed but retained and used for corporate purposes. May be tax-exempt. Also referred to as non-profit.

Officers: Manage the daily operations of a corporation. Generally consists of a president, vice-president, secretary, and treasurer. Appointed by the board of directors.

Par value: The face value assigned to shares of stock. Par value stock must be sold for at least the stated value, but can be sold for more than the par value.

Piercing the corporate veil: A legal decision that allows a court to ignore the corporate entity and reach the assets of the shareholders, directors, or officers.

Preemptive rights: A shareholder right that allows shareholders the opportunity to maintain their percentage of ownership of the corporation in the event that additional shares are offered for sale.

Preferred stock: Generally, stock which provides the shareholder with a preferential payment of dividends, but does not carry voting rights.

Proxy: A written shareholder authorization to vote shares on behalf of another. Directors may never vote by proxy (except in some close corporations).

Quorum: The required number of persons necessary to officially conduct business at a meeting. Generally, a majority of the shareholders or directors constitutes a quorum.

Registered agent: The person designated in the Articles of Incorporation who will be available to receive service of process (summons, subpoena, etc.) on behalf of the corporation. A corporation must always have a registered agent.

Registered office: The actual physical location of the registered agent. Need not be the actual principal place of business of the corporation.

Resolutions: A formal decision which has been adopted by either the shareholders or the board of directors of a corporation.

"S" corporation: A specific IRS designation which allows a corporation to be taxed similarly to a partnership, yet retain limited liability for its shareholders.

Shareholders: Own issued stock of a corporation and, therefore, own an interest in the corporation. They elect the board of directors and vote on major corporate issues.

Stock transfer book: The ledger book (or sheets) in which the registered owners of shares in the corporation are recorded.

Treasury shares: Shares of stock which were issued, but later re-acquired by the corporation and not cancelled. May be issued as dividends to shareholders. They are issued but not outstanding for terms of voting and quorums.

Index